THE FAR SIDE OF THE WORLD.
IRISH SERVICEMEN IN THE KOREAN WAR 1950-53.

Map
Brian Durney

Also by James Durney and published by Gaul House

The Mob
The History of Irish Gangsters in America

Far from the Short Grass
The Story of Kildaremen in Two World Wars

On the One Road
Political Unrest in Kildare. 1913-1994

The Volunteer
Uniforms, Weapons and History of the Irish Republican Army 1913-1997

Printed by the Leinster Leader Ltd. Naas
Design and Layout, Icarus Media
Cover Design Icarus Media

THE FAR SIDE OF THE WORLD.
IRISH SERVICEMEN IN THE KOREAN WAR 1950-53.

JAMES DURNEY

There is full many a man that crieth
War! War! that knows full little to what
war amounteth. War hath its beginning but
what befells thereafter it is not light to know
The Melibee

Dedicated to my father Jim Durney
and all UN soldiers who have served
their country honourably in peace and war.

Contents

Acknowledgements..5

Forward...9

Prologue..11

Chapter 1. The war begins..13

Chapter 2. Army of all nations...32

Chapter 3. On to the Yalu..42

Chapter 4. Red storm...52

Chapter 5. A winter of discontent...62

Chapter 6. War at sea...78

Chapter 7. American frontline. New Year and Spring Offensives. 85

Chapter 8. The Ulsters and Irish on the Imjin.......................................93

Chapter 9. Duty First...106

Chapter 10. To the trenches..121

Chapter 11. Over there...141

Chapter 12. The hills of Korea..148

Chapter 13. POWs. 173

Chapter 14. Dying for peace...199

Appendix 1 Irish Korean War veterans finally become US Citizens.............217

Appendix 2 Roll of Honour...221

End Notes...228

Bibliography..237

Veterans Interviewed..239

Index...240

Acknowledgements

Martin O'Dwyer, Cashel, Co. Tipperary; Packie O'Dwyer, Herfordshire, England; Liam O'Duibhir, Emly, Co. Tipperary; the late Brian McGinn, and John Leahy and Marilyn Knapp & *The Irish In Korea* website; John Hawkins, Enniscorthy, Co. Wexford; John Fitzgerald, Yonkers, N.Y., John Jennings, Long Island, N.Y.; Monasterevan Local History Group; Royal Ulster Rifles Museum, Belfast; Charles Dennehy, Straffan, Co. Kildare; Sean Taheny, Gurteen, Co. Sligo; Tom O'Keefe, Wexford; Jim Sullivan, Naas, Co. Kildare; Col. Robin Charley, President British Korean Veterans Association, Ireland branch; Spencer McWhirter, Hon. Secretary, BKVA, Ireland branch; Pam Alexander, British Legion, Dublin; Jack Clarke, Dublin; Henry O'Kane, Honiley, England; Gerry Fox, Dublin; Catherine, Defence Attaché's Office, US Embassy, Dublin; Pat Lynch, Dublin; Glen Foy, Post Adjutant, American Legion, Ireland; John Lee, Tralee, Co. Kerry; Paddy Healy, Castlegregorey, Co. Kerry; Pat O'Connor, Tralee, Co. Kerry; Pat Kelly, Killarney, Co. Kerry; Ray O'Hanlon, *Irish Echo*; Father Sean Dunne, Columban Fathers, Dalgan; Sarah Herlihy, Liverpool; Claudia Krebs, Office of Australian War Graves; Turtle Bunbury, Dublin; Roy Warke, Naas; Gerry Murphy, Norfolk, England; Mary Doody, Chicago; Tommy McConaghy, Ballymoney, Co. Antrim; Mike Kelly, Claregalway, Co. Galway; Michael McCormick, Loughrea, Co. Galway; Mrs. Joyce Green, Ballyvolane House, Co. Cork; Justin Green and Robert Leach; Anne King, Dundalk, Co. Louth, and Mary Woods; Marie and Joan Fahy, Drumnin, Co. Galway; Frank Stewert, Suncroft, Co. Kildare; Colm MacDonnchadh, Lucan, Co. Dublin; Michael O'Brien, Valencia, California; Martin McDonagh, Athboy, Co. Meath; Colm Ó Mongáin, Newstalk 106; Rachel Collier, Dublin; Tom O'Sullivan, Coilleach, Co. Galway; Seosamh Ó Cathail; Jack McCabe, Dundalk, Co. Louth; Patrick Lane, Cobh, Co. Cork; Susan Kirwan and Mrs. B. Coyne, Dunlavin, Co. Wicklow; Brian Gallagher, UCD Dublin; and Paddy Durney, Newbridge, Co. Kildare.

Special thanks to John Hawkins, who started the ball rolling, introduced me to Irish veterans of Korea, and has been my guide and mentor throughout the workings of this book; Col Robin Charley for his foreword, expertise, countless phone calls and correspondence and permission to quote from *The Royal Ulster*

Rifles In Korea; John T. Jennings for allowing me to quote from his address to The Mayo Society of New York's 125th Annual St. Patrick's Ball and Dinner (2004); John Lee for allowing me to use his story from *Dúthaigh Duibhneach* by Brendan Fitzgerald; Henry O'Kane for allowing me to quote liberally from *O'Kane's Korea: A soldier's tale of three years of combat and captivity in Korea 1950-53*; Richard Doherty for permission to quote from his interviews of fellow Ulstermen in *The Sons of Ulster. Ulstermen at war from the Somme to Korea*; Michael Clifford for permission to quote from *Dying for the love of God*; Mary Doody, Chicago, for allowing me to use a letter from her dear brother, the late Michael Fitzpatrick; William May, Clontarf, Dublin, for his unique collection of photographs from his time in Korea; Denis O'Shaughnessy for allowing me to quote from his interview of Paddy Sheehy in his book *A Spot So Fair. Tales from St Mary's*; and John Stephens for his patience, and list of Irish-born servicemen killed in action with the British armed forces. Thanks also to my wife and children for only they know what it is like when I embark on another project when my wife Caroline becomes a "book widow" and dad turns into a "computer hugger". Again my son Brian always turns up trumps with the layout of the book and the cover design. Thanks also to Philip Higgins, Mark Rogers and Tony Ryan of the *Leinster Leader.*

Of course, there is one group of people, above all others, who have made this book possible, the many ex-servicemen who fought throughout the Korean War and who so willingly gave their personal accounts. Interviewing or corresponding with these veterans has been one of the most fascinating, and emotional, times of my life. Most enjoyed the opportunity to tell of their experiences in the Forgotten War, while others were too distressed to delve into the past. I am pleased to be able to tell the story of Irish servicemen in the Korean War, in the best way a historian can provide: their story told in their own words.

Note: All military ranks given in the text are those held at the time of the events described. All times relating to military matters in the text are given in accordance with the 24-hour clock, i.e. 0100.

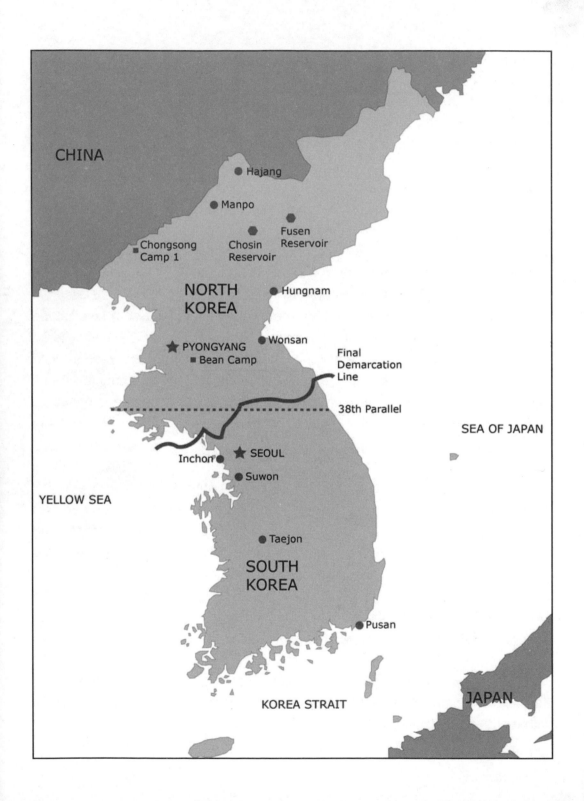

Foreword

By Colonel W.R.H. Charley, OBE, JP, DL.
Late The Royal Ulster Rifles
President, The British Korean Veterans' Association
(Ireland Branch)
(RUR Captain in Korea 1950-1951)

I feel very honoured to be asked by the author to write a foreword to this book, especially as I served alongside many of those mentioned.

This book gives an excellent insight, for historians and others, into the first United Nations war - the Korean War. This war began in the summer of 1950 and continued until 1953. It involved 60,000 members of the British armed forces, many of them Irishmen.

In June 1950, US President Harry S. Truman announced that the line against Communist aggression had to be drawn somewhere - the Korean War was a result of this political decision. The UK Prime Minister, Clement Atlee, agreed with Truman. He was determined never to use appeasement to buy off aggression, as Neville Chamberlain had done with Hitler in 1937. Thus British troops were sent to Korea alongside those of other nations.

The fighting was savage and the extreme weather conditions in Korea did not help our situation. North and South Korea are roughly divided by the 38th parallel. In Western Europe the 38th parallel goes across sunny southern

Portugal but in Korea it is not so pleasant along this line of latitude. In winter it is unbelievably cold as harsh winds from the steppes of Russia cover the country with ice and snow. In summer it is fiercely hot and humid with constant rain causing mud underfoot - not to mention the occasional addition of whistling typhoon winds.

The Korean War is often referred to as the 'Forgotten War'. For those Irishmen who fought in Korea and for the families of those who died, it will never be forgotten. In this book the great bravery and courage of the Irish soldiers involved in this war are vividly illustrated in the individual stories.

Adversity often leads to strong friendships - many survivors of the Korean War have a fierce bond of comradeship which has developed into the British Koreans Veterans' Association. The Irish Korean Veterans' Association meet on 23 April every year, the anniversary of the Battle of the River Imjin in 1951.

Robin Charley
September 2005.

Prologue

The country of Korea is a peninsula joined to northern China and stretches southward to within 120 miles of the islands of Japan. At about 600 miles long and 135 miles wide it is about the size of Britain. In 1950 it was home to about twenty million people, most of whom lived in the south. Known as the "land of the morning calm" its people were mainly peasants living rather poor and miserable lives. A Korean proverb for the country runs: "Over the mountains, mountains." The landscape is colourless, with very few flowers. The hillsides are gouged with thousands of dells and gorges; the hills steep, and speckled here and there with boulders, scrub oak and stunted fir. In the valleys streams meander past rice paddies, walled cities and pagodas. It was then a sleepy country sometimes known as "the Hermit's Kingdom." Despite its proximity to China and Japan few people in America, Britain, or Ireland could find Korea on the map. This, of course, was not their fault. Korea did just not feature in their education. Told it was in the East near Japan, it was assumed it was a warm country. When the Korean War broke out in June 1950 journalists, military men and ordinary people went rushing for their atlas. To the soldiers of Britain and America, who would soon be fighting and dying there, Korea was on the far side of the world.

The position of the Korean peninsula made it easy for Chinese and Mongols from Asia, as well as Japanese, to invade the country. For centuries, parts or the whole of Korea were under foreign rule. Japanese victory over China in the war of 1894 allowed them to obtain control of Korea, which became part of the Japanese Empire in 1910. After the defeat of Japan in World War II Russian and American troops entered Korea, dividing it for convenience into northern and southern parts separated by a line drawn along the 38th Parallel. The intention was that the United States and the USSR would with the Koreans make proposals for an independent Korean government. As the Americans and Russians could not agree the United Nations called for elections to choose a government in 1948. UN observers, whose duties were to see that elections were fairly held, were not allowed north of the 38th Parallel, so the government elected represented Korea south of the 38th Parallel only. The Russians, meanwhile, formed a Communist state north of the 38th Parallel and began to train and equip a North Korean army. The following year both the Soviet Union and the United States withdrew their military forces from Korea but the mutual antagonism between the North and the South only worsened. Skirmishes between both sides became quite common.

At 0400 (4 a.m.) on June 25 1950 without warning the North Korean Army invaded South Korea. The United States rushed troops to help the South Koreans and were joined by troops from the British Commonwealth and from several other countries belonging to the United Nations. When the American led UN force tried to re-unite the country by force of arms China joined in on the side of North Korea. For three years the fighting swayed up and down the peninsula, until a truce was signed in July 1953, with no victors on either side. Over one and a half million men and women died and two and a half million were wounded or injured. When the war in Korea broke out many people in Ireland, indeed in Britain and the United States, did not know where Korea was, or could find it on a map. But within weeks many Irishmen were fighting for their lives as they tried to stem the relentless blitzkreig of the North Korean army. Some of them were soldiers serving in British regiments, like the Royal Ulster Rifles and Irish Hussars, while others were recent emigrants to the United States, Canada, Australia and New Zealand. For all of them Korea, the country on "the far side of the world," would be an experience in modern war which would never be forgotten.

1

The War Begins

On the rainy morning of Sunday, June 25 1950, after a devastating artillery and mortar barrage, ten divisions of the North Korean People's Army streamed over the 38th Parallel. Four communist spearheads, led by their almost invulnerable T34s, raced southwards checked more by the terrain rather than the Republic of Korea Army. Under-trained, poorly-led and ill-equipped, the Republic of Korea (ROK) Army was no match for the well-honed military machine of the NKPA and were quickly sent reeling. The United States had no combat forces in Korea, but there was several hundred members of a Korean Military Advisory Group (KMAG) scattered across South Korea training the ROK Army and Coast Guard.[1] Because the opening rounds of the war were not unlike the usual spate of harassment and manoeuvres that had been going on intermittently for months more than seven hours elapsed between the start of the invasion and receipt of official notice from the US Embassy in Seoul by the State Department in Washington. Within hours orders began trickling through the chains of command and the US 7th Fleet began a blockade of the Korea coastline. USAF planes provided cover as around 600 American citizens and selected personnel from other countries were evacuated without incident. President Truman authorised the contribution of whatever forces and equipment might be available for "cover and support" of the ROK forces. Direct aid began on the second day of the war when the US transferred ten P-51 Mustang fighter planes to the South Koreans and convoys of military trucks started moving equipment and ammunition to USAF transport planes waiting at bases in Japan.[2]

At first the North Koreans blitzkrieg made rapid progress, quickly taking the South Korean capital of Seoul and driving back the South Koreans and their American advisors, but help was soon on its way. On June 27 a resolution sponsored by the American ambassador, Warren Austin, was passed by the United Nations Security Council, calling upon member nations to "render such assistance to the Republic of Korea as may be necessary to repel the armed attack and to restore international peace and security to the area." It was carried by a vote of seven to one, with Yugoslavia abstaining. That same day US Brigadier-General John H. Church arrived at Suwon airfield and quickly realised that the ROK army was in a state of impending dissolution. He informed General Douglas MacArthur that American ground troops would have to be committed to halt the North Korean advance and drive the invaders back to the 38th Parallel. (The USAF was already committed in a support role to the retreating ROKs.)

Two days later MacArthur himself flew into Suwon and insisted on driving up through the streams of fleeing refugees and disordered troops to the Han river, with its blown bridges, a barrier to the advancing NKPA. This trip convinced MacArthur that air and naval power alone would not retrieve the situation and requested the use of an American regimental combat team. He hoped to build this up to two divisions, but President Harry Truman, in a shock decision, gave MacArthur full authority to use whatever ground forces he had under his command in the Far East.[3] In a stunning reversal of its previous public policy Washington was moving to defend a country which was of negligible strategic value and posed no threat to US security. In less than twenty-for hours the first battalions of American infantry were being flown from northern Honshu to Pusan, in southern Korea. Five years after the defeat of Japan America was again at war.

The first Irishman to die in Korea did not belong to any of the many armies which fought up and down the peninsula, but was from the St. Columban's Order*. The Columban Father's had been in Korea since 1933 when nine Columbans on their way to missionary work in China received word to go to Korea instead. The previous year, Bishop Galvin, writing of the chaos in China, strongly advised,

"I think the society ought to look for some other field in which to work." Within five years of their arrival, the Columbans were entrusted with two missions, Kwangju and Chunchon. Their first years were dominated by harassment from the Japanese who occupied Korea since the turn of the century. This harassment culminated during World War II when all Columbans were either put in jail, placed under house arrest or deported. With the invasion of South Korea the Columbans saw seventeen years of patient effort wiped out as the advancing Communists spread terror, ruin and death over the land. Five Irish Columbans were murdered by the Communists and one died in prison; two survived the infamous "Death March" to North Korea.[4]

*The society, named in honour of St. Columban, an early Irish missionary monk, was founded in 1918 by Fathers Edward Galvin and John Blowick, at the celebrated seminary at Maynooth, Co. Kildare. The idea for the society began to grow in China, where Father Galvin, working under French priests, felt compelled to form an organisation in his native Ireland dedicated to bringing the Christian Gospel to the Chinese.[5]

When the surprise NKPA invasion began Monsignor Thomas Quinlan was saying mass a few miles from the border in Chunchon. "Our mission was only twelve miles from the border," he later said. "During the six o'clock mass we could hear the sound of the guns. Before last mass and benediction was over at 11 o'clock, the sounds had grown considerably louder." Tom Quinlan was from Borrisoleigh, Co. Tipperary. Born in 1896 he was one of the first students to start in the new mission seminary at Dalgan Park, Co. Meath, and was ordained in 1920 and sent to Hanyang, China, on missionary work. At this time there was a lot of turmoil in China and Fr. Quinlan was busily engaged in negotiating release terms for missionaries who were kidnapped or imprisoned. Following a visit to Ireland in 1933 Tom Quinlan was requested to begin a new mission in Korea in July 1934. During WWII Fr. Quinlan was put under house arrest by the Japanese. Following the war, Msgr. Quinlan was chosen as the Prefect Apostolic in Chunchon city. After a few years of relative calm Tom Quinlan's world was about to explode as Chunchon was in the direct line of the invading NKPA.

Throughout the day no mention of an invasion came over the radio, so Tom Quinlan attributed the sound of gunfire to just another skirmish, though a little more prolonged and intense than usual. At six o'clock that evening an official announcement of the invasion was made by radio and instantly the townspeople of Chunchon began to flee by train, truck and any means possible to Seoul. Later that evening Father Anthony Collier visited Quinlan from his parish across the city. Collier's church overlooked a bridge that would be a key position when the communists entered the city. He reported that a few of his parishioners had been hit by stray bullets, and he had given first aid to them. Tom Quinlan suggested he would be safer staying rather than returning to his parish. Collier replied: "I would prefer to stay with my own parishioners. Short of a direct hit by a shell I shall be safe in the residence. If the Reds capture the city, I might be of some help to my people." Fr. Collier returned to his parish, but Tom Quinlan never saw him again. Father Tony Collier was killed by North Korean soldiers, two days later.[6]

Tony Collier was in charge of the second Columban parish in Chunchon city. He was thirty-seven years old. Tony Collier was born in Cruisetown, Clogherhead, Co. Louth, on June 20 1913. He was educated in CBS, Drogheda, from 1921-1926 and St. Patrick's College, Armagh, from 1926-1931. He went to the St. Columban's Order, in Dalgan, Navan, in 1931 and was ordained there in 1938. Tony Collier was lively, humourous, talented, and an artistic cartoonist. In 1939 he went to Korea. On the day he left Tony's mother could not bring herself to say goodbye. According to his sister, Teresa, who died in 2004, their mother continued to make bread as the priest prepared to leave. Her husband came back into the house after Tony had left and said: "You should have said goodbye to him. We'll never have him home again." Tony's brother Kieran also became a Columban and served in Burma most of his life and died in recent years in Dalgan Park.

Back at the mission headquarters in Chunchon Tom Quinlan was visited by the American military attaché in the area. Colonel Hogge asked the Irishman to flee south to Wonju with him. Tom Quinlan thanked the American for his thoughtfulness but said his place was with his people. Then, Quinlan turned to his assistant Galwayman, Fr. Frank Canavan and said, "You're free to go. You are not responsible for this district. I'll give you my blessing and think of much of you as if you stayed." Fr. Canavan said he was staying. Col. Hogge said good-bye and left. So did most of the inhabitants of Chunchon. Fr. Quinlan said: "On Monday morning, (the second day of the war) the exodus of the townspeople was in full swing. People with bundles on their heads, in their hands, on their backs, people leading or carrying children, old people, young people. By noon, most of the 60,000 inhabitants had fled. I think not more than 500 people were in the town on Monday evening."

Earlier that day shells began to fall in Chunchon and in the course of the day several fell in the church grounds. Tom Quinlan was hit in the chin by shrapnel from one of them, but fortunately his wound was not serious. At dawn on Tuesday the communists stormed across the river, Chunchon's last natural line of defence, and forced the ROK troops to fall back. More shells landed in the mission grounds and both Quinlan and Canavan organised a fire-fighting team from the few mission servants and local Christians who had remained. As they fought one of the fires two North Korean soldiers appeared. They asked were the missionaries American and when the priests said they were Irish the soldiers' hostility diminished. They told the priests to carry on their good work - of trying to stop the spread of fires to neighbouring buildings - and left.

The immediate outcome of the communist invasion was a stunning success everywhere except Chunchon. Here determined ROKs held off three NKPA infantry assaults for three days. The North Koreans captured Chunchon only after ordering the tanks and the NK 7th Division heading south for Hongchon to turn back and close on Chunchon. When the communists arrived in Chunchon Fr. Tony Collier and his friend and helper, Gabriel Kim, a local convert to the Catholic faith, were walking to the post office when they were detained by NK soldiers. The two were tied together and marched down the street at gunpoint in the direction of the river. Without warning one soldier opened fire with a machine gun. Mortally wounded Fr. Collier fell to the ground, dragging Kim under him. The communists left the two men for dead, but Kim was still alive. Kim was wounded in the throat and shoulder and lay there beneath the body of his friend, for a day and two nights, trying hard to free himself from the stiffening corpse. He eventually broke free and lived to tell the tale of Fr. Tony Collier's last moments. He joined the throngs of refugees making their way south to Pusan and comparative safety.[7] News of Collier's death did not emerge until October of that year, when a cablegram from the Reverend Brian Geraghty, Superior of the Maynooth Mission in Korea, finally reached Dalgan Park. This sort of human tragedy stirred up Irish public interest in the Korean War and encouraged a natural anti-communism. *The Standard* added fuel to the fire with headlines such as Reds use tabernacle as target and running stories of Communist troops stamping on the sacred host.[8]

On Sunday, July 2, Tom Quinlan was saying mass when North Korean soldiers burst in. The few mass-goers fled in terror, but were forced to return. The soldiers were aggressive and abusive and demanded watches and fountain-pens. They hurled articles off the improvised altar and smashed the glass in cabinets. Both Frs. Quinlan and Canavan were led away, hands above their heads. They were brought to the local police station, interrogated and later put in the cells. They were sent on to Seoul where they joined other captive priests and missionaries, among them an Australian Columban, Fr. Philip Crosbie, who was arrested by North Korean police in Hongchon on July 6, and the Apostolic Delegate to Korea, Bishop Patrick Byrne. Sister Mary Clare (nee Clare Emma Witty) was also captured in Seoul on July 2. She was Irish by birth, having being born in Enniskerry, Co. Wicklow in 1883, but was a nun in the Church of England. She was Mother Superior in the Society of the Holy Cross, in the South Korean capital, when the communists arrived. The group of foreign missionaries were separated from the "unfortunate" Korean prisoners, who were daily harangued and tortured to "confess to crimes against the people." On July 21 the missionary group left for Pyongyang, the North Korean capital.[9]

Another missionary priest, Fr. James Maginn was killed a few days later, on July 4, two days after North Korean troops occupied Samchok, his parish on the east coast, about fifty miles south of the 38th Parallel. In the week between the outbreak of war and the occupation of his parish he had been urged by his people to leave but he refused to do so. Most of his parishioners were new converts who were afraid of the communists and Jim Maginn was not about to abandon them. North Korean soldiers took Jim as he was praying in his little one-room church. They beat him, and then three days later they shot him dead on a hill just outside the town. He was thirty-eight years old. It was not until March 1952 that his grave and body were located by Fr. Brian Geraghty. Jim Maginn was born in Butte, Montana, on November 15 1911 and was educated in St. Mary's Newcastle, Co. Down and St. Malachy's, Belfast. He went to Dalgan in 1929 and was ordained there in 1935, leaving for Korea the following year. He had spent fourteen years in Korea, including a brief term of imprisonment and eight years under police observation by the occupying Japanese. The North Koreans put pressure on Fr. Maginn's parishioners to declare themselves communists, but none went over to them.[10]

A few miles further down the coast in Mukho, Fr. Patrick Reilly went into hiding. Initially there was 1,100 Catholics in the town, but by the time the North Koreans arrived only about eighty remained. Fr. Patrick Reilly went to hide in the house of a catechist on June 28 or 29, when the NKPA occupied Mukho. The catechist's house was about five miles north-west of the town. After twenty-six days the North Koreans, acting on a tip-off, discovered Fr. Reilly's whereabouts. He was arrested and taken to the police station in Mukho. He was killed on August 29, though the exact details of his death are unknown. His body was found on a mountain path by an old man gathering wood. He had been shot through the chest. Paddy Reilly was thirty-five years old. He was born in Drumraney, Co. Westmeath, in 1915 and was ordained in Dalgan in 1940 and did pastoral work in the diocese of Clifton, England, for five years before going to Korea in 1947.[11]

Meanwhile, the Columbans further south felt safe. The action was hundreds of miles away, and nobody thought the communists would take over the whole country. On July 5, ten days after the invasion, Monsignor Patrick Brennan wrote from Mukpo to the order's superior general in Ireland. "There is no need to worry.

In fact, some of the padres are out digging up the ground for a good crop of tomatoes." However, within days the NKPA was outside Mukpo. An American officer arrived at the priests' house in Mukpo and advised them to leave. He assured them that it was only temporary, that in a few months the Americans would retake the area and everything would return to normal. The plan was to go by boat to the southern port of Pusan, where, if necessary, they could easily flee to Japan. Monsignor Brennan said it was his duty to stay. Fr. Thomas Cusack, the pastor in the area, also insisted on staying. The forty-year old native of Ballycotton, Liscannor, Co. Clare, had been in Korea since 1936, and had been imprisoned by the Japanese for four years.[12]

The assistant pastor, Fr. John O'Brien, said he too would stay. Born in Dunamon, Co. Roscommon, in 1918 Jack O'Brien was ordained in Dalgan in 1942. He served as a British Army chaplain from 1943-1948. Fr. Jack was chaplain to the 2nd Royal Ulster Rifles in the Normandy landings, serving with the battalion as it fought through France and Germany. The "tough rugby-playing padre" was much loved by all the ranks for his indomitable humour and unswerving courage. Jack O'Brien was well known for delivering "hot, sweet tea" on his motorcycle to the foremost frontline positions on operations. He continued to serve with the 2nd Ulsters in Egypt and Palestine until mid-1946. In 1949 he went to Korea as a missionary.[13]

About twenty, mainly Irish, Columbans and another dozen French missionaries left the area and headed to Pusan in a convoy. The Columbans were kept busy in Pusan. Every day three or four American troopships would arrive, many without chaplains, and so the refugee priests went to the piers to hear confessions and say Mass for troops about to go into battle. Some of the priests joined combat units as volunteer chaplains, adding to their duties that of interpreter. Probably the most famous volunteer was Father Frank Woods. A "late vocation" Frank Woods had been a barman in his native Dunleer, Co. Louth, before studying for the priesthood. Frank Woods volunteered his services as a chaplain to the US Army and joined the 2nd Battalion, 31st Infantry Regiment, of the US 7th Infantry Division because he knew the commanding officer from the military government days after WWII. For his conduct in action he received the highest decoration which can be given to a non-American citizen, the Medal of Freedom with Silver Palm.[14] Frank Woods' citation reads that he climbed a hill and shouted at a group of North Korean soldiers in Korean to give themselves up. It was thought only two wounded were there. About seventy-five men stood up, their hands over their heads. The citation concludes that with no thought of his personal safety Father Woods arranged for the surrender, reflecting the highest credit on himself and the US Army. After the war Frank Woods stayed on in Korea "working actively until his untimely death in 1973. Frank Woods' passing left a distinct vacuum in Columban life in Kwangju, representing as he did the popular idea of a missionary, as a tough out-of-doors type who could take things in his stride". [15]

Another Irish-born priest, Father Tom Neligan, and a fellow Columban brought two Catholic Korean families to safety in one jeep through 150 miles of guerrilla infested areas. In Pusan Fr. Neligan served as an auxiliary chaplain to thousands of American soldiers, sailors and marines. In the days of the Pusan Perimeter he heard confessions on the piers, troopships and camps of newly arrived GIs who were at the front a few hours later. He was one of the first band of nine Columban missionaries to enter Korea in 1933. During WWII he was imprisoned and later interned by the Japanese. He died just after the war ended after four months illness in an army hospital in Seoul.[16]

On July 24 a truckload of North Korean soldiers arrived at the church in Mukpo. Monsignor Brennan knelt down and began to say the rosary. The troops went away, but returned shortly and took Frs. Cusack and O'Brien prisoners long enough to march them around Mukpo. Then they brought them back to the rectory, saying they were not going to interfere with anyone's religious beliefs. But it was all a sham. The communists wanted the Catholics of Mukpo to feel at ease, so they could easily identify who the converts were. A few days later the three priests were detained and taken to Kwangju and then to the city of Taejon. An American prisoner, Lieutenant Alexander Makarounis, who spent some time in captivity with the priests in the following months, later wrote of them in the May

1951 issue of *The Far East.* "It would be hard to tell you what these men did for our morale - they boosted it by at least 500%...He'd (Monsignor Brennan) encourage Fr. O'Brien to sing us a song and do one of his Irish jigs. Fr. O'Brien had a good voice and the way he sang 'Far Away Places' sort of made you forget you were cooped up in a prison cell and sent your thoughts flying back home." On the way to a prisoner of war camp Fr. O'Brien helped the wounded Lt. Makarounis "along, and Father Cusack lent a hand to Monsignor Brennan. It was a sad procession!"

In Taejon the priests were separated from the military prisoners. "We do not know what happened," Lt. Makarounis wrote, "after we were taken from the cell. But wherever they are, I shall always remember them for the comfort, cheerfulness, kindness and courage they somehow communicated to us when they were no better off themselves." However, by late September, the American-led UN forces were advancing, driving back the North Koreans. The three priests, along with over a thousand other prisoners, were herded into a Franciscan monastery in Taejon. On the evening of September 24, all the prisoners were massacred in one of the worst outrages of the war. The bodies of Monsignor Brennan and Frs. Cusack and O'Brien were never recovered.[17]

Meanwhile up north Monsignor Quinlan and Fr. Canavan were taken into custody and took part in the notorious Death March to the far north of Korea. Along with them were many US POWs and some civilians, many of them missionaries. Commissioner Lord of the Salvation Army went to see the commander of the North Korean troops, who was known as "the Tiger.""These people will die if they have to march!" protested Commissioner Lord. "Then let them march until they die. This is a military order," said the Tiger.

The death rate from the hardships of the march was appallingly high. Many of the prisoners were old, and were weakened from months of captivity. They were marched north for nine days from dawn till dusk. Anybody who gave up was shot. Others just dropped dead from exhaustion, or died in their sleep. Most nights were spent in the open in the depths of the freezing Korean winter. Monsignor

Quinlan saw the Tiger himself fire a bullet into an American lieutenant's head. The lieutenant's offense was that he had allowed his men to rest because a guard had given him permission to do so.

Fr. Philip Crosbie, the Australian Columban, later wrote of the Death March in his book *March Till They Die.** "Our hearts ached with helpless pity as we came upon more and more sitting or lying exhausted by the roadside, attended always by guards, who waited ominously till we stragglers passed. Then, each time, we listened in dumb anguish for the sound that always came - the sound of a shot - behind us on the road."[18]

The three Columbans survived the march, but Sister Mary Clare did not. She died in her sleep on November 6 in Chunggang-jin, North Korea. Another nun who was present later wrote in the Catholic magazine, *Missions*, of the Irish sister's death. "This morning we found our dear sister Mary Clare, dead on her bed of straw. A person of deep Christian charity, she helped us in times of distress. With her companions who helped her so much on the forced march, we prepared her body for burial. We carried her on an improvised bier to the top of a neighbouring hill, quite close to the camp. We ourselves dug her grave, only so deep as our failing strength allows, and we laid her down there."[19]

The march ended on November 9 as the survivors reached the village of Chungkang more than a hundred miles farther north. Ninety-eight people had died from exhaustion, disease or were summarily murdered along the way. Within a month, on December 6, Fr. Frank Canavan, whose health was never robust,succumbed to pneumonia, as a direct result of hardships experienced on the Death March, In a prison camp In Hanjang-ni, North Korea. He had contacted pneumonia on the march and, although he was ill for some three to four weeks, he seemed to have recovered when suddenly he had a relapse. Born

*In Ireland the book was titled *Three Winter's Cold*, in America it was *March Till They Die* and in Australia the book was titled *Penciling Prisoner*.

in 1915 in Killursa, Co. Galway, he was known for his interesting stories about life in Ireland. He had only being in Korea for a year. Through great courage, self-sacrifice and determination, Monsignor Quinlan saved the lives of many prisoners. It was thought he died, too, but word filtered through in 1952 that both Quinlan and Crosbie were still alive.[20]

The first American troops to reach Korea were elements of the US 24th Infantry Division, one of four American divisions on occupation duties in Japan. (Each infantry division consisted of three fighting regiments, plus support troops. Field artillery and tank battalions were also integrated into divisions.) The 24th Division had been stationed in Japan since 1945 after battling through New Guinea and the Philippines. The other three divisions in Japan were 1st Cavalry, and 7th and 25th Infantry. The 7th Infantry Division had even spent some time in Korea as occupation troops and had only left the peninsula in 1948. However, as the occupying divisions remained in Japan on a whole, demobbed veteran troops had been sent home via the points system and were replaced by new inexperienced inductees and draftees. The divisions were undermanned and flabby; the men not even fit, because no one dreamed they would ever be needed. Japan was a comfortable posting, the troops, as one of their commanders said, had become accustomed to "Japanese girlfriends, plenty of beer, and servants to shine their boots." Five years before America had been militarily more powerful than any other nation in the world, but now it would be hard to push the NKPA back across the parallel. The atom bomb had made the American fighting man soft. GI's believed there was no longer any need for them to fight. Korea would be a rude awakening to the American military.[21]

The Americans assumed the fighting would take on a new aspect when they arrived. Task Force Smith, named after its commander, Lieutenant Colonel Charles B. Smith, arrived at the southern Korean port of Pusan and headed north on an exhausting odyssey by rail and truck to Osan, where on July 5 they encountered an armoured North Korean column. Smith's understrength battalion, committed against a far superior force, merely held up the communist advance for a few hours, for the loss of nearly two hundred men, a little less than a third of his strength. Out of condition and outnumbered by as much as twenty to one, the first US troops to arrive were for the most part green troops; fewer than twenty per cent of them had seen action in World War II. Their only anti-tank weapons were obsolete bazookas, hopelessly ineffective against the mighty T34 tank. Two more American battalions trying to block the NKPA advance were quickly brushed aside as the communists continued on to the important commu-nications centre of Taejon. One by one American units appeared in front of them and in a series of skirmishes were quickly battered and bruised and then hastily retreated in scenes of utter chaos and confusion, abandoning vehicles and equipment. In those early days many surrendered, but few prisoners were taken and American troops came across many cases of surrendered soldiers dumped in ditches with their hands tied behind their backs, shot and bayoneted. This had a sobering effect on American soldiers, who realised it was better to die fighting than to expect mercy from a ruthless and callous foe. (NK troops also slaughtered ROK troops, South Korean civilians and Western missionaries with regular abandon.)

The rout of the first American units stung the country's pride and helped recruitment. Patriotism was still strong in 1950 and many of the new recruits clamouring to join the armed forces were the younger brothers of men who had fought in World War II. America and its President were now truly aroused. Numerous reserve and National Guard units were being called up. Thousands of individual reservists not assigned to reserve units were called up and hastily assigned to units all over the globe, though most were destined for Korea. Recruiting drives were intensified and draft quotas increased, to put 600,000 men in uniform as quickly as possible. Many new immigrants to America, including hundreds from Ireland, were drafted to fight for their adopted homeland. Others did not wait to be drafted and volunteered for duty. However, few of the recruits were enthusiastic about fighting in Korea, a country few of them could find on a map. One GI, Stephen Zeg from Chicago, doubtless spoke for many of them, when he told a reporter: "I'll fight for my country, but I'll be damned if I can see why I'm fighting to save this hellhole."[22]

On July 19 the communists launched their attack on Taejon. The 24th Division lost 1,150 men in the disastrous battles around Taejon, but managed to hold the communist advance. On July 22 the battered division was finally withdrawn handing over the front-line positions to the 1st Cavalry Division. Despite its name the 1st Cavalry was equipped as an infantry division. The 25th Infantry Division also arrived but in its first encounter with the North Koreans its 24th Infantry Regiment broke and fled. On July 29 the 1st Cavalry Division, outflanked around Yongdong, began retreating towards Kumchong. The 25th Division held its positions until July 30 before being compelled to fall back. A North Korean division then hooked around Taejon and sped through the defenceless countryside southwards to the port of Pusan. The 25th Division was rushed to Masan, thirty miles from Pusan, to block the communists and stop them from encircling the Americans and South Koreans. In the first days of August American and ROK units headed south and east to a new line, known as the Pusan Perimeter. The next stop was Pusan and the sea. Here on the high ground behind the loop of the Naktong river, on the last mountain mass before the sea, the fate of the American Eighth Army, and of the United Nations in Korea, would be decided.[23]

The Pusan Perimeter was a rectangle about 100 miles long north to south and about fifty miles east to west. The south flowing Naktong river formed the western boundary except for a fifteen-mile stretch from the confluence of the Nam river and the Naktong to the Korea Strait in the extreme south. The northern flank ran from near Naktong-ni eastward through the mountains toward Yongdok on the Sea of Japan. Here the American and United Nations build-up began. There were now three American divisons, 1st Cavalry and 24th and 25th Infantry divisions, plus the 5th Regimental Combat Team and the 1st Marine Provisional Brigade. Both the 5th RCT and the Marines brought with them M26 Pershing tanks, finally giving the Eighth Army tanks to counter the T34. Complete air superiority and powerful tank and artillery reinforcements gradually helped the infantry forces effectively secure the perimeter.

Serving with the Headquarters Battery, 90th Field Artillery Battalion was Tipperary native, Sergeant Thomas J. O'Brien. Arriving in Korea with the 25th

Divisional Artillery in July 1950, the 90th Field Artillery Battalion furnished general supporting fires for the 25th Division's infantry regiments. On August 13, in the Pusan Perimeter fighting, while in support of the attached 5th RCT the 90th Field Artillery came under fierce attack by infiltrating North Korean infantry. The 105mm guns of their sister battalion, the 555th Field Artillery Battalion, were no match for the North Korean T34s and anti-tank guns and their positions were overrun by NK infantry. The 155mms of the 90th FA could not depress their tubes low enough to engage the NK tanks and guns and they had to withdraw losing all six of the howitzers it had emplaced. Under intense pressure the 90th FA was forced to withdraw while bringing out all their wounded. They lost ten killed, sixty wounded and thirty missing. For its gallantry the 90th was awarded a Presidential Unit Citation. Sgt. O'Brien was awarded a Bronze Star for leadership and gallantry. Born in Ballyvistea, Emly, Co. Tipperary, in 1927 Tom O'Brien emigrated to America after World War II and arrived in New York City to stay with an aunt and uncle. After a time he joined the US Army. A neighbour, Liam O'Duibhir, remembers attending school with Tom Joe, as he was known in the small village. He was a "very nice fellow, one of two brothers." An uncle of Tom O'Brien's was killed in action with the National Army during the Irish Civil War in the nearby Glen of Aherlow.[24]

By August 7 Eighth Army commander, General Walton Walker, was confident enough to begin offensive action and the first American counterattack began to recapture Chinju, west of Masan. Involved in the attack was the 35th Infantry Regiment, 25th Division. Serving with the 35th Regiment was Pfc. Thomas J. Ward, a native of Ireland, and the first Irish soldier to die in the Korean War. On 13 July 1950, the 35th (Cacti) Infantry Regiment, 25th Division, had landed at Pusan. Commanded by Colonel Henry G. Fisher the Regiment initially set up defensive positions with one battalion near Kyong-ju and the other at Pohang Dong. The 35th, like most other regiments coming from occupation duty in Japan, was minus its third battalion. In August the 25th Division was given the assignment to defend the southwestern sector of the 150-mile Pusan Perimeter. The Cacti Regiment was ordered to hold the Chung-ni-Masan route into the perimeter. On August 18 a strong communist attack hit the 1st Battalion, 35th

Infantry. A North Korean battalion struck Company A pushing it back, but rein-forced by Company C the battalion line was restored. Tom Ward was killed in action on August 22. Thomas J. Ward was born on October 20 1926 in Osman Street, off the Falls Road, Belfast. His father, Tom Ward, had served in the US Army in WWI. The family moved across the border to Carrickmacross, in County Monaghan, where Tom Ward Senior opened a shop and pub in the town's main street. Tom Ward emigrated to America, where he became an American citizen and was drafted into the US Army. His family received a letter of sympathy from General Douglas MacArthur, Commander-in-Chief, US forces. It read:

"Dear Mr. Ward,-
The untimely and tragic death of your son, Thomas, who met his death on the field of battle in Korea, has shocked all of us deeply. Some measure of comfort may be derived from the knowledge that he died in the service of his country and in defence of a peace-loving people.

"I am confident that in his devotion to duty, as the cost of all he held dear, will hasten the day when ruthless aggression will disappear from the face of the earth and free men will live together everywhere in peace and harmony.

"Our faith enables us to withstand the shock and grief of death. It is my earnest prayer that Almighty God will sustain and strengthen you in this hour of trial. While the loss of your beloved one will be a hardship, we know that no life is real-ly lost for those who have faith in God.
Sincerely yours, General MacArthur."[25]

As the United Nations build-up continued two regiments (the 9th and 23rd) of the US 2nd Infantry Division arrived in Pusan in August, along with the first elements of a promised British brigade: the 1st Battalion Middlesex Regiment and the 1st Battalion Argyll and Sutherland Highlanders. The 3rd Battalion Royal Australian Regiment soon arrived from Japan where it was conducting occupation duty and the three regiments were at first known as the 27th Infantry Brigade. They initially served with the US 24th Infantry Division. The 27th Brigade was re-designated the 27th Commonwealth Infantry Brigade in October when a Canadian regiment arrived. The Commonwealth Brigade was transferred to the US 1st Cavalry Division. Commonwealth troops serving in Korea eventually included British, Canadian, Australian, New Zealander, and South African contingents. At its highest strength the Commonwealth contribution amounted to 20,000 men. Thirteen countries had promised troops to the UN cause and while their the number of men produced was small - 44,000 in total compared to 300,000 Americans - their presence boosted American morale and did much to demonstrate the effectiveness of the United Nations when faced with a crisis.

With the arrival of more troops the North Korean command, knowing that its chances of breaking through to Pusan were declining day by day, unleashed a desperate general offensive along the Pusan Perimeter. The North Koreans assembled nearly 98,000 troops for the offensive, over a third of them raw recruits with little training. They were thrown at the American, British and ROK troops, who numbered 120,000. In the fierce battles that followed the North Koreans broke through at several points. In one of five main thrusts two divisions attacked the US 2nd Division, which had only recently gone into the line. Corporal Bartholomew Galvin was serving with the 23rd Regiment, 2nd Infantry Division. A native of Gorticurrane, Annascaul, Co. Kerry, Bart Galvin emigrated to America and settled in Weymouth, Massachusetts. He was drafted into the US Army and arrived in Korea from occupation duties in Japan. On September 1 North Korean troops crossed the Nam and Naktong rivers at numerous points and overran Company C of the 23rd Regiment, killing most of its members; only twenty men survived. Company B, emplaced north of Company C, also lost heavily and withdrew to the east. As the 9th and 23rd Regiments were sent reeling Cpl. Bart Galvin was reported missing in action. His body was later found.[26]

It took a further week of fierce fighting before the North Korean offensive was thrown back. This was the watershed of the North Korean advance. On September 3 the Americans counterattacked the Naktong Bulge and pushed the NK back two miles. A further three miles was gained the following day, but the

NK were still pressing hard north and west of Taegu and were still threatening near Masan. The success of these attacks panicked the American command in Taegu and there was talk of a last ditch stand at defensive positions just north of Pusan, the Davidson Line, which was laid out in August. As early as July 4 Gen. Douglas MacArthur had planned an amphibious landing at Inchon in the communists rear. Final plans for the assault were completed on September 4 and over 70,000 men were ready for the landing on September 15. However, if the NK offensive broke through the Inchon attack would have to be abandoned. As Eighth Army Headquarters prepared orders for the retreat to the Davidson Line to start on September 6 Bulldog Walker made a final decision: there would be no withdrawal. Eighth Army would stay and fight. As fierce battles continued the British 27th Brigade was committed to battle for the first time. Walker placed it north of the 2nd Division to block NK movement across the Naktong at the Yongpo bridge on the Koryang-Taegu road. With the British 27th Brigade were many Irishmen, regular soldiers with British regiments and support units.

On September 22 the 1st Battalion of the Argyll and Sutherland Highlanders moved across the Nantong River to support the left flank of a new American offensive against the North Koreans. The next day the Argyll and Sutherland Highlanders were engaged at Hill 282. After fighting their way to the top of the hill the Argylls were pounded by North Korean mortars. Waves of NK troops began attacking up the hill and the battalion CO called for air support. Recognition panels were laid out to warn American planes that two companies of friendly forces were on the top of the hill. The American Mustangs radioed back to their base that there were markers out but they were told there were no friendly forces on the hill and to proceed. The planes dropped napalm on the hill and strafed the occupiers who were, unfortunately, the Argylls. After several strafing runs the attack was called of as the Argylls managed to fire a recognition flare. Seeing the confusion the North Koreans counterattacked up the hill and a fierce battle ensued. The Argylls, by now outnumbered and trying to care for their many wounded, some of them horribly burned, had no choice but to retreat. The situation was quickly restored, however, when Major Muir, who had taken command of both companies, collected some thirty men and led them back.

Fierce close-quarter fighting followed, in which Major Muir showed the greatest courage and resourcefulness. He was eventually mortally wounded, and later posthumously awarded the Victoria Cross. As there were barely twenty men left unwounded in the two companies, it was impossible to hold Hill 282, and the Argylls reluctantly withdrew.   In this engagement the Argylls lost two officers and eleven men killed and four officers and sixty-nine men wounded.[27] One of those killed was Private Michael Dempsey, twenty-one, from Waterford. He was the first Irishman killed in action with the British armed forces.

2

Army of all Nations

Following the end of World War II Irish immigration began to renew to Britain, America, Canada, Australia and New Zealand. Apart from the natural course of hopping across the water to Britain, America remained the first choice of Irish immigrants. They arrived in their thousands to traditional Irish areas like New York, Boston, Chicago and San Francisco. Little had changed since the mid-nineteenth century when the country's most rural southern and western counties - Cork, Kerry, Galway, Mayo, Tipperary and Limerick - alone provided nearly half of southern Ireland's emigrants. By the mid-1950s, in an Ireland marked by economic stagnation and emigration, Cork, Kerry, Galway, Mayo, Donegal and Limerick provided fifty-five per cent of the emigrants from the Irish Republic. All these counties had large rural populations, poor quality land divided into numerous small land-holdings and few large towns. Between 1946 and 1961 over 500,000 people left Ireland - more than half of them women. Most went to Britain but 68,000 immigrated to America.

Until the 1930s, most emigrants from Ireland's western counties were more likely to emigrate to America than England. However, with the Depression work there became scarce, and Irish emigrants to America were required to provide £100 in capital or a guarantor. By the mid-1930s, England was, by necessity, the choice of many who had to leave Ireland. While the economic war with Britain further depressed the Irish economy, England's wartime economy (1939-45) and post-war boom attracted many Irish people to Britain. Even after the war there was so much work available that the flow of immigrants across the Channel continued unabated. In 1946 more than 30,000 from the Twenty-six Counties received travel permits to go to employment in Britain. Immigration continued in the following year at the same pace forcing the Catholic Hierarchy to issue a statement saying that the Bishops of Ireland "view with great alarm the excessive degree to which (emigration) has increased in recent years".[1]

With World War II over few Irish emigrants to America believed their services would be required by Uncle Sam. However, on March 17 1948 President Harry Truman signed the Selective Service Act requiring all males between the ages of eighteen and forty-five to register for the military draft. In due course all who did were called in for examination, and when the Korean War broke out in 1950 many young men were called up. As all Irish emigrants gave an American address it is hard to calculate how many served in the Armed Forces. Many Irish emigrants could have opted out of armed forces service by taking advantage of the special exemption which was included in the 1950 Irish American Treaty of Friendship, Commerce and Navigation, but most decided to discharge what they regarded as their duty to their newly adopted country. By taking advantage of the waiver the Irish could have refused to serve, but in exchange had to waive the right to become American citizens. Obviously, most wanted to become US citizens and thought their new home was a country worth fighting for. Gerry Fox felt if he was "happy enough to earn his bread and butter there" he "was happy to serve his adopted country" in its time of need. Gerry Fox emigrated from Dublin to Chicago in 1950 and was drafted the following year. He served a year in Korea with the 2nd Infantry Division and "was very, very proud of being involved in the US Army."[2]

When the Korean War broke out the US military, according to General Mattew B. Ridgway, was in a state of "shameful unpreparedness".[3] The US Army had ten combat divisions, the equivalent of another division occupying Germany, and nine separate regimental combat teams. Most of these units were understrength. In addition the US Marine Corps had the Fleet Marine Force, which was less than the equivalent of a single war-strength marine division. Reserve and National

Guard units were hastily called up and the men sent to fill up vacancies in standing units. Most were headed for Korea and many officers and non-commissioned officers who had served in WWII found themselves back in uniform and flung into their second war. While it seemed unfair, without them the US Armed Forces would not have been able to train men quick enough to "hold the line".[4] Not everybody waited to be called up. As in previous calls to arms men from all walks of life flocked to recruiting stations. Other recruits came from newly arrived immigrants, eager to prove themselves worthy of American citizenship. (However, you had to wait five years before becoming a US citizen and those who were killed in action before that happened never gained their citizenship. It was not until 2003 and a lengthy campaign by other Irish veterans, that twenty-eight Irish-born soldiers killed in action, or died in accidents, in Korea, were finally granted citizenship.)

John T. Jennings, from Knockmore, Co. Mayo, emigrated from Newtown, Enfield, Co. Kildare, where his family had settled, in 1948 to live and work in New York City. He was drafted into the US Army in early 1951. "I was not yet a citizen nor was I not the only Irishman drafted. There were numerous other recent arrivals from Ireland who, like me, felt it would be an honour to serve our newly-adopted homeland. We believed as deeply then as we do now that with sacrifice and hard work America would provide ourselves and our families, here and in Ireland, with the greatest rewards. What we didn't know was that a number of us who left for Korea in 1951 would never get the chance to experience the American Dream. The following is a brief version of my experience as a young Irish American soldier in Korea. For those of you who have had husbands, fathers and relatives who served in the US Army during that time, I hope it sheds a little light on their experiences in that faraway land so many years ago. Volumes have been written describing the Korean War as the 'Cold War', the 'Forgotten War', the 'Korean Police Action', the 'Korean Conflict' when, in fact, it was a fully-fledged war engaged in by the United Nations to prevent Russia from spreading its brand of Communism to other parts of the Globe.

"At the outset of the invasion, Reserves and National Guard divisions were activated in the United States and all men under the age of 26 had to register for the draft. When leaving Ireland in 1948 in order to qualify for a permanent visa I took an oath that if called upon I would bear arms in defence of the United States. Draft registration for me took place on December 20, 1950, at Morris High School on Arthur Avenue in the Bronx. The next day I was sent to 185 Whitehall Street in Manhattan for my physical. I was classified 1A, which qualified me for induction into the US Army on February 20, 1951. All those inducted on that day were transported by bus directly to Fort Devens in Massachussetts.

"The first morning at Fort Devens we were up at 5:00 am and ordered to go next door to the barbershop. One didn't have to tell them how you wanted your haircut - they already knew! Crew-cut starting at the forehead - the hair flying in all directions reminded me of forting hay on a windy day. This was followed by two days of multiple choice tests and interviews. Following the results of the tests we were assigned new classifications and transported to training divisions all over the United States. I was sent to Fort Jackson, South Carolina - from the snow in Fort Denver to the scorching heat of South Carolina. Several hundred of us were assigned to the 31st Infantry Division, also known as 'All White' Dixie 31st, a National Guard Division from Mississippi and Alabama. They were activated two weeks earlier. It was like the blind leading the blind. All but the draftees - eight of us in a unit - had rank. The Southern boys were no more familiar with assembling the trigger mechanism of an M-1 rifle than we were.

"Basic Training - Rifle, pistol, bazooka, machine gun, hand grenade and hand-to-hand combat. Up at 4:00 am, roll call, march, chow, more marching, inspections, bivouac, more marching ... through swamps in torrential rain, through swarms of fire flies, reminding me of "Willie the Wisp", infiltration courses where we crawled on our bellies under rows of barbed wire while live rifle and machine gun fire whizzed and pinged directly above our heads. During the constant daily marches we eight Yankee draftees had an insubordination problem in that the Southerners spoke a dialect we had never heard before. A Southern non-coms command for 'Right flank' generally had the Northern conscripts carrying out a

'Left flank' or the opposite of the Southern soldier. An officer standing nearby would roar 'Halt'. He understood the sergeant's command but we didn't. The first Saturday the lieutenant speaking through his nose while reading the Articles of War from a book picked me to explain the article such and such. My response was: 'Sir, I do not understand a word you are saying but if you give me the book I will answer all of your questions by tomorrow.' He gave me the book.

"At the end of the fourteen weeks basic training convoys of trucks took us to the Citadel in Charleston, South Carolina - roughly 100 miles away - to go swimming in the lake. When a dark-skinned Cuban draftee from our company entered the water all the locals jumped out of the lake and began shouting about the black solider dirtying the lake (they didn't use the word black). Senior officers eventually convinced the locals that the soldier was Caucasian (Cuban) otherwise he could not be a member of the All-White Dixie Division. A few days later I was given $127 and ordered to report to Fort Lawton, Washington State, within two weeks, my first trip west of NYC and now I was on my way to Korea. I returned to New York and eventually Penn Station to purchase a ticket to Seattle at the cost of $115. Travel time was three days. I asked an agent about meals and he said: 'No meals'. A gentleman further back the line shouted: 'Soldier! Contact Flying Tiger Airlines in Connecticut'. This I did and ended up booking a flight at the cost of $109. From there it felt like I joined the US Air Force. My flight from Newark, New Jersey to Seattle took 28 hours that included seven refuelling stops in seven different cities along the way.

"Fort Lawton, Washington, was a 'pipeline to Korea' camp, where they took away clothing and re-issued battle clothing and newer weapons. One memory from the camp was that while waiting on the chow line, all of us were inoculated in both arms with six different vaccines to protect us from every known disease on earth. Three days later I was transferred to Fort Lewis, Washington where 3,100 of us boarded, by number, a 'small' troopship the *Marine Phoenix*. The sleeping compartments were laced with canvas bunks, four high. The ship broke down twice leaving us bobbing about, poor sea legs and all in the middle of the Pacific Ocean. Two weeks later we disembarked in Yokohama, Japan. On arrival I was handed a letter all the way from my mother in Ireland, which began, 'Ye are like the wild geese agraw, one son in Korea, one in the U.S. waiting to be drafted, one at home, one in England and I don't know where APO 7 SF is!' We billeted (slept in tents) at Camp Drake, Japan. Up at 6 am, breakfast at 6:30 then on two days later back again on the *Marine Phoenix* and on to Korea, that is Inchon, Korea." J.T. Jennings arrived in Korea in August 1951 and was assigned as a medic to the 32nd Infantry Regiment, 7th Infantry Division. His two brothers, Tom and Ned, were also drafted. Tom served in Korea with the 1st Cavalry Division, while Ned served his time in the US. In his time in the service J.T. Jennings met several fellow Irishmen in the Armed Forces: Captain Michael Kavanagh, Westport, Mayo, 32nd Infantry Regiment, 7th Infantry Division; Mark Rowland, Larthdrane, Co. Leitrim, 17th Regt., 7th Infantry Division; and Paddy Boyle, Balla, Co. Mayo, who was later wounded in action.[5]

The American replacement system in Korea was known as the Pipeline. Unlike the British army practice of creating a home for the officer and soldier in the regiment, whose individual battalions were kept intact as much as possible, the American system was in direct contrast. In practice an American unit might remain in combat situations for weeks or months, while individual soldiers were rotated in and out. The British practice was to rotate whole battalions in and out, while the individual men in each battalion remained together. Replacements came from a home depot where soldiers were taught the identity and traditions of their regiment. The American system was to fill up depleted units with replacements from across the United States, which left little sense of identity and loyalty to fellow soldiers who they did not know and might have no geographical ties to.

Most American units remained in Korea for the duration of the war and were topped up with replacements as men rotated home or were killed or wounded. A collection of strangers is not a cohesive and viable combat entity and to create such an organisation needs time, familiarity and a common sense of purpose. The American system did not promote this or security for the individual soldier. Especially in the first weeks of the war when replacements were assigned to units, thrown into battle, and killed or wounded before anyone even knew their name. However, combat bonds men together quickly and in platoons and companies an amazing and mutually supportive system closely akin to a family develops. The longer soldiers were together, plus the quality of their officers and non-coms, tended to mould individual units into a "band of brothers".

Some Irish emigrant draftees were luckier than those sent to Korean war zone. Pat Healy was sent to Germany, while fellow Cork man Tom Daly, who joined the army on the day the Korean War broke out, was sent to England. Mike Keating, from Mitchelstown, Cork, was sent to the Far East, but his posting was Japan. He left Ireland in 1949, was drafted the following year and in August 1951 arrived in Japan. After "four-five months training in Aberdeen Proving Grounds, in Maryland, some were sent to Germany, Japan or Korea." Mike Keating had a "flair for mechanics and was sent to Japan to an ordinance unit, 8186 Army Unit, repairing tanks, trucks and ammunition carriers damaged in Korea, at Camp McGill outside Yokohama. It was a large garage with 1,500 Japanese personnel and six to eight Americans looking after them. It was a nice assignment. After our work was done we had *carte blanche* liberty to do what we wanted. I was glad to do it, though I was hoping I wouldn't be sent to Korea, but if I wound up in Korea, so what. That's the way it was. No matter where I wound up, it was all an adventure."[6]

The United States emerged from WWII richer and far more powerful than it had ever been, while Britain emerged practically bankrupt, no longer a world power. When Germany and Japan surrendered in 1945 most people in Britain thought there would be many years of peace. Unfortunately after the war ended, the victorious nations were soon divided into two opposing groups, and Britain felt bound to maintain large military forces and spend immense sums of money, which it could ill afford, providing them with modern equipment. The army kept about four divisions in Germany and in addition large numbers of troops were kept in India, the Middle East, Malaya, Kenya, and Aden, together with garrisons in places like Malta and Gibraltar. To keep the forces up to the strength required the government had to continue conscription and from 1945 about half the regular army consisted of "national servicemen" conscripted for eighteen months. With the outbreak of the Korean War this was extended to two years, in order that conscripts over nineteen could serve in Korea. After serving with the regular army national servicemen had to do a year's part time service with the Territorial Army or the Army Emergency Reserve. Anyone living and working in Britain who had a National Security number were entitled to do their National Service and many Irish who had crossed the Irish Sea to work on the rebuilding of war-torn British cities ran the risk of being conscripted. (Ireland was not declared a Republic until 1949 and until then all citizens of the country had, under the terms of the Anglo-Irish Treaty of 1921, dual membership and could hold an Irish and a British passport.)

Korea was an unpopular posting, as indeed was Palestine or Malaya, or anywhere young conscripts were at risk. The main reason for poor recruitment to the army, apart from the lure of high employment outside, lay in poor conditions of service. Pay was derisory. Living conditions in worn-out and poorly maintained barracks were hardly conducive either to extension of existing regular engagements or as an inducement to sign-up. The youth of Britain had had their fill of war and were not eager to fight in a country that few could find on a map and was not even part of the Empire. The main effort of the regular soldiers was devoted to training conscripts, a task heartily detested by many. However, the outstanding performance of national servicemen in Korea and elsewhere would show, that it was performed with remarkable efficiency. Young conscripts - eventually around 16,000 - fought well in Korea and adapted quickly to the rough conditions. Jimmy Durney emigrated from Callan, Co.Kilkenny, to live and work in England and was conscripted and sent to Korea.

William May left North Wall, Dublin, to stay with his sister in London when he was fifteen. At eighteen he had to register for conscription and in early 1950 he received a letter detailing him to an enlisting depot. At the time he was working in a leading London advertising agency. Friends advised him to apply for the Inland Transport. He was sent to Seaforth Barracks in Liverpool and assigned to the Royal Irish Fusiliers training depot in Ballykinlar, Co. Down. (Back in Ireland anyone who did not want to stay in the army simply got the bus or train across the Border on their first leave and never returned.) After three months basic training Billy May was sent to Germany to the British Army of the Rhine. While there he heard of the outbreak of the Korean War and the extension of National Service from eighteen months to two years. "The (radio) speaker was taken off the wall and kicked around - but we had to pay for it later." Billy May was sent to Korea with a reinforcement draft for the Royal Ulster Rifles and served four months on the frontline. He "didn't mind doing his National Service as everyone was doing it. I just wanted to get it over with it, and wanted to stay in England."[7]

There were many Irishmen serving in the British armed forces after World War II. Some were war veterans and some had joined after the war. The reasons were as diverse as they had always been: some were escaping poverty and unemployment, others were following a family tradition, while some were just looking for adventure. A few Irishmen serving in the British forces were not too far away from Korea. Joe O'Connell, left Newbridge, Co. Kildare, after the war looking for work and ended up in the British Army. After service in Germany he was in India when the war broke out and was sent on to Korea. Tom Lane, from Moneyvroe, Cappoquin, Co. Waterford, was in the Royal Air Force at the time and transferred to the Royal Irish Fusiliers. However, he did not arrive in Korea until 1954 by which time the war was over. He had joined the RAF in 1946 after serving two years in the Irish army. At twenty shillings a week for a British private soldier the pay was twice that of the Irish army.[8]

Gervase Murphy, from Bangor, Co. Down, joined the Royal Ulster Rifles at the end of World War II, but after three years soldiering left to further his education. He went to Trinity College, Dublin, where the Government Further Education Scheme paid his fees. In Ireland at the time he said there "was a lot of talk about the Royal Ulster Rifles and a lot of admiration for what they accomplished." He felt "emotionally connected, as my old regiment was involved." However, there was not a lot of talk in Trinity about the Korean War, except among ex-servicemen."Ex-servicemen are always interested where a war is concerned," Gerry Murphy recalled. "You felt lucky not to be involved and also a bit sorry, a bit of regret at not been there. At that time I didn't really know I would be returning to the army." Gerry Murphy was ordained in 1952 and in gratitude for his further education returned to the army as a chaplain. In 1955 he was sent to Korea with the Royal Army Chaplain Department ministering to British troops serving on the 38th Parallel. While there he made a special journey to pay his respects to the memorial for the men of the Royal Ulster Rifles who died in Korea.[9]

In keeping with Australian tradition conscription was phased out as soon as WWII ended. Three battalions of volunteers were raised for service with the British Occupation Forces in Japan, and they became the nucleus of Australia's post-1945 army and its first regular field force for immediate action in a national emergency. When South Korea was invaded Australia was one of the first member states to promise aid to the UN mission. On August 21 1950 the K (Korea) Force recruiting campaign was initiated in Australia. Recruits could join the Australian Armed Forces just to serve in Korea. The raising of K Force was the last time that a volunteer force was raised in Australia to serve in a particular conflict. The following year National Service was introduced. All Australian males aged 18 had to register for 176 (later 140) days of training. The three regular battalions of the Australian Army saw service in Korea and by the time the Armistice was signed in 1953, 278 Australian soldiers had been killed in action, two of them were natives of Ireland.

While thousands of Irishmen were heading for Korea under the United Nations banner there did not seem to be any faith in the workings of the UN in Irish political circles. The Korean War was the first test of the United Nations and would show whether the organisation could overcome its divisions and be an effective body. Russia used the war to test the resolve of the Western powers and the United Nations and found neither wanting. Irish confidence in the UN was renewed by its actions in Korea and the United Nations success in Korea ensured that Ireland still sought to join it. If it had falled In Korea than it would have been seen as a doomed organisation. Two years after the ending of the Korean War Ireland joined the United Nations.[9]

3

On to the Yalu

On September 15 the 1st Marine Division and the 7th Infantry Division landed at Inchon, some 30km from Seoul. Codenamed "Operation Chromite," the landing at Inchon was the largest amphibious operation undertaken since World War II. It was a bold and daring attack - MacArthur's masterstroke. Writing in his acclaimed biography of Douglas MacArthur, *American Caesar*, William Manchester wrote Inchon is "about as large as Jersey City, as ugly as Liverpool and as dreary as Belfast".[1]

More than 230 ships were assembled for the invasion. Most came from the United States, but others came from the Royal Navy, the Royal Australian, Canadian and New Zealand Navies, the ROK Navy and the French Navy, as well as specially chartered merchantmen. Rear Admiral James H. Doyle, an Irish-American from Jamaica, New York, was commander of the amphibious group. It was decided to use the 1st Marine Division and the 7th Infantry Division for the landing.

The 1st Marine Division had two regiments fresh from America, while it's 5th Regiment was extricated from the Pusan Perimeter for the operation. The 7th Division was the sole remaining formation of the US occupying troops in Japan, as the other three divisions were already fighting in Korea. The division had been constantly milked to build up the numbers of its sister divisions in Korea and had to receive a total of 390 officers and 5,400 men, almost all of them from training establishments in America and of high quality, when the division was alerted for the Inchon operation. A further 8,000 South Koreans were pressed-ganged into service with the division and given only the most basic training.[2]

The marines made the initial landing against light opposition, while the 7th Division landed the following day and advanced inland to the south and east of Seoul. The first in were the 3rd Battalion, 5th Marines, who captured Wolmi-do Island only sustaining seventeen wounded. The 1st and 5th Marine Regiments landed at Red and Blue Beach and by nightfall had reached the main road from Inchon to Seoul. At the end of D-Day all objectives had been taken for the loss of twenty-one men killed, one missing and 174 wounded. The North Koreans lost a large number of men, including 300 prisoners. The Inchon landings took the North Koreans completely by surprise. Aware of the extreme difficulty the UN had been operating in the Pusan Perimeter, they did not dream that they would be able to launch a full-scale invasion of the north. It took the NKPA two days to realise that the invasion was real and not a feint. By that time Inchon was secured and the vital airfield at Kimpo was falling into the hands of the marines.

Charles Dennehy, Staigue, Cahirdaniel, Castlecove, Co. Kerry, went ashore with the 7th Infantry Division. He was serving with K Company, 3rd Battalion, 32nd Infantry Regiment. Born in 1930, the youngest of fourteen children, Charles only met his older siblings when he emigrated to New York in 1947. He remembered there was plenty of work around Kerry, but no money. A friend and schoolmate of his, John White, also emigrated and served in Korea with the US Marines. They went to school together and made their communion and confirmation together. After a period living and working in the Bronx and Queens Charles Dennehy joined the US Army at the Times Square recruiting station in July 1949, signing up for three years. Charles went through his sixteen weeks basic training at Fort Dix, New Jersey, with the 9th Infantry Division, and then was posted to the 3rd Infantry Division at Fort Devens, Massachusetts. He had applied for duty in Germany in May 1950 from where he planned to visit home.

The process usually took about a month but the Korean War broke out before his application went through and instead he found himself shipping out to the other side of the world. After a period of amphibious training in Norfolk, Virginia, and more exercises in the Caribbean, Charles Dennehy was sent to Japan to the 32nd Regiment, 7th Infantry Division. (At the time the 32nd Infantry Regiment was formed in Hawaii it was given the title "The Queen's Own Regiment", by the last Queen of Hawaii. In Korea the 32nd Infantry Regiment was known as "The Buccaneer", because of its ability to move quickly and strike hard.) In Japan the 7th Division were earmarked for the Inchon invasion and the division underwent six weeks of intensive training for the purpose. Charles Dennehy recalled his intensive training day and night and remembered sleeping in an old Japanese pillbox on Mount Fujiyama.

At that time the 7th Infantry Division had already posted almost 10,000 of its officers and men to divisions in Korea and was seriously understrength. Over 8,000 South Korean civilians were rounded up, and press-ganged into the 7th Division and Charles Dennehy remembers the "recruits" forced to sing the Republic of Korea national anthem day and night. One South Korean was teamed with one American who was supposed to teach the Korean how to be a soldier. (This was known as the "buddy system.") American and Korean habits and characteristics were greatly different leading to much confusion and misunderstanding.

American infantry and artillery reinforcements from the US were also allotted to the division and some were combat veterans. Others had being on occupation duties in Japan and had a good knowledge of Japanese, a language which, because of the long history of Japanese occupation, most Koreans could speak. Sitting in a foxhole at night the South Koreans learnt their American "buddy" basic Japanese so they could communicate. However, the ROK soldiers were not known by their names but by a number, usually in Japanese. Charles Dennehy "really liked the Koreans. They were a very humble people. The men always walked ahead of the women to protect them." While by September the division was at full strength (24,845), less than half of these were effectively trained for the battle. After six days of loading supplies and equipment the division embarked at Yokohama for Inchon. The laced canvas bunks onboard ship were nine high. "The ROKs were put in the top bunks and the Americans on the bottom bunks. But when the ROKs got seasick, it came down on top of the Americans, whose language was choice."

On the second day of the invasion troop transports carrying the 7th Infantry Division arrived in Inchon Harbour. As many of the GIs expressed it in the letters they wrote home. "You could sure smell Korea a long time before you saw it!" General Almond was eager to get the division into position to block enemy movement from the south. On the morning of September 18, the 2nd Battalion, 32nd Infantry Regiment, landed at Inchon and the remainder of the regiment went ashore later in the day and immediately began moving toward 1st Marine positions on the Seoul Highway. "We landed by landing craft, running left and right. You never run straight out of a landing craft, as the ramp might hit your legs," Pvt. Charles Dennehy said. "Just as we landed they opened up. The North Koreans had tanks. Russian T34s. As we went up to the front we met loads of wounded coming back in jeeps - Americans and ROKs covered in blood." Using the Seoul-Inchon highway as its route the 32nd Infantry moved up against Tongdok Mountain. The North Koreans had planted a field of box mines along the road, and the 32nd lost three tanks in moving through. By evening the 32nd Infantry had relieved the 1st Marines on the south side of the Han river. The regiment suffered forty-three casualties in its first day of fighting. The next morning, the 2nd Battalion moved up to relieve marines occupying positions on the right flank south of Seoul and responsibility for the zone south of Seoul highway passed to the 7th Division.[3]

On September 20 the battleship *Missouri* directed its huge 16-inch guns inland in support of the 7th Division, moving south to protect the marines flank and blocking any NK troops coming up from the Naktong front. The 32nd Infantry Regiment captured Tongdok Mountain and Cooper Mine Hill as the 7th Division swung east and south out of the Inchon beachhead, while the 1st Marine Division crossed the Han River, the last natural barrier to the capitol city, Seoul. The 32nd

Infantry was held up by minefields as it attacked to Anyang-ni, but by September 21 they had captured Anyang-ni and Yongdungpo cutting the main supply lines to NK troops in the south. K Company joined an armoured force sent to Suwon. The lead American tank was knocked out by a T34, but American M26s soon knocked out two NK tanks while the remainder fled. The next morning the armoured column drove through the deserted town of Suwon, passing the bodies of several Americans killed in the previous day's encounter. The big event of September 22 was securing Suwon Airfield and opening it to United Nations traffic. This field, twenty-one miles south of Seoul, could accommodate the large C-54 transport planes with its 5,200- foot runway. Charles Dennehy witnessed his first combat action near Suwon airfield. "I remember one North Korean coming at a tank with a shovel, screaming. The tank's fifty calibre machine gun cut him to pieces."[4]

Dissatisfied with the marines' progress General Edward "Ned" Almond, MacArthur's chief of staff, ordered the 7th Infantry Division and its 32nd Regiment into the battle for the envelopment of the enemy defences in Seoul. Twenty-one year old Irish native Pfc. John Corcoran was also serving with the 32nd Regiment. (Despite the fact that both Charles Dennehy and John Corcoran were serving in the same regiment, neither was aware of the other's presence. Charles Dennehy said he never met any other Irishmen while serving in Korea.) Born in Coolikerane, Millstreet, Co. Cork, John Corcoran had emigrated to the US and settled in Lafayette, Louisiana. He had joined the US Army in 1949. As the marines faced stiffening resistance around Seoul the 7th Division prepared to envelop the NK defences from the south by crossing the Han river into the capital city. On the cold morning of September 25 the 32nd Regiment and the ROK 17th Regiment crossed the Han at the ferry-site of Sansa-ri, three miles east of the main rail and road bridges over the river. After a heavy artillery and mortar barrage, the 2nd Battalion assault force, mounted in marine amphibious vehicles brought in especially for the crossing, churned over the river without the loss of any men or equipment. The infantrymen moved quickly up Nam-sam (South Mountain) and captured it without loss.

The 1st and 3rd Battalions moved across the Han behind the assault force, then turned eastward toward the nearest hill objective. Here the Americans became victims of a "friendly fire" incident. Their forward observer erred in the range and American 4.2in mortars fell on their positions wounding and killing many in the company. John Corcoran was mortally wounded. He landed on his buddy, Paul Olivier, also from Lafayette, literally saving his friend's life. John Corcoran was evacuated to Japan, but died of his wounds in Osaka Hospital on October 2. His friend Paul Oliver survived and tends John's grave at home in Lafayette.[5]

On the morning of September 26 the 3rd Battalion, 32nd Infantry moved out from a position east of South Mountain to capture Hill 106, which was two miles away. After a brief fierce battle the North Korean defenders were routed and the drive up the hill became relatively easy. The Americans set up a roadblock at the bottom of the other side of the hill and spent the day clearing up isolated groups of North Koreans. It was dangerous and deadly work and the 32nd suffered another fifty or so casualties. By now the marines were fighting in the suburbs of Seoul and the ROKs had captured the hills east of the capital. E Company established contact with the marines on the regimental left at the western base of South Mountain. The city was soon sealed off with the 32nd Infantry on the southern route. The North Korean commander in Seoul decided that the city was doomed and began the withdrawal of certain units while leaving others to fight desperate delaying actions. The main North Korean forces evacuated the city and streamed northward by every unguarded road and path, but its delaying force launched desperate counterattacks at every point of the American advance into the city.[6]

After three days of sporadic fighting Seoul was cleared of NK troops and the Inchon landing ended in total victory. MacArthur's vision had been proved accurate and the doubts raised by his superiors proved to be unfounded. Douglas MacArthur's stature rose precipitously. On September 29 he led South Korean president Syngman Rhee through cheering crowds to Government House in Seoul and personally returned Rhee to the center of power in Korea on "behalf of the United Nations Command." Seoul after the fighting, recalled

Charles Dennehy, was a "heap of rubble".[7] The civilian populace had suffered heavily and thousands were killed and injured in the bitter fighting as most of the remaining defenders had chosen to fight to the death. The next day the 1st Marine Division assumed responsibility for the 32nd Infantry zone in Seoul and the Buccaneers crossed back to the south side of the Han river.

With the capital in the bag, the 7th Infantry Division turned its attention to the south. The Division continued to drive toward the southeast to seize key terrain, and also to cut off possible enemy escape routes. At Osan, site of the Communist tank breakthrough against the 24th Division some sixty days earlier, the 7th Division linked up with the flying column from the 1st Cavalry Division, which had raced 102 miles from the Naktong, through enemy-held country, to clear the way for the joining of the two American forces. With the arrival of troops from the Pusan Perimeter the mission of the Inchon landing force was complete, and the 7th Infantry started a long overland truck drive to the port of Pusan. Since the Inchon landing the 32nd Infantry Regiment had captured 1,203 prisoners and intimated it had killed 3,000 enemy troops, for a loss of sixty-six killed, 272 missing and forty-seven missing.

However, the commanders of 7th Infantry were not entirely satisfactory in the division's performance. In the later stages of the drive on Seoul the 7th Division had not kept in touch with the 1st Marine Division on their left, which had cost them the marines' trust. This was a problem of command, not of the fighting men. The 7th Division had performed very well against stiffening opposition and were just fresh from the US and no better trained than the rest of the American army at the time. A hasty field-training programme was initiated, but this ended abruptly when sixteen men were killed and eighty wounded, from 17th Regiment, by white phosphorous bombs from their own 4.2in mortar company during a demonstration exercise. At Pusan more amphibious training began for the next phase: the drive to the Yalu river. In a badly thought and ill-planned operation to cut off retreating NKPA forces MacArthur withdrew both the 7th Infantry Division and the 1st Marine Division for a planned amphibious landing on the north-east coast of Korea.

As the Inchon landing was getting underway Eighth Army began its offensive to break out of the Pusan Perimeter. However, the NK troops had heard nothing of the landing in their rear and put up determined resistance to the US, ROK and British Commonwealth attacks. (With the arrival of the 3rd Battalion Royal Australian Regiment, that month, the British 27th Brigade was renamed the 27th Commonwealth Brigade. The brigade was attached to the US 1st Cavalry Division. Other allied elements arrived throughout the month, including Thai, Greek and Dutch forces.) By September 23 word had filtered through to NK lines of the Inchon landing and their units were soon in full flight northward. Signs of panic and disintegration began to quickly appear. All across South Korea, desperate North Korean soldiers tried every means to escape northwards as all sense of cohesion disintegrated. Some fought tenaciously while others simply just watched the Americans drive by in their tanks and trucks and made no effort to stop them. In other cases some laid down their arms and meekly walked to the POW camps, while others disappeared into the hills to conduct a guerrilla campaign in the UN rear. Advancing Americans and South Koreans found many cases of communist massacres and murders of American and ROK military personnel and of civilians. Between 1,000 and 2,000 civilians were killed in the city of Wonju alone.

On September 28 ROK troops advanced north of the 38th Parallel. American units waited impatiently for the signal to follow them. While American and British politicians wangled MacArthur declared that unless the North Koreans laid down their arms he would take "such military action as may be necessary to enforce the decrees of the United Nations."[8] On October 7 the UN General Assembly endorsed an American proposal that the UN objective was the establishment of "a unified, independent and democratic government" of all Korea.[9] However, as the Russians tried to distance themselves from events in Korea, alarming signals began to appear from Peking. The Chinese foreign minister declared that the People's Army would not stand aside if the UN crossed the parallel and would send troops to defend the Korean frontier. The Americans thought they were bluffing. US Defence Secretary George Marshall wired MacArthur to "proceed" and "let action determine the matter".[10] On October 9 Eighth Army advanced in full force across the Parallel at first encountering fierce resistance. Within a week the North Koreans broke and headed northward in full flight. The Americans, South Koreans and British began a headlong pursuit. It looked like the war would finally be over in a few weeks and the troops would be home for Christmas. The Chinese declared the UN resolution as illegal and said American troops were menacing Chinese security. While MacArthur wired Washington that he saw no indication of "major Soviet or Chinese Communist forces" Mao's divisions began to slip across the border to prepare a counterattack.[11]

On October 19 Pyongyang, the North Korean capital, fell, while an airborne regiment was dropped thirty miles to the north, cutting off the fleeing NKPAs escape route. The advance continued and by late October some UN forces were only forty miles from the Chinese border. While the American and British Commonwealth forces on the west had hard but successful going against tough but deteriorating North Korean opposition, the ROKs on the central and eastern fronts, encountered a wholly new situation. The ROKs were the weak link, under-strength and unable to maintain contact with Eighth Army on the west and X Corps on the east because of the mountainous spine that divides Korea vertically. On October 25 the ROKs with a company of American tanks encountered a roadblock south of Chosan, fifty air miles from the Yalu river, the frontier with China. After a fierce firefight the ROKs captured a Chinese prison-er. Under interrogation he said there was 10,000 Chinese troops in front of them and another 10,000 east of them. Dismissing these revelations as ridiculous the ROKs pressed ahead. Within the next three days four South Korean regiments were virtually destroyed. When the US 1st Cavalry Division passed through the ROKs to take up the attack, the division was savagely mauled and driven back to the Chongchon river. (This was the Chinese First Phase Offensive.) In the east the 7th Marine Regiment destroyed the Chinese 124th Division, which left 1,500 dead on the field, in the only major UN success.

The 25th Infantry Division took part in the break-out from Pusan and the drive into North Korea. Sgt. Tom O'Brien, Headquarters Battery, 90th Field Artillery Battalion, was killed in action on October 26. The circumstances of his death are vague and his body was never found. He is posted as missing in action. A school friend, Liam O'Duibhir, remembers attending a memorial mass for Tom in the village church when news reached home of his death. Attached to the 25th Infantry Division, the 90th FA furnished general supporting fire for the Division's infantry regiments and had fought with the 25th since July.[12]

On the night of November 5-6 the Chinese attacked the 27th Commonwealth Brigade's bridgehead position just south of Pakchon, forcing the brigade to withdraw. As quick as the Chinese attacks began they ended. Australian troops could see the Chinese marching northward away from the battleground. By the end of the day the Chinese were all gone - back into the mountains. It was the same everywhere else. The Chinese just simply disappeared. It was a warning to the UN not to continue its advance. MacArthur, flush with victory and his own ego, took it that the Chinese had striven their hardest to overcome his forces, and failed. He flew to Eighth Army headquarters at Chongchon and predicted the war would be over shortly and that "we can get the boys home by Christmas". Later MacArthur lamely explained that the remark was meant to encourage his troops and to reassure Peking that he had no ambitions beyond the Yalu. Meanwhile, the UN forces would continue their drive to the Yalu and complete the reunification of Korea. In the mountains, 250,000 Chinese troops waited for them.

4

Red Storm

After linking up with US troops pushing north from the Pusan Perimeter the 7th Infantry Division was relieved of the responsibility for the Seoul area and taken 350 miles south to Pusan, to begin training for another proposed landing, this time at Wonsan, North Korea. On October 28 the division was loaded onto troop transports and sent instead to the east coast village of Iwon, in North Korea. After an unopposed beachhead landing on October 29 the 7th Infantry Division started driving north to the Yalu, the river boundary between North Korea and Manchuria. In bitter cold weather the 1st Battalion, 32nd Infantry moved quickly northward to the east coast of the Chosin reservoir to relieve the marines in their sector, while the 2nd and 3rd Battalions moved to the Fusan reservoir area to prepare for the drive to the Yalu river and the Manchurian border.

Morale was high as General MacArthur's Headquarters predicted that the "boys" would be home by Christmas. However, there were definite indications of a Chinese presence in the area. Major General Edward Arnold, the X Corps commander, believed them to be "remnants fleeing north" further fuelling his plans to attack to the north. On the drive north of the 38th Parallel MacArthur had deliberately separated Eighth Army, from the operations of X Corps. The two divisions of X Corps - 1st Marine and 7th Infantry - landed on the east coast and moved north separated from Eighth Army by the central spine of the North Korean mountains. (Attached to the US Marines were 235 British marines of 41 Independent Commando, Royal Marines.)

As the 32nd Infantry pushed north they were involved in a "sharp skirmish at Pungsan and a harsh firefight at Kapsan". The push continued in arctic-like cold weather, and on November 20 the 17th Infantry, 7th Division, slogged into Hyesanjin village on the Yalu river - the first and only American unit to reach the Manchurian border. This was to be the northernmost point of advance by the United Nations command in three years of bitter warfare. Fifteen miles to the west the 3rd Battalion, 32nd Infantry, was moving along a parallel road leading to Singalpajin. Once at the Yalu, the 17th was to march west from Hyesanjin to Singalpajin; the 3rd Battalion, 32nd Infantry was to push westward to meet marines coming north from the Chosin reservoir. Cpl. Charles Dennehy remembered "looking across towards Manchuria. The cold was awful. One morning it was minus thirty-eight degrees, impossible to dig in, even with a pick-axe. There was only one thing worse than the cold and that was the tiredness. We climbed mountain after mountain in extreme cold, each one higher than the next. You never knew where you were. Place names on a map meant nothing."[1]

The 3rd Battalion, besides being temporarily short one rifle company guarding a power plant, was operating all by itself. Forty-four miles north of the regimental headquarters, it was rather alone in enemy territory and somewhat in a vacuum. No one had much information about friendly neighbouring forces, or whether enemy forces might be nearby. The ground was covered with snow, a dreary landscape almost bare of growth. Streams were frozen so thick the ice could support tanks. Of the three enemies in Korea - the weather, the terrain and the North Koreans - the weather was probably the worst. If the sun was shining, the temperature in winter might get up to twenty degrees below zero, while thirty and forty below were more normal. The troops wore every piece of clothing they could manage - woolen long johns, cotton pants, two pairs of socks, pile jacket over wool shirt, parka with hood, trigger-finger mittens with wool insert, scarves around their heads under their helmets to protect their ears. Anyone who was sitting or standing was usually stamping his feet to keep them from getting numb. The cold affected equipment. Artillery shells did not always detonate completely when fired. Engine motors had to be started every hour and run at least fifteen minutes. Men had to shoot their weapons periodically to be sure they worked.

There was no point waiting until the enemy was on top of you to find out whether your weapon worked. Charles Dennehy was a 60mm mortarman and they had to build fires in empty 55-gallon drums and put them against mortar base plates to keep the metal from crystallising and snapping.[2]

The M2 60mm mortar was first used in World War II. The light weight and quick set up of the M2 made it an excellent indirect fire support for mobile platoon and company level action for use in between the effective range of hand grenades and the 81mm mortar. The "sixties" were the rifle company's miniature artillery, providing close-in support for attack and defence. They fired high-explosive, white phosphorous, and illumination shells. HE would demolish enemy soldiers, their weapons and light earthworks within a twenty-yard diameter of impact. WP, or Willy Peter, sent up a plume of white smoke where they hit, and were used for smoke screens and for marking targets. Illumination rounds, fired at night, lit a diameter of one hundred yards with high-intensity light for twenty seconds. Each mortar weighed forty pounds and broke down into three parts for carrying - tube, base plate and bipod. The bipod was often left attached to the tube for speed in bringing the mortar into action, and two men readily carried the combination, with ammunition in complete rounds being carried by supporting troops. A good mortar team could assemble the components, sight in, and be ready for a fire mission in less than thirty seconds. The CCF initially had no artillery, but made great use of light mortars.

As UN forces continued their advance to the Yalu Chinese forces avoided contact, fading to the left, right and rear of UN troops. The Chinese moved only by night and preserved an absolute camouflage discipline by day. Air observation saw nothing and the UN moving in columns had not sufficient troops to patrol the outland where the hidden enemy watched their every movement. On November 26 the Chinese suddenly attacked. (This was known as the Second Phase Offensive.) The first blow struck on the weakest point in the UN line, the juncture between Eighth Army and the ROK II Corps at Tekchen. Here the Chinese virtually wiped out the improperly aligned South Koreans. The Chinese attack widened the gulf between Eighth Army and X Corps, sent the US 24th

Infantry Division reeling back across the Chongchon, and enveloped the right wing of the US 2nd Infantry Division, which had been backing up the ROKs. Meanwhile 150 miles to the east the X Corps front was in extreme crisis. In most of the northeastern sector the ROKs, the 3rd Infantry Division and most of the 7th Infantry Division were positioned out of range of the Chinese attacks and were able to withdraw to safety along the east coast. But most of the 1st Marine Division and elements of the 7th Division, which had reached the hills overlooking the Chosin reservoir, were surrounded and cut of from their base, the port of Hungnam. When the Chinese offensive began on the night of November 27 the marines were advancing north of Yudam-ni at the western extremity of the Chosin reservoir. That night the Chinese launched attacks on the forward elements of the marines and on thirty miles of their main, and only, supply route to the coast, seventy-eight miles away to the south at Hamhung. Outnumbered and in danger of being cut-off the marines and the rest of X Corps had no choice but to fight their way back to safety.

MacArthur continued to urge his commanders forward until its was obvious that the Chinese outnumbered his forces sometimes ten to one and had enough troops to surround Eighth Army and X Corps and continue on to Seoul. Realising at last that there was no way to salvage his offensive MacArthur issued instructions for a series of Eighth Army delaying actions while the marines and army troops of X Corps fought their way to the coast, where they could be picked up by the Seventh Fleet. Peking announced that the UN were in "wild flight", but in reality the withdrawal of X Corps was superb. The marines and army troops at Chosin formed a column and fought their way out of a trap, through waves of Chinese, moving ever eastward over an icy corkscrew trail in subzero conditions. At one point they seemed utterly lost, confronted by an impassable chasm, until US pilots arrived overhead with a huge suspension bridge and parked it in the gap.

Corporal Charles Dennehy, as a rifleman and mortarman, attached to the 60mm mortars was "closest to the frontlines. We never knew the Chinese had entered the war. There was no sign of them during the day. They were packed tight into

Korean huts, because of our air force. They only moved at night. We thought we were still fighting the North Koreans until the firepower increased. We were wondering where they got all the firepower. But it was the Chinese. The Chinese came in hordes. The cold was just awful. When bringing back our wounded, under fire, at the Fusan reservoir they began to freeze. It was that cold a man's arm held up to signify he was wounded could freeze in that position." On the morning of November 28 a radio message informed the troops at Singalpjin that their plans to link up with the 17th Regiment had been changed. Instead they were to return to Samsu. The marines had been attacked at the Chosin reservoir and a general retreat was under way. On November 29, when the full force of the Chinese Communists struck the UN forces, the 2nd and 3rd Battalions, 32nd Infantry, stood their ground until UN elements further north moved to join the battle. Together all these UN elements made an orderly withdrawal from the Fusan area. During the withdrawal Cpl. Dennehy was wounded in the arm and leg by shrapnel from a Chinese grenade. A piece of grenade shrapnel went straight through his arm. Shrapnel wounds are worse than a bullet as they had jagged edges and did not make a clean exit hole. He was still able to walk and when the 32nd Infantry reached the safety of Samsu Charles Dennehy was evacuated to the naval hospital in Kove, Japan.[3]

On the day following the crushing attack by the Chinese on the ROK II Corps assigned to protect the right flank of the Eighth Army, General Almond ordered the 1st Marine Division to attack northwest and cut the enemy lines of communication at Mupyong-ni. But before the Marines could execute the mission, the CCF began the second phase of their counteroffensive with the objective of destroying X Corps. Six Chinese divisions swarmed down on the Marines and the 7th Infantry Division. The Marines were attacked by two CCF divisions as they went forward to relieve the army troops at the village of Yudam-ni. Fighting continued into the night and Gen. Almond authorised General Smith to abandon his heavy equipment if it would help his withdrawal. Smith announced he would not abandon any equipment he could use and he would withdraw only as rapidly as he was able to evacuate his men.[4]

On the day the Chinese attacked the US 1st Marine Division a group of British Commandos, men from 41 (Independent) Commando, Royal Marines, were due to leave Hungnam to join the division where they were supposed to serve as a reconnaissance unit. In early August the British Admiralty had called for volunteers for raiding duties in Korea. The first men of the Royal Marines trained with the US Marines learning how to handle American weapons and were then attached to a US Army Raider company. Their task was to survey the Inchon landing beaches for the 1st Marine Division. With the success of this mission the British Admiralty raised a larger force for raiding duties in Korea, designated 41 (Independent) Commando, Royal Marines. Led by Lieutenant Colonel Douglas B. Drysdale, an Anglo-Argentinian with extensive combat experience in Burma and Malaya in WWII, the unit was not to be a full Commando, but a small unit of around 200 men.[5]

As the Chinese continued to advance 41 Commando instead took up positions around Koto-ri in bitter cold weather. Col. Drysdale was ordered to take his men, a company of US Marines and a US Army company, and some USMC tanks and "hack through" the Chinese defenses from Koto-ri to the main base at Hagaru-ri. This battle group, known as Task Force Drysdale, fought their way through ten miles of Chinese by leapfrogging each unit ahead starting with the Royal Marines clearing one hill, then moving the US Marines through on to the next, then putting in the US infantry, then bringing the British Marines forward once again. Hundreds of Chinese poured down on them from the hills and Task Force Drysdale fought every inch of the way. Massed Chinese attacks succeeded in cutting the task force in two, managing to cut off Captain Ovens troop and the US infantry company. Only a few survivors made it back to Koto-ri. As one group of US infantrymen prepared to surrender Capt. Ovens turned to Corporal Dave Brady of the Assault Engineer platoon.

"Look, here," said Ovens, "never mind what they do ... We're British, and we're not going to surrender." "Well, actually, Sir," Cpl Brady replied, "I'm half-Irish." They both fought their way back to Koto-ri with about twenty other Royal Marines. The rest of Task Force Drysdale entered the US Marine perimeter at

0130 that night. They had lost 321 men - out of a total of 900 - and 75 vehicles.[6] Dave Brady was an assault engineer (expert in demolitions, mines and defence works) and had volunteered for raiding duties in Korea. He established himself as the unit `wag', always ready with an apt remark, usually at an inappropriate moment. After the Korean War Dave Brady joined the London Metropolitan Police and was awarded no fewer than twelve Commissioner's Commendations, the Queen's Award for Bravery and the Queen's Gallantry Medal.

On December 6, after a week at Hagaru-ri, the Marines began the move to Hungnam . About 10,000 men and 1,000 assorted vehicles set out for the sea, bringing with them their heavy weapons, their wounded, and even their dead. The Royal Marines, now reduced to 100 men, formed up with the US 5th Marines as part of the rearguard. Irish-American Father Cornelius J. Griffin served as chaplain with the 7th Marine Regiment and was present with the leathernecks from the landing at Inchon and the advance into North Korea. During the long retreat (the word retreat is not in the Marines vocabulary so they referrred to it as "an advance to the sea".) he was an inspiration to the men and was present up and down the column helping and cajoling his "boys". One time Fr. Griffin came along the column and found a marine shivering on his exposed perch of a truck. The young chaplain reached into the deep pockets of his parka and pulled out a small bottle of whiskey. "You look like you could use this," he said. The marine cut the seal of the bottle with his fighting knife and emptied the tiny bottle in one swallow. He felt the warmth course through his body. "You're a Godsend, Padre," he said.

"Thank you, for saying that, son," answered Fr. Griffin. "This is not the way I had expected to be doing His work." Then he moved down the column looking for more frozen Marines. As the Chinese attacked the column Fr. Griffin rallied the men with a rush of profanities that would make a gunnery sergeant proud and when the marine sitting on the back of the truck caught a piece of shrapnel in his foot the chaplain was back with him. Fr. Griffin cut off his boot, bandaged his foot and slipped him another little bottle of whiskey. The marine thought of it as holy water.[7]

Fr. Griffin was badly wounded as the column approached Koto-ri when   when a mortar round exploded in front of his jeep. The jeep swerved off the road and a young marine pulled Fr. Griffin out of the wreckage as Chinese soldiers fired grenades and burp guns at them. The marine threw himself over the chaplain and took a full burst. Fr. Griffin was wounded by shrapnel in the jaw and upper body. The driver was killed. A group of marines drove off the Chinese attack and put Fr. Griffin in a truck which took him to the aid station. He was one of the hundreds of wounded who were flown out of another air strip that the engineeers had blasted from the frozen ground at Koto-ri.[8]

General Smith and his half-frozen, exhausted Marines reached the Hungnam perimeter on December 11 as the nearly 200 vessels organised for evacuation of the beachhead got underway. General MacArthur flew to the beachhead on the same day and praised the men for their "high morale and conspicuous self-confidence" throughout the heavy fighting. MacArthur added that, "Although highly outnumbered, you have come through in a superior manner." The Marines not only brought out their wounded and all movable equipment but prisoners and captured enemy equipment.[9]

The withdrawal of the UN from North Korea that winter saw the collapse of Eighth Army as the troops fled by every means available. This is nothing unique. Men of every army run away when their front is broken or they find themselves enveloped by superior forces. Eighth Army and X Corps lost 13,000 killed, wounded and missing in the first days of the Chinese offensive. Some American units fought courageously, while many just collapsed. In their fear to get away from the Chinese "hordes" some soldiers threw away their heavy weapons, ammunition, spare clothing and even abandoned their wounded.

"Bug-out" fever gripped the American army. The sight of an oriental face was enough to sent them into panic - some even fled when they saw South Korean troops coming behind them. As the supply system cracked, men became desperately hungry. Cpl. Charles Dennehy remembered the hunger, fatigue and cold. They were living on C rations and had not seen bread since leaving Japan.

"C ration tins* had to be prised open with our bayonets and each bean had to be prised apart one by one to be eaten." While Walker's Eighth Army fled south in panic the 1st Marine Division and the 7th Infantry Division had salvaged at least a portion of honour from one of the most inglorious moments in American military history.

The retreat from the Chosin reservoir to the port of Hamhung was heroic. The marines - with elements of the 7th Division - had retired from the Chosin reservoir in column of units, with virtually all their heavy equipment and transport intact, maintaining the cohesion of the division to the end. (Of the 967 men who fought at the Chosin Reservoir as members of the 1st Battalion, 32nd Infantry Regiment only 3 officers, 18 enlisted men and 4 KATUSA** soldiers survived.) X Corps had suffered 4,418 battle and 7,313 non-battle casualties, the latter mostly minor cases of frostbite. Chinese losses were staggering, including 35,000 against X Corps alone. The marines had taken 2,665 casualties, including 383 dead, fought off three Chinese armies and captured the imagination of the American public and the admiration of all. (The ten Chinese divisions attacking in Chosin were so wasted they never again saw action in the Korean War.)

Admiral James Doyle, who had put the marines ashore at Inchon, also commanded the Hungnam withdrawal - an amphibious landing in reverse. In an operation characterised by ingenuity and superb Naval gunfire support, the 1st Marine Division, the 3rd and 7th US Army Divisions, and 100,000 Korean civilians were evacuated under the sweep of heavy enemy gunfire without a single allied casualty. For these masterful exploits Admiral Doyle was awarded

* C rations contained various small cans of food (lima beans, hamburger patties in gravy, etc.) that could be heated up over the solid fuel cake of wood alcohol/with stand included in each box with dessert in cans (usually fruits in syrup) and a small efficient can-opener. Each box also contained a pack of cigarettes, Camels or Lucky Strikes.

** Koreans augmented to the US Army.

the US Navy Distinguished Service Medal decoration and the US Army Silver Star decoration. Despite the defeat of the UN MacArthur's winter retreat was one of his most successful feats of arms. Against overwhelming odds the fallback had been orderly. Of the US divisions hit by the Chinese steamroller only the 2nd had been badly mauled, suffering twenty-five per cent casualties - compared to sixty per cent losses in some American units in WWII's Battle of the Bulge. The Korean War had now entered a whole new phase.

5

A Winter of Discontent

At the outbreak of the war in June the British Army was, as was nearly always the case, unprepared. The army was stretched to its limits providing garrisons all over the ever-shrinking Empire. It was decided that a brigade would be sufficient to please American demands for a token force in Korea. Two infantry battalions were dispatched in great haste from Hong Kong, while the rest of the self-contained Brigade Group was gathered together in England. Designated the 29th Infantry Brigade it would include two Irish battalions, the 1st Royal Ulster Rifles and 8th King's Royal Irish Hussars. In the summer of 1950 the 1st RUR was stationed at Sobraon Barracks in Colchester. The 1st RUR - in British Army terms this would be 1 RUR - was at a peacetime footing of half battalion strength, so 400 reservists, mainly from the North Irish and Lancastrian groups, were mobilised. The 8th King's Royal Irish Hussars were also part of the Brigade and were in Tidworth, having returned from overseas in 1948. (The 1st Battalion, Gloucestershire Regiment and the 1st Battalion, Royal Northumberland Fusiliers, had not yet joined the Brigade.)

The 8th King's Royal Irish Hussars were to go to Korea with the brand new Centurion Mk3 battle tank with its 20 pounder gun and highly secret stabilising system. The Centurion was Britain's first attempt to produce a universal tank and do away with divisions between Infantry Tanks and Cruiser Tanks. First developed just at the end of WWII, the Centurion arrived too late to take part in the war. The early version was equipped with a 17 pounder main gun and a

20mm cannon, but these were replaced by a 20 pounder, fully stabilised, main gun, and a Besa machine gun. It was reputed that the performance of the 20 pounder gun - when firing APDS - was twice that of the 88mm gun of the German Royal Tiger Tank. The Centurion Mk3 first saw action in Korea and soon proved itself to be the best performing tank in this theatre of operations. Particularly notable was its excellent cross-country performance. However, there was almost no time for familiarisation with the new tank, training being curtailed by the need to get them to the docks for transport to Korea in slow-chartered merchantmen. The Hussars had to be brought up to strength with reservists and officers borrowed from virtually every other cavalry regiment.

After a brief period of training - most of the men were veterans of World War II - the 1st RUR left Colchester and on October 1 embarked on the Trooper *Empire Pride* in Liverpool bound for Korea. Rifleman* Henry O'Kane recalled vividly in his book, *O'Kane's Korea*, the scene on the Liverpool docks as the Rifles boarded the troopship. "Many friends of the Regiment came to wave us goodbye and the landing stage was crowded with well wishers - many from Ireland. Not since before the war when the great troopers sailed was such a scene witnessed on the docks of Liverpool. All during the war the docks were closed and the departure of troop ships were not seen by the public. Since the war troop ships mostly sailed from Southampton. Now the people of Liverpool gave us a great send-off - dockers clambered on cranes and buildings, the Band played and one large Irish group of men and women danced about waving the bottles they were sipping as they sang with the band the traditional songs of the 'Rifles'. Another group stood apart silent, subdued and bewildered by it all. These friends, sweethearts and wives of the reservists just stood around silently, bewildered, and must have wondered what was happening to them, that their men torn from their homes, should be part of such a joyful gathering of wild Irish going to a war that was causing so much grief and hardship to so many reservists' families."

*A Rifleman is the term used in the Royal Ulster Rifles for a private soldier.

Henry O'Kane, from Tully, Eglington, Co. Derry, was on garrison duties at Colchester when the Korean War broke out. He immediately went to the unit library and read up on his new destination: Korea. Unknowingly, Henry would spend the next three years in the Land of the Morning Calm. O'Kane originally joined the Royal Inniskilling Fusiliers, as did his father and grandfather before him, but was transferred to the Royal Ulster Rifles in 1947, on a re-inforcement draft.

"It took a long time, many years," O'Kane wrote, "for me to discover the RUR's like the rest of the North Irish Brigade were full of eccentric, nostalgic Irish Officers, some of which supported and encouraged a weird brand of Irish Patriotism, who, on occasions like St. Patrick's Day, allowed and encouraged the Irish Tricolour to be flown. However, because of the battalion's effectiveness these activities were disregarded by higher authority." O'Kane spent nearly a year with the Rifles as part of the British occupation force in Austria and returned to Ireland in the spring of 1948, going to Colchester the following year for garrison duty.

According to Captain Robin Charley, from Newtownards, Co. Down, one reservist, who lived in Liverpool, "decided not to report back to 1 RUR in Colchester at the end of embarkation leave but appeared at the back of the crowd to wave the ship goodbye. His company sergeant major, Andy McConville, rushed down the gangway, grabbed him by the scruff of his neck and brought him on board. This same reservist, in spite of not wanting to be called up was a good soldier in action in Korea, on one occasion repelling a Chinese attack with tincans and stones after his ammunition ran out."[2]

The trip out to Korea was uneventful but a troopship "was no cruise liner," according to Rfn. Henry O'Kane. "...it was a trip with plenty to do, boat drill and weapon training... There was never enough room in the canteen and duties kept us busy most of the day."[1] Sergeant Hans Milligan agreed. "I should say the *Empire Pride* had nothing to be proud of," he wrote. "There were no beds only a number of hammocks which were slung on hooks above the wooden tables and benches. When we were almost cast off another (troop) train pulled into the dock and the powers that be decided to take them on board. This added another four hundreds to the fourteen hundred already on board. These extras had to sleep on the tarmac floor which was painted green."

"When they slept the green paint came off on their clothes and bodies. The Minister for War came on board to say farewell and at the end of his message we heard the end of the weather forecast which was gales in the Irish Sea. This proved true as soon as we crossed the Mersey Bay. The gales lasted until we entered the Mediterranean. The only break was when one man jumped overboard and we had to circle in the Irish Sea for six hours. His body was washed up on the Channel Isles a week later.

"Things on board improved greatly after Gibraltar. We stopped for a short spell in Aden, then Sri Lanka, then Singapore and finally to Pusan where we entrained for Seoul." Steeped in a military tradition Hans Milligan had joined the Royal Ulster Rifles on August 1 1945. His father was wounded at Gallipoli and his uncle was killed on July 1 1916. Another uncle was an RSM in the Royal Irish Rifles and was awarded a Military Cross on July 1 1916. He was eighteen when he was first sent overseas to Palestine.[3]

Most of the troops on board the *Empire Pride* believed the war would be over by the time they got there and the Rifles would be assigned as part of the occupation force. However, just before they reached Pusan the whole character of the war was changing and a completely new phase of operations was beginning. But the full implications of the Chinese advance across the Yalu river were not yet realised on board, for news was very scarce. On the morning of November 5 the battalion adjutant, Captain H. Hamill, wrote "the mountainous coastline of Korea came into sight, although partly hidden by driving squalls of rain. By midday the *Empire Pride* was anchored in Pusan harbour and, while she waited her turn to go alongside, the men on board took their first look at the bleak harbour, the squalid township beyond, and, in the distance, the dark and rugged mountains stretching away inland to the north.

Soon after midday the ship went alongside and Major John Shaw, who had been in command of the advance party, came aboard to give us his news. In the meantime, below on the quay-side, the 56th United States Army Band, composed entirely of American Negroes, gave us a resounding and martial welcome, playing Sousa marches and "hot" jazz alternately. In the late afternoon the Battalion disembarked and marched to the railway, station, there to entrain for Suwon, where the Brigade was to form up." As each man stepped off the gangway on to Korean soil he was handed an apple by a Korean schoolgirl, part of a group who stood in their school uniforms. The schoolgirl gave each soldier an apple, a solemn bow and murmured "Thank you, sir," as they passed.[4]

The 1st RUR was assigned to the village of Uijongbu, about fifteen miles northeast of Seoul where in the surrounding countryside North Koreans left behind in the retreat, had formed themselves into large, well-organised, guerrilla forces. These guerrillas were beginning to constitute a serious menace to Eighth Army's lines of communication. The village of Uijongbu itself lay across the main railway and road communications from Chorwon and Kumwha in the north to Seoul. From their base the Battalion sent out foot patrols into the mountains, accompanied by interpreters, and information about guerrilla movements began to accumulate. "The first few days at Uijongbu were a very good opportunity for acclimatisation," H. Hamill wrote, "in more senses than one. The various forms of battle procedure were practised and made perfect, although there was no contact with the guerrillas.

"Physical fitness developed quickly with the hard foot-slogging of patrolling the hills; and at the same time we got our first taste of what the Korean winter was like. Although there was very little snow, the temperature was continually well below freezing and a knife-like wind blew constantly down the valleys, bringing with it the iron cold of the Siberian plains to the north. No winter clothing or equipment had yet been issued, nor was there any form of stoves or heating to be found. The ruins of Uijongbu offered no shelter, and men learned quickly to line their trenches with rice straw and wood reverting to keep out some of the cold. Shaving was a torment, especially as razor blades were scarce and a blunt blade in this climate usually removed a good deal of skin with the beard. However, never at this time or later, except in actual battle, did officers or men go unshaven, and there was a good deal of satisfaction in presenting a clean chin to our frequently bearded Allies."[5]

The tropical kits supplied to British soldiers exemplified the lack of knowledge of the climate in Korea. The predicament of the two battalions sent up from Hong Kong in August 1950, on the assumption that they would return there on the arrival of 29th Brigade was even worse. At the end of October, as the thermometer slid below zero, they were still clad in jungle green, with only their greatcoats and blankets. For them it was essential to barter NAAFI goods with the Americans for their excellent winter clothing, sleeping bags, tents and tent heaters. The "clothing was inadequate," Sgt. Milligan wrote. "Our pigskin boots were made for the invasion of Norway in 1940 and never used until Korea."[6] Rfn. James B. Dunwoody wrote: "The weather was very extreme. Very cold in winter and very hot in summer, but I seemed to adapt to it, maybe because I was young."[7] Company Sergeant-Major Sean Fitzsimons, Dublin, said, "At night, once you touched the metal with your hands, your bare hands, you left the skin on the metal. You used to stand on sentry, you always had a couple of sandbags, filled them with straw, stuck the feet in, and that's what kept you going."[8] Major Gerald Rickord was embarrassed when an aunt presented him with two pairs of longjohns before he departed for Korea. Within days of arriving in Korea he was eternally grateful.[9]

Major Archie Braithwaite, of 176th Battery, passed on his experience on cold-weather warfare and gave the Ulsters many tips on how to wear the newly issued winter clothing. This consisted of a string vest, worn next to the skin; a heavy woollen pullover over the one normally issued; heavy woollen vests and longjohns and oiled socks; and frost-proof ski-type boots. Over all was worn a loose windproof suit. This was of a light very closely woven camouflaged material. The trousers were tied close at the ankles and waist by cords. The jacket was similarly pulled tight at the hips, buttoned close at the wrists, and had a hood, the rim of which could be drawn tight round the face. It was, in fact, windproof and, if worn properly, kept one fairly warm in the sub-zero temperatures. It did not keep out the rain or snow, and was only really effective in dry cold. Major Braithwaite was the first to adopt the local form of head-dress - a fur-lined dog-skin cap with peak and earflaps, which later became very popular and was eventually replaced by an American ski cap of a similar but standard pattern issued to all ranks.[10]

Because of the reports of communist guerrillas operating behind the lines the Ulsters sent out sweeping patrols into the nearby hills. On November 25, "We went off down the road," Capt. Robin Charley recalled, "...the sergeant-major and myself in the middle and three paltoons out in front and we suddenly met about 250 guerrillas ... carrying bandoleers of ammunition, weapons and holding green flags. They wanted to surrender to us. I lined them up to take their photograph which I thought would be a great scoop for the regimental journal. Unfortunately, the freezing temperature made my photograph blurred which was most disheartening. The guerrillas were escorted back to Btn. HQ and handed over to the Regt. Police."[11]

On November 28 the Ulsters were ordered to move north to Anju about sixty miles north of Pyongyang, their destination: the Yalu river. Thanksgiving Day, November 24, had passed bleak and blustery and the British and the other Allies laughed at the lengths the Americans had went to make sure every GI got his Thanksgiving dinner. The following day Eighth Army began to move forward once more. By nightfall the US 2nd Infantry Division had encountered massive Chinese troop concentrations and by the following night had been driven back two miles. On the right of Eighth Army the ROK II Corps, three divisions in strength, had collapsed almost literally overnight, and was fleeing southwards leaving a gap eighty miles wide in the Allied lines. An attempt by the Turkish Brigade to move to the support of the South Koreans was thwarted by Chinese troops well behind the American flank.

Gen. Walker ordered his forces to began an immediate retreat. As the trucks of the 1st RUR and the rest of the British 29th Brigade ground their way north of

Pyongyang "they were continually slowed or halted by the increasing volume of southbound traffic," Capt. Hamill wrote. "It was beginning to be apparent that the Battalion and, behind it, the rest of 29 Brigade were going north alone, for it seemed that the whole army was moving southward as fast as it could go. This, in fact, was the truth. The U.N. forces, operating under a divided command, had been met, checked, and split apart by the Chinese counteroffensive. Both the British 27th Brigade and the Turkish Brigade were fighting a desperate rearguard action in the Chongchon river area, while the rest of I and IX Corps were in full retreat, having suffered severe losses in the first clash with the new enemy."[12]

After leaguering that night near a Korean village the Ulsters set off north again the next day against the traffic stream. While the Battalion was still moving up, however, the orders were again changed, and finally a position was taken up at Chai-Ri, ten miles south of Sukchon. The main road ran through the centre of the Battalion area, and the headlong nature of the retreat was soon obvious. All manner of vehicles were driven recklessly, and with full headlights blazing, through the Ulsters blocking positions. By day and night a continuous stream of vehicles, tanks, and troops passed southward in a thick pall of dust. Information about the enemy was scarce and it was only as the traffic thinned and occasional bodies of battle-stained Turkish troops, on foot, began to pass through, that there was any indication that contact with the enemy might be imminent. The order for 29th Brigade to join in the general retreat came through on December 2, and "the Battalion, bewildered and half ashamed of this curious method of waging war, turned southward again." The 29th Brigade halted on the outskirts of Pyongyang, and the Ulsters took up positions on a line of hills just north of the town, with orders to cover the withdrawal of the last elements of I and IX Corps across the Taedong.

Here, on the morning of December 4 they first met the men of 27th Brigade. "As their column passed through our lines," Capt. Hamill wrote, "the riflemen ran out to the roadside to shake hands and to make the usual ribald remarks, and to throw to the troops in their vehicles some of the "PX" stores and comforts which the retreating Americans had abandoned in Pyongyang and which had that morning been rescued from the burning city. There was a strange feeling of relief at the sight of this British Brigade - a return to reality after the bewildering spectacle of the unfamiliar American army in retreat."[13] The previous night groups of men had went into the North Korean capital to salvage loads of clothing, boots, rations and cigarettes before they were destroyed by the Americans. The enterprising Ulsters had not forgotten the Pyongyang brewery and the water truck was filled up with North Korean beer. "I never saw so many buckets and jerry cans move so swiftly," Rfn. James Dunwoody wrote, "and then vanishing so fast." James Dunwoody was already in the Sea Cadets and Royal Navy Reserve when he decided to join the Royal Ulster Rifles in 1948 "probably because my uncles were in the RUR". He had two uncles in WWI, one in the British Army and the other in the Canadian Army. He also had uncles serving during WWII, as did his older brother who was in the Royal Navy.[14]

By dusk the last elements of the United Nations army were south of the Taedong. Luckily the Chinese were unable to follow up at the same pace and the next morning 29th Brigade was ordered to abandon its positions and to follow the remainder of the Eighth Army south across the Taedong. Just before midnight they boarded their trucks and drove through the blazing city of Pyongyang. The withdrawal was carried out without incident, except for a strafing attack by a lone aircraft on the Ulsters column as it crossed the Taedong bridge. Only one rifleman was slightly wounded in the attack.

The Ulsters took up positions in an area about six miles north of Seoul known as Compo Canyon. "In Compo Canyon we spent our first Christmas in Korea." Rfn. Henry O'Kane, C Company, wrote. "It was celebrated in comfort and as is usual in an Irish Battalion with a good deal of conviviality. The QM, Capt. Tom Smith, had succeeded in securing enough turkey to feed the Battalion extremely well. Christmas pudding, a double ration of rum, an issue of canned beer plus a good supply of Korean Sake completed the feast. All the Korean houseboys were grouped together to sing Ari-sang and other Korean melodies. They also managed a bit of Silent Night and White Christmas. The Pipes and Drums gave a rendering of Irish tunes and the Korean hills echoed to the sounds of Paddy

Carey, The Wearing of the Green and similar Irish patriotic tunes. A good time was had by all."[15]

On the last day of 1950 the Chinese attacked across the Imjin at Korangpo-Ri, penetrated the defences of 1st ROK Division, and established a bridgehead, from which they quickly broke out. On New Year's Day a warning order was received to the effect that the Ulsters, with the rest of the 29th Brigade, was to be prepared to counterattack in the sector held by 1 ROK Division. They were in defensive positions in the area of Chaegunghyon village, which they called Happy Valley, when straggling groups from 1st ROK Division passed through their lines. There was also a continual stream of refugees moving south.

However, it was impossible for British troops, new in the country, to differentiate between Korean and Chinese and enemy soldiers mingled with the civilians to gain information on the British defences. "Word came through that the enemy had crossed the 38th Parallel and was approaching our area. B Coy moved to prepared positions already dug on Point 195.[16] We took up positions about midnight," Captain Robin Charley recalled, "and then at about 4.00 in the morning one of our platoons was approached by some people up the side of a hill saying, 'South Koreans, we surrender.' And the boys stood up out of their slit-trenches and then got rushed and these were actually Chinamen , they weren't South Koreans at all, it was a ruse.

"We then organised a counter-attack against this position on top of the hill. One of our officers, called Ivor Daniel, who was platoon commander of the reserve platoon of B Company, was ordered by the company commander to do a counter-attack and it was ... just as we'd learned in the School of Infantry. He said 'Fire Section there, numbers 2 and 3 Sections, follow me', and he did a right flanking, charged the enemy with covering fire from the Fire Section and the Bren guns and it worked exactly as per the book. I was there standing watching it with the sergeant-major. I remember we were thinking how well it was all done, and they suffered no casualties at all. They drove the Chinese off the top of the hill and we reoccupied Hill 195."[17]

"Snow lay thick on the ground," Henry O'Kane wrote, "and on the 2nd of January we awoke to the bitterness of the cold in the exposed positions across this stretch of hills with the valley between. A howling wind literally blew ice into our faces as we felt the full force of the Manchurian winter. During the day we tried to keep warm by fortifying our positions and later I went out on patrol to contact the Glosters on our right. All was quiet on their sector."[18] On the night of January 2 the Chinese began probing the Ulsters positions but were driven off by machine gun fire. The next morning the Chinese attacked in strength. Their approach up the rough scrub covered hillside had been made under cover of darkness with considerable skill, and their initial assault was made from the very edge of the Ulsters positions.

The confusion of this sudden attack was increased by the trickery of the Chinese who came on shouting, "South Koreans, we surrender," and led by a man with a white flag, to the accompaniment of much shouting and blowing of bugles. Two platoon positions were penetrated in the first assault, and there was confused close-quarter fighting for some minutes, until both platoons were forced to fall back on to their main Company's positions. A Chinese bugler, in quilted winter uniform and dog skin cap, was seen on the very summit of Hill 195 sounding his success signal, and small parties of the enemy began to work along the ridge south and south-west, with the obvious intention of striking at the mortar position and Battalion HQ. The Ulsters fiercely engaged the advancing enemy and stopped them in their tracks. Heavy artillery fire and supporting fire from the tanks of the 8th Royal Irish Hussars came down on the hilltops. This was followed by an air strike, called up by the Americans on the left. "With great elation," Adjt. Hamill wrote, "the Riflemen watched the four Shooting Star jets circle once low overhead and then dive screaming into the valley, hurling rockets, napalm, and cannon shells upon the massing enemy."[19]

In the meantime the Ulsters were rapidly planning a counterattack, but it now appeared that, owing to refusal of the Rifles to budge any further and the very heavy and accurate fire by the supporting weapons, the enemy had been halted and virtually destroyed where they stood. The battle was over, but, for some time afterwards, small groups of Chinese withdrawing northwards were raked by artillery, and many more casualties were inflicted. A physical count showed about thirty dead Chinese inside the Battalion position. Two prisoners were taken, but only one lived long enough to be sent back for interrogation. Casualties in the Battalion were light: around twenty, with only four killed, the first fatalities in the Battalion. The Brigade settled down to see what the night would bring, and throughout the Battalion morale was high. According to Capt. Hamill: "The Chinese, this almost legendary enemy, whose "hordes" had sent the Eighth Army south in headlong retreat, had been met, fought, and sharply defeated in this action. The puzzled resentment of the British troops against a type of war in which they had done nothing but retreat ignominiously before an enemy they had never seen, changed now to a confident realisation that they, at any rate, were more than a match for their opponents."[20]

However, two Chinese divisions were in front of the Ulsters and despite the success in recovering their lost ground the 29th Brigade were informed that they were to retreat south of the Han river. There was no time to lose, because the US 35th Infantry nearby had already withdrawn, leaving the British flank unprotected. The tanks of "Cooperforce," led by Captain Donald-Astley Cooper, 8th King's Royal Irish Hussars, were to form a rearguard. Cooperforce was composed of six Cromwell and eight OP tanks of 45th Field Artillery Regiment. The Ulsters commanding officer, Lt. Col. Jack Carson, was medically evacuated several days earlier and Major Tony Blake took over as acting CO. The route of withdrawal lay first to the west behind the present British positions and then south by a pass over a low range of hills. The track itself was icebound and treacherous, and for some distance was commanded by a high curving cliff overhanging the river bed along which it ran; the pass was a sheet of ice and only just negotiable by vehicles in daylight. Chinese troops soon commanded both sides of the road down which the Ulsters were to retreat. General Ridgway was desperate to secure their safe withdrawal, but the local British commander made a harsh decision that the Ulsters must fend for themselves. To send other units to their rescue would simply have been to dispatch all to a common ruin.

The Mortar Platoon fired off its remaining dumped ammunition into probable enemy assembled areas as the engines of the battalion's vehicles coughed into life. The night was bitterly cold. As the men walked silently and the vehicles bumped and slithered through the snow and ice flares, dropped by friendly aircraft, broke out overhead, and the column of men and vehicles was brilliantly illuminated against the surrounding snow. By the time the flares went out the damage was already done. A hail of mortar and machine-gun fire burst from the heights. The fighting which developed became confused. The attack broke on the centre of the column, while a Battle Patrol of Ulsters and the tanks of Cooperforce at the rear had still not moved off. The only chance of extricating the rear of the column from the trap was for men and vehicles to keep moving. This became more difficult as vehicles slid off the track in the confusion and blocked the way of those behind. In the riverbed the fighting was at close quarters. The Chinese established a machine-gun post in the riverbed in front of the Ulsters, and began to stream down from the cliffs using grenades and automatic weapons. Maj. Tony Blake and Major Joe Ryan were last seen here making every effort to keep the column on the move and under control.[21]

Both Maj. Blake and Maj. Ryan were captured along with several dozen other ranks. A Chinese officer, furious that the bulk of the British troops had escaped, asked for the Ulster's commanding officer to identify himself from the ranks of the captured. Tony Blake stepped forward, as did his batman. The Chinese officer drew his pistol and promptly executed them both. Tony Blake was thirty-nine years old. Anthony Howell Bruce Blake was from Meelick, near the shores of Lough Derg, Co. Galway, and was the son of Major Cecil Bruce Blake, a Boer War and WWI veteran. Tony Blake attended Sandhurst when he was seventeen, was Military Attaché in Poland in WWII, and parachuted into Arnhem with the HQ and Defence Platoon of 1st Airlanding Brigade.

Tony Blake was holder of the Polish decoration of the Military Cross, the Czech decoration of the Military Cross and the US Decoration of the Distinguished Service Cross (DSC), but was refused the British DSO, allegedly because of the huge losses occurred by the 1st Airborne Division. He was fluent in Czech,

Polish and Russian. Tony Blake left behind a wife, and daughter, born in 1949, and a son who was born some weeks after he died. For the surviving Ulster POWs, ahead lay a mid-winter death march to prison camps in North Korea.[22]

Meanwhile, a section under Lt. McCord, with Sgt. Campbell and Cpl. Blackstock, moved forward and attacked the Chinese machine-gun with grenades, and then returned with one Cromwell tank to help the main body forward through the gap they had just made. A troop of Cooperforce under Lt. Godfrey Alexander, 8th KRIH, escorted by 7 Platoon of C Company, was ordered by Capt. Astley-Cooper to try to break out along the river bed to the west towards the main road. The tanks came under very heavy and accurate mortar fire as they moved, and Lt. Alexander was killed by a mortar fragment. Godfrey Alexander was twenty-two and a native of Dublin. Also killed was twenty-one year old Trooper Joseph Collison, from Athy, Co. Kildare. None of the troop got through. Astley-Cooper's tank cast a track on the rough ground. His crew bailed out and escaped. He was never seen again.[23]

"Confusion reigned. The Chinese came swarming down the sides of the cliffs then calling on us to surrender," Henry O'Kane wrote, "shouting, blowing whistles and bugles. The noise echoing in the hills. The machine guns and small arms mowed them down but they came relentlessly on as if drugged or drunk. They swarmed around the vehicles and carriers pulling men off and fighting at close quarters. Intense small arms fire was everywhere. At this stage a number of men, including myself, were wounded." Henry O'Kane had suffered a shrapnel wound in the head and had also been peppered with fragments about the face and head. "Many acts of heroism were performed that night. Cooper Force were heavily engaged at the rear in the riverbed where, greatly outnumbered, they inflicted very heavy casualties upon the enemy before being overwhelmed. In another incident a bayonet attack was put in by about fifty men of Support Coy who then fought their way out over the hills. In my particular area a fierce counter attack was put in against the Chinese machine guns. This heroic action enabled some of us to escape in the darkness. My group, which consisted of men from various companies, stumbled along the track or limped across the terraced paddy fields. Some with wounds needing urgent attention were carried on the backs of fellow riflemen, all tired, grim and grimy, until we reached the main highway where "Wags Truckers" awaited us.

"This gallant Negro trucking company of the US Army, commanded by the huge Capt. Wagner had come further forward and stayed there longer than anybody had the right to expect. These guys, on permanent attachment to the 29th British Brigade, were as happy to see us returning as our mothers would have been. We boarded their trucks and jolted together in comradeship, over the pontoon bridges and across the sand flats of the Han river while Seoul burned. Of the UN Forces the Royal Ulster Rifles were the last unit to cross the Han before the bridges were blown and the last unit to leave the Seoul area was the Argylls of the 27th British Brigade." Henry O'Kane was later evacuated to the British Commonwealth Hospital at Kure, on the east coast of Honshu, where he spent a month recovering from his wounds.[24]

By now the last of the Ulsters had broken contact and were doggedly moving south. Major John Shaw, realising that the situation in the valley was beyond control, decided to gather together all the men he could find, and made a single determined effort to break clear. He abandoned most of the vehicles, which were now either ditched or without drivers. He succeeded in collecting together about sixty men, and broke through the Chinese-held village of Pulmiji-Ri, and out into the hills to the south. They made their way south to the main road where they came under fire from a delaying force of US infantry. The Americans were eventually persuaded by the efforts of Sgt. Campbell and Major Shaw that the party was British. Shaw's party was the last group from the Ulsters to escape and they wearily mounted the two vehicles which remained, and drove south. The remainder of the Battalion had marched in during the early hours of the morning to the embossing area and were by dawn back in the old billets at Suwon, where they were later joined by Major Shaw's party. Capt. Robin Charley wrote, "When B Coy reached the transport area I always remember the American driver seeing my three captain's pips (and asking) 'Are you a three star general?'"[25]

On January 4 the Battalion was assembled at Suwon, and the casualties were counted. They had lost 208 officers and men killed, wounded, or missing. During the next few days the figures dropped, as men made their way back, either from American hospitals where they were given treatment, or even from the area of Pulmiji-Ri, where an American helicopter pilot brought out a total of seven survivors. In all the Ulsters lost thirty-three killed in action, or died of wounds. The 8th KRIH lost four killed, and nineteen wounded and missing. All the tanks of Cooperforce were lost and all the crews, save one, were killed or captured. On January 5 the Ulsters moved again, riding on the Centurion tanks of the 8th Hussars, and dismounted about forty miles south, at Pyongtaek.

6

War at Sea

On June 29 1950 the British Government placed the ships of the Far East Fleet directly under the authority of Gen. Douglas MacArthur for operations in support of the UN Security Council Resolution to repel aggression. Naval forces from Britain, Australia, Canada, New Zealand and France which happened to be stationed in Japanese waters at the outbreak of the war, were in action off the coast of Korea from early July. At this period British naval power in the Japanese Sea was temporarily stronger than that of the Americans, as the main body of the US 7th Fleet was based at Pearl Harbour. Britain's Far East Fleet consisted of twenty-two ships at sea between Malaya and the China coast. Among the first ships to see action were HMS *Belfast, Triumph, Cossack, Jamaica, Black Swan, Cockade* and *Consort* with HMAS *Bataan* and *Shoalhaven.* On July 6 HMS *Jamaica* was hit by a shore battery. Two men died, while ten others were injured, four of whom later died of wounds. These four were army personnel on familiarity duties with the Jamaica and with the two seamen they were the first British servicemen to die in the Korean War.[1] *Jamaica* and *Cockade* were the first British ships to sight and sink mines.

Serving on board HMS *Cockade* was Tom O'Keefe, who had left his home in Wexford in 1947 to join the Royal Navy as a boy seaman. Tom O'Keefe and his twin brother, Michael, both joined the Royal Navy on May 6 1947. They came from a seafaring family and an uncle, Raymond O'Keefe, was killed on the *Ark Royal* during WWII. Tom O'Keefe was born in London in 1931. His parents were from Wexford and they returned to Ireland during the Blitz. Tom signed up " basically to look after his brother, Michael, who was mad to join the Royal Navy." As boy sailors the twins had to continue their ordinary schoolwork and also learn the rigours of seamanship. Officially, at that time, they could still be caned, and while neither felt the lash, others were not so lucky. It was part of the old navy now long gone. The two brothers never served together, but often met up in Malta. In May 1949 Tom O'Keefe was serving on board HMS *Comet* as a boy seaman when it collided with HMS *Chevron* during exercises in Malta en route to the Far East. He was transferred to HMS *Cockade* where he finished his com- mission and was rated up Ordinary Seaman.

HMS *Cockade* was a war emergency "C" class destroyer launched on March 7 1944. Commissioned for service in the Far East she served throughout the Korean War. (*Cockade* was scrapped at Newport in 1964.) Armed with four 4.5in guns, two 20mm Oerlikons (designed for aircraft defence), and a single Bofors gun, *Cockade* had a crew of 240. (There were several other Irishmen on board, but only one from Southern Ireland. He was serving as a stoker, so he and Tom O'Keefe rarely met.) *Cockade* left Dartmouth in 1949 for operations in the China Sea, but was diverted to Korean waters when the war broke out. Operating out of the southern Japanese port of Sasebo *Cockade* was assigned to the United Nations Blockading and Escort Force. *Cockade* began duty on July 2 as a destroyer screen, along with other British, Australian and American ships, protecting the US aircraft carrier *Rendova* during daily flying operations against enemy targets on the west coast of Korea. The British Commonwealth and Allied ships were formed into the West Korean Support Group and the US ships into the East Korean Support Group. The British flagship was the cruiser, HMS *Belfast.* No. 827 Squadron, RAF, flew anti-submarine patrols.

Korea is largely mountainous and its coastline particularly indented - especially on the west and southern coasts. The peninsula is surrounded by water on three sides and without the absolute command of the sea, the UN campaign could scarcely have been fought, since all troops and supplies were brought in by ship. Command of the sea was crucial to the UN, as the communists outnumbered their ground forces. The UN forces soon took advantage of their superior naval forces and seized control of Korea's long coastlines, using many ships to transport large numbers of troops and supplies throughout the war. As the communists never really challenged the UN's naval forces, the principal role of the navy became that of floating air bases in support of the ground troops. The use of aircraft carriers increased the numbers of aircraft available to UN ground forces and battleships were able to range up and down the coast in support of the infantry.

Sasebo in Japan was the main base for logistics and the *Cockade* was part of the great Allied fleet when MacArthur launched his surprise attack at Inchon. On September 12 *Cockade*, *Charity* and *Concord* accompanied the aircraft carrier *Triumph* from Sasebo. Their objective, though unknown to the crews of the ships at that time, was to cover the landings at Inchon. The group, part of Commonwealth Task Force 91, was joined by the cruiser *Ceylon* and HMAS *Bataan*, and was now known as the Northern Group. "There were mines that had to be cleared." Tom O'Keefe wrote." Individual ones laid by the North Koreans particularly in the Inchon river. They were usually blown up or sunk by rifle fire."

"A couple of engagements stand out. We were on patrol off the west coast and our brief was to go in close to the shore drawing the fire of shore batteries. Our info on that was positive. Also there were still Japanese laid mines from World War 2. They were still active. We were to go in at daybreak and I remember that night everyone on board was very quiet. No joking or skylarking around. I suppose in our mess the average age was 19. I could sense there was a lot of silent prayer that evening. Just before dawn *Cockade* pointed her bows at the purple land and silently headed in close. The word Korea means 'land of morning calm'. The sea was flat the sky leaden coloured. Not a sound aboard. The daylight broke suddenly and I remember feeling that every enemy eye was watching us. Then we spotted a junk some miles ahead that appeared to be laying mines.

"Then a couple of loud bangs and 4 shells from the guns ashore straddled us. I remember the deck vibrating madly as we went from slow ahead to full ahead. Captain Jack Lee ordered the battle ensign to be hoisted and our guns under director control engaged the shore batteries. I was a cordite supply on X gun. Out of the corner of my eye I saw a C.P.O. running along the deck when he was drenched with water from a shell that didn't explode long side. Then a large black mine passed down our port side within feet. We were aware of a Neptune seaplane circling overhead and we could hear the shells from the larger guns of HMS *London* passing over us. The seaplane was acting as spotter for the *London*. I can't remember how long the engagement lasted. It seemed like just minutes. The *Cockade* silenced the shore batteries. No fatalities or injuries in that engagement, apart from minor dents in the ships superstructure due to shrapnel. In fact the only death from enemy action was a member of Y guns crew killed in an engagement off Taewha-Do in the Yellow Sea. Mick Skelton." (Able Seaman Mick Skelton was killed on January 12 1951, but by that time Tom O'Keffe had returned to England.)

"The 2nd incident which stands out was on the 9th of August 1950 when we rescued U.S.N. Ensign E. A. McCallum. On his first combat mission he was flying a Corsair. During a low strafing run he was hit by enemy fire. He managed to keep the aircraft in the air and cleared Inchon, but crashed in the approaches. He swam to a rock called South Watchet Rock. He was there several hours. North Korean gunboats were trying to find him. They knew he was there. They were all night taunting him with loudspeakers. Also the rock was below water at high tide and "Mac" could see several sharks circling it. We got to him in time blowing up a gunboat en route."

Ensign McCallum, interviewed by US newspapers, said: "I knew it was the Royal Navy. They came in with all guns blazing." In fact, HMS *Cockade* only fired one round from its 4.5in gun, which blew one gunboat out of the water. The rest quickly fled. McCallum was met by the ship's doctor who gave him a huge glass of whiskey, to ward off shock and cold. By the time he reached the bridge he was nearly drunk. (Unlike the Royal Navy, US ships were 'dry' and ships crews denied alcoholic refinements.) He remained firm friends with the ship's company and attended several of *Cockade's* reunions. (E.A. McCallum died in 2004, a retired Commander.) In October as UN troops crossed the 38th Parallel *Cockade* was assigned to 8th Destroyer Flotilla operating on the east coast of Korea. "(A) mission I vaguely recall was during the Inchon 2nd front." Tom O'Keefe wrote. "Marines going ashore at Wonsan. This time we were about 10 miles out at sea doing Asdic Patrol (Anti Submarine Patrol). The North Koreans hadn't any sub-marines, but the Russians had! The main British ship engaged there was HMS *Belfast*." (HMS *Belfast*, an Edinburgh-class cruiser, was built at the Harland & Wolff shipyard in Belfast and launched on 17 March 1938 - St Patrick's Day. It was commissioned into the Royal Navy on August 5 1939, just under a month before the outbreak of World War II.)[2]

After MacArthur's stunning victory at Inchon he came up with an astonishingly bad plan for the destruction of the remnants of the NKPA and the occupation of North Korea. Instead of sending some forces in hot pursuit for the North Korean capital of Pyongyang, or dispatching strong forces overland to Wonsan to cut off NK troops in the Iron Triangle, MacArthur decided to withdraw X Corps from the Seoul area and send it on a long circuitous and time-consuming voyage to an amphibious landing at Wonsan. On October 15 UN naval forces, including *Cockade*, began concentrating in the Wonsan area in support of mine-sweeping and the amphibious landing. The amphibious landing was held up because of delay in lifting about 3,000 mines laid in Wonsan harbour under Russian supervision. Five minesweepers were lost before the minefield was cleared. The marines, and their escorts, steamed back and forth in the Sea of Japan for six days in what the leathernecks called "Operation Yo-Yo." Finally, on October 25 the marines LSTs went into Wonsan harbour and began unloading. By the time the marines landed at Wonsan the ROKs were already there. So too, was Bob Hope. He had staged a USO show the night before the marines came ashore.[3]

With the entry of China into the war, naval pressure was increased against Communist ground forces by bombardments and blockades. "HMS Cockade with other destroyers," Tom O'Keefe wrote, "made up the 8th Destroyer Flotilla, i.e. *Concord, Cossack, Constance, Comus, Consort*, etc. *Cockade* had what you might call a roving commission. Seeking out Korean shore batteries. Engaging them and sometimes bombarding the railway line that ran north-south from Wonsan, picking up isolated targets. Our patrols off the east coast of Korea usually lasted 56 days, refuelling at sea from RFA tankers. Then back to Sasebo in Japan, then out again. The watches were usually divided 4 hours on and 4 hours off, unless we were closed up at action stations." The main north-south road and railway lines on the east coast of North Korea were only a mile or so inland and therefore highly suitable targets for Allied ships in the Sea of Japan.

"We were involved with three aircraft carriers *Theseus, Triumph* and *Glory*. Often we were assigned to crash boat, picking up pilots who either overshot the carrier or when returning from a mission were damaged and crashed in the sea. One day a British Sea Fury ditched in the sea a hundred yards away. We could see the pilot as he tried to open the cockpit canopy. Suddenly the plane sank like a stone. I don't know how long we circled hoping he would resurface. But, nothing. Again the ships company were quiet that evening. The only time we were up close to death was then and at Mak Po when we came across white clad bodies floating at the mouth of the river. You didn't know whether they were men or women and I wondered 'Did we do that?' That was personal."

"The cold in winter was awful. We had to put heaters on the guns to stop them freezing. We were given long johns that looked like they were knitted on broom poles, but we were glad of them. We discovered that they were surplus stores left over from the Crimean War... Our greatest fear was to be attacked by aircraft. During action stations we wore anti-flash gear - white linen gloves, helmet and duffel coat, not much protection. It was more psychological, I think... We had a few bad typhoons, bad food, but thanked God we were not ashore as a soldier. No one joined to die. Their lives were not given, but taken. On deck, on watch, all talk was of home. All my thoughts were of home. Wouldn't I like to be at home having a pint of Guinness and eating some of my ma's bacon and cabbage. These things were important to us as nostalgic links to home.... Our food was rationed, but sometimes we got food from the Americans; minced beef and white bread."

"And so it went on." Tom O'Keefe wrote. "Dawn and dusk action stations. Below freezing most of the time. Endless patrols up and down the coast. We were hardly more than boys, but we matured quickly. Lasting friendships were forged on board that has lasted over fifty years."

At the end of November 1950 the crew of *Cockade* were relieved - service on board was two years. (In March 1951 *Cockade* was again on duty in Korean waters, though with a different crew.) The crew transferred to the luxurious troopship *Dilwara*, which brought them to Singapore. Here they were transferred to that "venerable old cattle boat" *Devonshire*, which brought them to Liverpool. Tom O'Keefe left the Royal Navy in June 1956 after nine year's service as Able Seaman Radar Plotter Second Class. He then joined the Merchant Navy, served another four-and-a-half years, and "fed up with the sea" returned home to Wexford town, where he resides today.[4]

HMS *Consort* was also one of the first ships to see action in the Korean War. Tony Lynch joined the crew of *Consort* in November 1951. Joseph Anthony Lynch, left Cobh, Co. Cork, in 1947, when he was seventeen and travelled to Belfast to join the Royal Navy. He spent most of his time stationed in the Persian Gulf. In 1951 he was hoping to return to England after an eighteen month tour in the Gulf, when he was sent to Korea for a further eighteen months. "Only two of us were sent to Korea," Tony Lynch said. "My abiding memory of Korea was the cold." As a leading electrian's mate he was assigned to HMS *Consort*, a "C"class destroyer, known as "The Galloping Ghost of the Korean Coast." *Consort* was based at Sasebo and was involved in operations along the North Korean east coast bombarding the railway lines and engaging communist shore batteries. Tony remembered only one other Irishman on board the *Consort*. After an eighteen month tour on *Consort* Tony Lynch returned to England on the *Dilwara*. He was demobbed in 1955 and emigrated to America in 1960. He now lives in Southern California.[5]

7

American Frontline
New Year and Spring Offensives

After the rapid retreat of the UN forces following the intervention of the Chinese, the frontline was eventually stabilised slightly below the 38th Parallel. Gen. Walker had been killed in a jeep crash on December 23 and was replaced by General Matthew B. Ridgway, a more aggressive commander. A division and corps commander in Europe during WWII Ridgway was regarded not only by his fellow-countrymen, but also by their British allies, as one of the outstanding American soldiers of the war. With his arrival MacArthur abandoned his direct leadership role, assuring Ridgway he had full authority to command Eighth Army. From this point on MacArthur did not interfere with field operations. Ridgway stepped into a demoralised command. Having being decisively defeated by the Chinese Eighth Army commanders talked of retreat and even withdrawal from Korea. Ridgway dismissed all this and talked of counterattacking. His aggressive attitude boosted the morale of Eighth Army.[1] But while he was working at his task of reorganising his army the Chinese launched their winter offensive along a forty-four mile front, stretching from Kaesong on the west to Chunchon in the center.

The main drive of the Chinese offensive was towards Seoul and the ROK forces north of the capital broke and fled. Seven Chinese armies and two North Korean corps penetrated deeply toward Seoul in the west and toward the rail and road center of Wonju in the central sector. The recently evacuated X Corps troops were reorganising in the southern part of Korea and were rushed to the eastern flank of IX Corps. Private Billy Scully had arrived in Korea in December 1950 where he was assigned as a replacement to the 31st Infantry Regiment, 7th Division. The 31st Regiment had taken heavy casualties in the retreat from North Korea and on December 21 was evacuated from Hungnam to Samchock. Here the division received much needed replacements, among them Private William Scully. Billy Scully had emigrated to America in 1947 when he was twenty-three, with his older brother Jack. Billy was from a large family of fourteen and already had three sisters living in the New York area. The Scullys originally lived in Kilgrena, Galbally, but moved to Deerpark, where Billy was raised. He played Gaelic football and was a very skilful hurler. A year after arriving in America Billy Scully was called up to serve a tour of duty as an infantry trainee in the US Army. He was given a choice, enlist or be deported to Ireland. He was honourably discharged into the Enlisted Reserve, but was recalled to active service in October 1950.

Two months later he was sent to Korea. The 31st Regiment were in action with the rest of the division during the New Year's Offensive as the UN forces were steadily pushed back from the 38th Parallel. On January 14 1951, only weeks after his arrival, Billy Scully was killed by a sniper's bullet. He was barely a month short of his twenty-seventh birthday. Billy's family, and in particular his parents, were grief-stricken when the news of his death was reported back to the little town of Galbally. His body was shipped back to Ireland in accordance with his wishes for burial in Galbally cemetery. Pvt. Billy Scully was posthumously award-ed the Purple Heart. Denis Scully, Billy's father received certification of this, as well as a letter from President Truman, in which he was thanked for the honourable service his son had rendered to America in time of war.[2]

Seoul had fallen on January 3 as Eighth Army withdrew to positions on a line running from Pyongtaek on the Seoul-Taejon highway east through Ansong, northwest to Wonju to the east coast town of Samchok. As Eighth Army withdrew the primitive supply lines of the Chinese slowed their offensive. Ridgway quickly realised the immense advantage of his own shortening supply lines, while those of the Chinese were now extended to the limits. By mid-January the Chinese supply lines were over-stretched and Ridgway, confident that his forces could turn the tables on the Chinese, began a serious of cautious probes. As the UN forces slowly stemmed the Chinese-North Korean offensive Ridgway began planning a counterattack. The communists had lost heavily in the first days of the offensive and began withdrawing to refit and replenish their divisions as contact between the two armies virtually ceased. In early February, with the Chinese offensive stalled, UN commanders prepared a counter assault across the center of the Korean peninsula. Unknown to the UN was that Communist forces also were launching a major offensive and had moved four Chinese and two North Korean divisions into the area north of the village of Hoengsong.

The Chinese tactics of almost always beginning major attacks by descending on less well equipped ROK divisions was brought forth on February 11 when the ROK 5th and 8th Divisions ran into strong Communist forces, quickly forcing the South Korean's to backtrack. The ROKs relied for fire and armoured support on American units and at one point, American artillerymen of the supporting 15th Field Artillery (FA) Battalion, encamped for the night, relying on ROK infantry for protection. When the Chinese attacked in the dark, the South Koreans, who had an inordinate fear of the fighting qualities of the Chinese, fled. The enemy swarmed over the American position. According to a *Time* war correspondent, "It was part of the most horribly concentrated display of American dead since the Korean War began." Some 133 artillerymen were killed along with 328 men from the 38th Infantry Regiment trying to rescue them. Two of the dead were Irish natives, Michael Gannon and Michael King, while another Irishman, William Murphy, was captured and later died in captivity.

Retreating ROKs had streamed south past American support forces, allowing the Chinese to flank the US positions. Soon, the Chinese were in control of the narrow, twisting valley north of Hoengsong and the road that ran through it - the only escape route. Steep hills rose up on both sides of the road, turning the valley into a shooting gallery. The Chinese relentlessly rained mortar fire down on the withdrawing and vastly outnumbered Americans. US rescue forces fought their way north from Hoengsong to the besieged units only to find that a river of Chinese soldiers poured in behind them. Points secured just an hour or so earlier reverted quickly to enemy hands. US infantrymen tried to clear an escape route for the howitzers, supply trucks and other vehicles, but enemy soldiers were everywhere. The American artillery fired point blank into ranks of attacking enemy, but it did little good. As soon as the withdrawing Americans pushed through one Chinese strongpoint, they would run straight into another, while enemy forces reformed behind them. Some 2,000 Chinese troops manned one enormous roadblock. But the route south was the only way out. So the Americans continued to run the gauntlet toward Hoengsong, taking heavy casualties all the way. Finally, the column of weary survivors reached Hoengsong. Those who made it to the village joined a more general and less hazardous retreat farther south.

Among those killed was Michael Gannon, who was born in Achill, Co. Mayo in 1927. He arrived in Korea with the 15th Field Artillery Battalion on July 15 1950. The "Fighting Fifteenth" went into action in August on the Pusan Perimeter. Corporal Gannon was killed in action in the fighting around Hoengsong on February 13. Michael Thomas King, from Elphin, Co. Roscommon, was also killed in action on February 13. He had emigrated to America, and was serving as a Pfc with the 38th Infantry Regiment, 2nd Infantry Division. Also in the 38th Infantry Regiment was William F. Murphy, from Shandon Street, Cork City.

He had emigrated to New York in 1948 where he stayed with his aunt, Mrs. May Moore. In 1950 William enlisted in the US Army and was expecting to be sent to Germany from where he hoped to visit home. Instead he was shipped to Korea in January 1951 and sent as a replacement to Company C, 1st Battalion, 38th Infantry Regiment. He was captured on February 12 and with hundreds more prisoners was forcibly marched north to a POW camp on the Yalu River in North Korea. To avoid air strikes the column of prisoners and their Chinese guards marched by night in bitter cold weather. However, William Murphy never reached the POW camp. He died on May 18 1951, of pneumonia, before reaching his destination. His body was never recovered.[3]

Another Irishman, John Lee, Company L, 38th Infantry, was also captured at Hoengsong. Coy L came up against a Chinese roadblock in a valley that reminded John Lee of Loch Corraili in his native Kerry. Communist troops were hidden on both sides of the road in caves and makeshift bunkers. They opened up with machine guns and grenades and quickly overcame the Americans. As his comrades fell on either side of him a ricocheting bullet or piece of shrapnel knocked John Lee's helmet off his head. The attack stopped as soon as it began and Communist soldiers descended on the road to take captive the few survivors and loot the bodies of the dead Americans. "After being taken prisoner we were rushed through rice paddies with muck and water up to our knees," John Lee said. "The snow was heavy on the ground. Some of the wounded who were able to walk had to move along with us. The badly wounded men were left behind to die, as there were no medics allowed to help them. Some prisoners in my group tried to get away by running from the guards but they were shot in the back and some were killed or wounded and left to die. The guards were rushing us fast.

"After a while US jets came overhead and started strafing along the mountain. I pretended I was hit and fell to the ground. Some guard came over to me and shouted at me. I did not understand Korean but I knew they were telling me to get up. I made a sign to them that I was hit in the leg by a bullet from the jets. I thought they might move off if they thought I was wounded. I was thinking that I might be able to make my way back to the American front line. That was not to be as one of the guards pulled back the bolt on his burp gun and aimed it at me. I got up quickly, as I knew what would happen. I made a bad mistake to pretend I was hit as the guard would have killed me right away."[4]

On March 7 when the 7th Marines re-entered the area north of Hoengsong, for the first time since the rout three weeks earlier, they found the battle scene eerily preserved. Hundreds of US soldiers remained frozen where they had fallen. The enemy had stripped some Americans naked. In many trucks, dead Americans lay behind the wheel or hung out the doors. A Sherman tank with one of its tracks blown off blocked the road. Two Americans were found with their hands tied behind them. They had been shot in the back of the head. Powder burns were clearly visible on the back of their caps. Marines, sickened by the sight, erected a sign along the body-strewn road. It read: "Massacre Valley, Scene of Harry S. Truman's Police Action. Nice Going, Harry!"[5] John Lee survived the Death March to a POW camp in North Korea. He remained a prisoner until August 1953.

By the beginning of March as the UN forces pushed on methodically the communist forces fought delaying actions until the last minute and then withdrew. While it looked like a general retreat by the communists it became increasingly clear that they were merely redrawing for a massive counterstroke: the Spring Offensive. John Murray, from Quignashee, Ballina, Co. Mayo, arrived in Korea on March 1 and celebrated his first St. Patrick's Day away from home by moving to the front. John Murray had worked in the Ballina Flax Mill before leaving for America in 1948. He was drafted in September 1950, at the age of twenty-two, and shipped out to Korea the following February. He arrived at the front just in time for the Spring Offensive, and had his first experience of long-range warfare when the Chinese, as a preliminary to an attack, began an artillery bombardment that lasted a week. Later, a sniper put Corporal Murray out of action for a number of months. He was supervising a road repair crew when he was shot in the left leg. After recovering from his wound, he was promoted to sergeant and sent back to the front. In April 1952 he was shipped home via Japan and demobbed that June. John Murray returned to live in Ireland in 1971.[6]

Another Irish emigrant, Michael Patrick Hardiman, was not so lucky. On March 6 Private Hardiman, serving with the 17th Infantry Regiment, 7th Infantry Division, was killed in action. Born in Moyne, Ballaghaderreen, Co. Roscommon, in 1926, Michael Hardiman emigrated to America in 1948 and settled in Philadelphia.[7] At that time the 17th Infantry was under the command of William "Buffalo Bill" Quinn, an Irish-American veteran of WWII from Crisfield, Maryland. When the Korean War broke out Col. Quinn was serving on MacArthur's staff in Tokyo and was appointed chief of intelligence for the amphibious assault at Inchon. He then served as intelligence officer for X Corps. In January 1951 he was given command of the 17th Regiment. The unit had just received a new radio call sign

- "Buffalo" - and he decided to call his troops "The Buffalos." Two newspaper correspondents gave him the name "Buffalo Bill" and the nickname stuck. The Buffalos were taking part in Operation Killer, Ridgway's plan foe IX and X Corps to advance and clear the communists from Chipyong-ni and mountains to the east. Designed to kill as many of the enemy as possible the operation also accounted for many UN casualties. Michael Hardiman was killed in action on the last day of Operation Killer.

Another casualty of that spring was Douglas MacArthur. Unable to accept that fact that the war was unwinnable and that Korea would remain divided he had pressed for a widening of the war, including bombing Chinese bases in Manchuria and the use of atomic bombs. Truman, who did not wish to embroil the United States in a full-scale war with China, a war whose outcome could scarcely be conceived, was left with no choice. He ordered MacArthur relieved of his command and to be replaced by Gen. Ridgway. Lieutenant General James A. Van Fleet was chosen as Ridgway's successor. (Van Fleet was a regimental, divisional and corps commander during WWII and headed the US military mission that aided the Greek army in its successful campaign against Communist guerrillas from 1948 to 1950.)

MacArthur's dismissal came as a shock. He was America's most decorated war hero, the liberator of the Philippines, the tamer of Japan. The American Legion went on the record as backing MacArthur. In New York, protesting Irish groups who had been picketing the British consulate for two years set aside their anti-British placards for those in support of MacArthur.[8] On the frontline soldiers were undismayed. Ridgway had become a commander to rival MacArthur's popularity. Commonwealth Brigade British officers were so happy they threw a party to celebrate MacArthur's dismissal. (MacArthur loathed the British and they him. The British Ambassador in Tokyo said, "To me, personally, MacArthurs's departure is a tremendous relief as it is, I think to nealy all my colleagues.[9]) In Europe Truman's decision was well received and the British and French press lauded the President for standing up to MacArthur.

By March 15 Operation Ripper had taken the UN forces back to the 38th Parallel and across the Han river in the west. Seoul changed hands a fourth time in less than nine months. Much of the city was rubble and there were no utilities and only 200,000 ragged civilians remained of the once bustling city's normal population of 1,500,000. By the end of March, Operation Ripper was declared a qualified success. The geographical objectives had been achieved but the enemy had not been destroyed. The communists forces had lived to fight another day.[10]

8

The Ulsters and the Irish on the Imjin

In mid-February after a fierce battle for the town of Chipyong-ni, American morale rose considerably when they saw that the Chinese "hordes" could be defeated. The US 2nd Division, which had been so crushingly handled at Kunu-ri, held against a massive Chinese attack, and won a much needed victory. Making use of their massive weight of firepower the UN forces gradually began pushing the enemy back. By March 15 Seoul was recaptured and twelve days later the UN forces re-crossed the 38th Parallel. Matthew Ridgway had assumed command of all UN ground forces - the Eighth Army, with which X Corps had just been merged. Four days before Walker's death MacArthur had said he would need four more fresh divisions to stablise the UN lines. Ridgway disagreed and said he could hold the 484,000 communist troops with the 365,000 soldiers under his command. He had studied Chinese Communist tactics in the Chinese Civil War and again in the fighting north of the 38th Parallel. Ridgway's plan was to punish the Chinese, while keeping his own casualties low. He was concerned with "the good opinion of his troops and never played to the greatAmerican audience as MacArthur had always done."[1] In a little over three months Ridgway had turned a beaten and demoralised army into a confident fighting force. Not only was the UN line straightened out, the forthright Ridgway inspired his men to advance and meet the communist threat head-on. For weeks the UN moved forward mile by bloody mile. After crossing the 38th Parallel Ridgway ordered the advance to continue to establish a line slightly north of the Parallel.

The US I Corps advanced on the left of the UN formation and the British 29th Brigade found itself occupying temporary positions on the line of the Imjin river. The 29th Brigade covered an unusually long frontage of about 11km (6 miles). The 1st Battalion of the Gloucestershire Regiment (the Glosters) were the left forward battalion with the 1st Royal Northumberland Fusiliers in the centre and the Belgian Battalion on the right. The Belgians were the only battalion deployed to the north of the river. The 1st Ulsters were in reserve. Because of the temporary nature of the positions and the expectations of moving north, their positions were neither deeply dug and no mines had been laid nor barbed wire defences constructed. The brigade relied for fire support upon the 25- pounders of the 45th Field Regiment, but lacked ready access to medium or heavy artillery. To make matters worse at that season the Imjin was fordable almost everywhere on foot.

Meanwhile, the Ulsters were lucky enough to spend St. Patrick's Day in reserve. A football match against the 8th Hussars was arranged and invitations issued for a Sergeants' Mess Smoker and an Officers' Mess Dinner. St. Patrick's Day dawned clear and sunny, and the war seemed far away. Rfn. Henry O'Kane was just back from hospital in Japan in time for the celebrations. Brigadier Tom Brodie "visited the Battalion to take part in the celebrations which in every Irish Battalion is laid on no matter what part of the world they are in... In the evening a concert party was an overwhelming success and it was made all the better by the appearance of my late comrades in arms, the laundry girls of Brigade HQ plus the plentiful supply of Guinness courtesy of the QM, Capt. Tom Smith."[2]

Adjutant Hamill wrote: "The day was an unqualified success, there being a good supply of turkey and various luxuries obtained by the Q.M. together with a very fair share of liquid refreshment, including Guinness. Brigadier Brodie dined with the officers and various guests, while the Sergeants' Mess Smoker opened the eyes of many visitors from other less fortunate units of the Brigade. Church services were held during the morning, and in the evening the Concert Party gave a very good show with a pronounced Irish bias, the football team clinched the pleasure of the day by beating the 8th King's Royal Irish Hussars by five goals to three. Early in the morning of the 19th of March a signal was received from

H.M.S. *Belfast*, saying that she was lying off shore at Inchon, on the west coast, and inviting a party of officers to visit her that day. Owing to the visit to the Battalion of General Sir Richard Gale, the Commanding Officer was unable to go, but a party, consisting of Major Rickcord, the Q.M., Capt. Ivor Daniels, and Lt. Mervyn McCord, was quickly, assembled and set off on the 75-mile jeep drive to the coast. With the co-operation of an American L.C.T., the party was able to get out to the ship and was royally entertained by Captain Sir Aubrey St. Clair Ford, D.S.O., R.N., and his officers. Much was done to further the close liaison between the Ship and the Regiment, and when the time came to leave, the party was played over the side by the Royal Marine band to the tune of Off, Off, Said the Stranger."[3]

On April 14 the Belgians and tanks of the 8th Irish Hussars skirmished with a Chinese patrol four miles north of the Imjin river, and took one prisoner. A week later an "armoured swan" drove eighteen miles north. "Lowtherforce," led by the C.O. of the 8th Hussars, again skirmished with a small Chinese force, which withdrew at once under pressure. Aerial reconnaissance reported little enemy activity on the British front. On April 22 patrols out north of the river contacted the enemy. Aerial reconnaissance that same afternoon reported that roads and tracks leading south towards the Imjin were packed with vehicles and troops on foot. By dusk Chinese forward elements had reached the river and had been engaged by 45th Field Artillery.

The standing patrol from the Glosters on the river bank opened fire on large numbers of Chinese troops grouped closely together, who began to ford the river at 1830. At around the same time the Belgians also reported contact with the enemy. The brigade adopted a fifty per cent stand-to for the night. At 2200 Brig. Brodie ordered the Battle Patrol of the Ulsters to secure the bridges at Ulster Crossing, the ford by which they had been passing the Imjin for the last three weeks, and to protect the Belgians line of retreat. It immediately appeared that, on the right, the enemy were trying to force their way round the Belgians' left flank.. Three Chinese divisions were actually on the move against the British front and within hours the 29th Brigade would be fighting for its life.

At midnight the Battle Patrol of around fifty men set off in their Oxford carriers to Ulster Crossing with orders to dismount on arrival and send the carriers back, to withdraw if pressed, and, if in serious trouble, to fight their way through to join the Belgians. The remainder of the Battalion was put at short notice to move, while reports of heavy fighting continued to come in from the other battalions. The Battle Patrol, according to Henry O'Kane, consisted of "all the hard drinking, hard fisted elements of the Battalion and must have been hand picked by the administration staff. Each man had a reputation of being a potential troublemaker and the sooner they got killed it would be all the better for unit discipline, nevertheless most were volunteers."[4] As time went on the Ulsters Battle Patrol proved to be one of the best compact fighting units in the 29th Brigade. At 0200 hours an Oxford carrier of the Battle Patrol returned to Battalion H.Q. and the driver reported that the patrol had been ambushed on their arrival at Ulster Crossing and that the enemy was already in strength at the bridges. After a brief, violent firefight the patrol had retreated on foot. They paused for the survivors to regroup.

Lieutenant Hedley Craig, the Battle Patrol commander, realising his task was hopeless, decided to stay behind with ten men to cover the withdrawal of the rest of the patrol, under 2/Lt. P. J. Kavanagh. The group found themselves surrounded and decided to surrender. They were assembled on a hillside with six other captured Belgian soldiers. Without warning the Chinese suddenly opened fire on the prisoners. Three RUR men and five Belgians died, while the rest, most of them wounded, made their escape in the confusion. When the bodies were found a month later, it was discovered that two of the Ulsters had been shot in the back of the head and one of the Belgians had been shot or bayoneted in the back. Lt. Kavanagh, wounded in the shoulder, rejoined the Battalion in the early hours of the morning, with five Riflemen, all of them wounded. He was evacuated to hospital in Japan and then sent home. Lt. Craig arrived back in the British lines two days later.[5]

The full attack on the Glosters came just before midnight, preceded by heavy artillery and mortar fire not previously available to the Chinese forces. By first

1. 8 Section 12 Platoon D Coy wait for dawn attack on HIll 614. John Hawkins is fourth from left standing beside Charley Thorburn (right). 2. John Hawkins, early days in Korea. 3. John Hawkins in his foxhole, winter 1951. Note his combat knife and hand grenades in easy reach. 4. John Hawkins looking anxious as 27th Commonwealth Brigade approach the Yalu.
(Photos J. Hawkins.)

1.Kapyong after the battle. Note broken rifles in the foreground.

2. Air and artillery strikes Hill 614, before 8 Section attack. (Photos J. Hawkins.)

1. Medic J.T. Jennings, poses alongside a US Army helicopter, Korea 1952.

2. A typical frontline US Army bunker, 1952. (Photos J. T. Jennings.)

1. HMS *Cockade* in Hong Kong.
2. Exploding of mines in Korean waters by marksmen on *Cockade*.
3. Tom O'Keeffe (right) and pals on HMS *Comet*, 1949.
(Photos T. O'Keefe.)

UN armour on the move, 1st Commonwealth Division area, 1951.
(Photo W. May.)

1. Machine gun post,
Ulster Rifles, 1951.

2. Pusan harbour, 1951.

(Photos W. May)

1. Bren gun carriers of the 1st Ulster Rifles, 1951. (Photo W. May)

2. Jack Clarke in his machine gun position facing no man's land, the Hook 1952. (Photo J. Clarke)

Michael Fitzpatrick, Claremorris, Co. Mayo, killed in action Korea, August 18 1951.
(Photo M. Doody.)

light the forward companies of the Northumberlands and the Belgians had been withdrawn and confused fighting continued throughout the day. By dusk the Ulsters had been deployed to the rear of the Belgians and succeeded in covering their withdrawal south of the river. The 45th FA were to the right of the Glosters and laid down supporting fire around the British battalions' positions, including a barrage on Chinese cavalry in the valley below them. Chinese infantry concentrations were shattered again and again by devastating British artillery fire, but although the 25 pounders of the 45th FA were fine guns and the crews very professional, they possessed limited killing power. There was a desperate need for the support of heavier artillery, but the British battalions' establishment of heavy weapons was inadequate and they possessed no way of calling in American 155mm fire. The 45th FA lost six men killed in action on April 23: one officer and five gunners. The officer was Lieutenant A. Bruce Samuel Hudson, a twenty-six year old from Dublin.[6]

By midnight, April 23-24, the Glosters were effectively surrounded. All companies had suffered severe casualties and the whole battalion was concentrated on one main hill feature - later to be known as Glosters Hill. A determined attempt was made to cut a way through to the Glosters by infantry of the Filipino Battalion, backed up by the Centurions of C Squadron, KRIH, but the track was virtually impossible for tanks, even without opposition. A mine blew off the track of one of the three Filipino M24 light tanks. Chinese troops strung out atop the hills bordering both sides of the defile swept the road with fire while others armed with pole charges worked their way down the steep banks toward the disabled tank. The other two M24s made no attempt to pull or push the damaged tank out of the defile or to rescue the stranded crew, but two less cautious Centurion tanks squeezed past the Filipino armour and went as far as the narrowing road allowed. Their covering fire allowed the crew of the disabled tank to escape. Meanwhile, the Filipino infantry became involved in a fierce fire fight with the Chinese occupying two hills abutting the road to the rear. Maj. Henry Huth, in command of the Centurions, radioed back to brigade headquarters that the road was blocked and the wide Centurions could not get through the defile. He was given authority to withdraw and the relief column headed back the way it had come. Leapfrogging rear guards, alternately tanks and infantry, held off Chinese who followed part of the way back as the rescue force withdrew to its starting point.

On the night of April 24-25 the Northumberland Fusiliers and the Belgians also withdrew, covered by the tanks of C Squadron. The withdrawal was very difficult and costly but was finally completed by midday on the 25th. C Squadron were busily engaged in battle with infiltrating enemy troops in the ditches, and paddy-fields along the road, and on the slopes above. The rest of the Brigade was ordered to withdraw to prevent the Chinese encircling them. The Glosters, however, were completely surrounded and could not withdraw. They were ordered to split up and break out as best they could. One of those killed on Gloster Hill was Private William Synott, a thirty-three year career soldier from Dublin. He was posted as missing in action but a repatriated POW witnessed his death on April 24. The Glosters suffered 243 killed and missing, and 530 captured. Rifleman James B. Dunwoody was a young nineteen year old from Belfast serving with the 1st RUR. "As a sniper," he wrote, "I was present in all of the Ulster Rifles engagements and I had a close up view of the capture of the Glosters. I was on a OP and I had a close up view of all the action when they were nearly all killed or captured."[7]

The order for withdrawal came as a great disappointment to the Ulsters, who had held off the Chinese attacks for last forty-eight hours, for the loss of one man killed, and several wounded. No ground had been lost and the enemy had been very severely punished in every attempt he had made to capture the hill or break through into the valley. Although tired, the men had every confidence that they could continue to hold the position and fight the Chinese attack to a standstill. The Acting CO of the Ulsters, Major Gerald Rickord was dismayed by the plans for the withdrawal, which called for his men to leave their positions on the high ground, and descend four miles to the valley road where transport awaited them. The Ulsters would have preferred to walk out along the ridges, keeping the enemy below them. But Brig. Brodie ordered otherwise. It seemed like a repeat of the withdrawal from Happy Valley, and this said Henry O'Kane "was still vivid in our minds".[8] By 1200 the Ulsters were assembled in the valley and moved out thirty minutes later. All their vehicles, except two Mortar carriers had already been sent back. Unfortunately, C Company, in moving off their hill to the assembly area, suffered four casualties from friendly fire, which was being laid on the vacated positions. As it was impossible to move the wounded men, Lt. Max Nicholls and a medical orderly gallantly stayed behind to look after them, while a request was made for an armoured ambulance to come forward to pick them up. The ambulance, however, was knocked out on the way up and never reached them. The valley was suspiciously quiet as the leading Company moved off, except to the south, where the battle for the saddle continued unabated. After a few minutes automatic fire from the western slopes began to sweep the valley and, after the column had covered about half a mile, the volume of fire from light automatics and machine-guns hidden on the west of the road became intense. The infantry were completely in the open, with little cover save that afforded by occasional paddy bunds and clumps of bushes. Casualties began to occur at once and movement was soon limited to short bounds from cover to cover. Wireless communication, which had hitherto been good, gave out and soon broke down completely as signallers or sets were hit or separated from their commanders. Lt. John Mole, in command of the remaining section of 3in mortars, dismounted his guns in the open and began to reply with rapid mortar fire on to the slopes from which the fire came, but the hail of machine-gun fire still swept the valley floor.

"It was one long bloody ambush," said Major Henry Huth, commander of C Squadron, 8th Hussars. He won a DSO for his direction of the tank actions during the retreat, and for the personal example he set as his was the last Centurion out of the valley. Captain Peter Ormond and Gavin Murray resorted to machine-gunning each other's tanks to dislodge Chinese infantry scrambling onto the hulls. Sergeant Jack Cadman drove his tank through a mud hut to dislodge a Chinese soldier who was battering on his turret hatch. The tanks ranged up and down the valley firing their 20 pounders and Besa machine guns against swarms of attacking infantry swarming down the slopes to the west.[9] The rear of the column, consisting of A Company (less one platoon), Main H.Q., and

D Company, had swung out of the low ground into the hills to the east and were moving up on to the eastern ridge-line in a long column. The Commanding Officer, with between twenty and thirty men who remained of B Company, also turned south-cast and moved up into the hills. The tanks, laden with infantry who had reached the saddle, turned south and drove fast down the road to run the gauntlet. But the road for a mile-and-a-half south of Hwangbang-Ni was teeming with Chinese. Every bank, ditch, and house was filled with them and some were actually crushed under the tracks of the Centurions. The unprotected infantry riding on the outside came under a continuous rain of small arms fire, grenades, and mortar bombs. Many were killed on the tanks and many of the wounded, lost their grip on the wildly, pitching hulls and fell to the ground. Two tanks were knocked out by pole charges rammed through their tracks, but the remainder, with their load of dead and living, broke through to the comparative safety of the Brigade Headquarters in the valley.

Rfn John Dyer recounted his escape on the back of a tank: "Coming out of Gloster valley, we were actually on the hillside on the banks of the other side of the valley and it was literally covered with men. They were running, not hither thither, but they were running straight for us and straight down the valley. They'd cut us off once already and were intending to cut us off again. Unfortunately they achieved it with many of them, but some of us were lucky enough to escape. I actually came out of the valley on the back of a tank. The backs of the tanks were basically kept for the wounded. We'd already loaded up the backs of the tanks with the wounded to try and get them out and there was one tank there with nobody on, so we just took a chance and took a ride on it. We were told there was a chance that we wouldn't get through and that we'd be safer going up the hills, but anyway two or three of us took the chance and climbed up on the back of the tank. The Chinese were still running alongside the tanks, throwing grenades on to the tanks, trying to disable them. I mean we couldn't do a lot about it because we had nothing left, we just laid there quiet and still, watching them, listening to them actually being crushed by the tank tracks ... As we came out we were taken up to an Indian field ambulance, the injured were lifted off and we were hoping to go back with the Hussars back to the HQ. No such luck!"[10]

"There wasn't anything to do," Rfn. Henry O'Kane wrote, "but to stop at intervals, return fire and keep on going. We were without cover at some point. The fire became strong. Mortars joined in. Suddenly I was hit in the leg. After crawling to a paddy bund, I ditched my gear, except for my rifle, and managed to keep on going. We began taking further casualties as we dodged from cover to cover, bund or brush, thought there was very little of either. Later on we seemed to put our heads down and keep on going. The fire was intense but we did not seem to notice it. I remember a group of Royal Engineers, acting as infantry, hunched under the lee of a Centurion tank that had shed a track shouting to us to get down, but we kept on going. We passed two more tanks, knocked out and on fire, and further down the road an RUR Oxford carrier lay with its dead crew spilling out. The name on the side read Ballymacab." O'Kane and the other wounded were loaded on the tanks of the Irish Hussars for the final run to Uijongbu. "It was a wild swaying, bouncing ride on the Centurion. It didn't last long - but I shall never forget it. The dust, the rattle of the tracks, the Besa machine gun, the screams of the wounded men as we were repeatedly hit. Suddenly we were surrounded by the Chinese again. They came along the road with Molotov cocktails and polecharges. Many of their men were killed by the tanks. Later, how much later I don't know, I came to in a ditch by the side of the road. A few yards further on the tank was slewed across the paddy, its tracks off and the petrol tank burning. I was covered in blood, my nose and ears were bleeding from concussion. I had lost my rifle - it was the only thing at that particular moment that worried me."

Henry O'Kane lay half submerged in a small stream by the side of the road, surrounded by small groups of wounded and those who were beyond help. Chinese soldiers ran by them in hot pursuit of the rest of the retreating men. After awhile some of the wounded began moving around, helping each other. One put a bandage around Henry O'Kane's head and gave him a swig of rum. The sound of gunfire receded. Three Chinese soldiers appeared and one who appeared to be of higher rank said, in careful English, "I think it is a good fight. For you the war is over." The wounded men were disarmed and given safe conduct passes. The wounded who were able to walk were marched down the road, hands on their heads. Those unable to walk were left behind. "They were never seen again," Henry O'Kane said. After walking about a mile the Chinese guards called a halt near a dry gully. One prisoner said it was an ideal place for executions and O'Kane and another Derryman, Tommy Spears, sat down and proceeded to smoke all their remaining cigarettes, seventeen in all, or eight and a half each. (Tommy Spears was a regular soldier who had served with the post-war Irish Brigade, in the 2nd Inniskillings in Austria, the Royal Irish Fusiliers in Trans-Jordan and Egypt, and the 1st Inniskillings in the West Indies.) Instead of being executed the prisoners were handed over to a second set of guards, given a leafy branch as camouflage to carry over their shoulders, and marched off to captivity. "So this is how the Chinese did it," O'Kane wrote, "advancing the length of Korea in daylight without being detected by our Air Force. Soon we were struggling around the now familiar slopes of Kamak San, around the long curve of the mountain, through positions now held by the Chinese, positions that had been strafed and blackened by napalm, past hundreds of dead Chinese and others still alive who stared at us seemingly without seeing - it was all very uncanny."[11]

Meanwhile, in the hills to the east of the saddle, about two hundred men from the Ulsters A and D Companies and Battalion H.Q., halted to reorganise, and then moved south along the ridge-line towards the lateral valley leading out to the main road to the south. Small parties of Chinese had already made their way across the valley floor and up into the eastern hills. These were engaged as the column moved along and only one group got within close range, where they were promptly driven back down the hillside. It was afternoon as the head of this column reached the escarpment overlooking the lateral valley. To the east, two miles away, was the MSR (main supply route) and, on the low hills through which the road passed, an American regiment was dug in.

"I stuck to the hills," Corporal Norman Sweetlove, Belfast, said, "and it must have been for miles and miles with the Chinese shouting down from the tops of the hills, 'Tommy, this isn't your war. British Tommy, hand your rifle up, this isn't your war.' But we just keep plodding on and then we came to where all the firing was behind us. I saw this pool of mucky water, I was dying of thirst and I dived into it and the next thing was ... Chinese burp guns opened up into the pond of water. We got ourselves out, we rolled away from that, (ran) another few thousand yards until we came to the top of the hill, looked down and (saw) the withdrawal ... the American convoys. We mostly fell down the hill, we'd no power in our legs, threw ourselves down the hill onto the MSR. I jumped on the mudguard of an American Red Cross ambulance, and he took us a few miles where the convoy was going."[12]

Groups of British, Belgian and American troops headed towards the MSR, covered by two Centurions, their guns pointed eastwards. In front of them, the paddy fields swarmed with Chinese moving east in open order and rapidly closing on the tanks. The weary Riflemen, now again under heavy fire from Chinese who had gained the ridge, plunged down the escarpment, through a small village at the foot of the slope, where machine-gun and mortar fire was intense, and east towards the road. The tanks, hard pressed by the advancing Chinese, withdrew, slowly in turn as the infantry passed behind them, while a few officers and men at the very rear of the column made a final dash across the paddy and clambered onto the tanks. Within another hour the battle was over. The last stragglers of 29th Brigade passed through the American block on the road and marched south. The tanks rallied on the road and followed the Brigade towards Uijongbu. At Tokchon cross-roads, four miles down the road, the Brigade was ordered to occupy a further blocking position.

In the Battalion, the count showed a total strength of 14 officers and 240 men. As darkness fell, this force, with the Northumberlands and the Belgians, began to dig in, and were fed for the first time in the day. They were told they would have to soon fight again, but later that night fresh orders came. It was realised the Brigade was exhausted. Sufficient American forces were now in the line to hold it against any new Chinese pressure. The Ulsters, utterly weary, marched a further six or seven miles towards Uijongbu until, at last, transport picked them up and carried them south through the night to Yongdungpo, on the south bank of the Han. Just before dawn the men dismounted in the disused Japanese

Ordnance depot from which the Battalion had moved up to the Imjin. Here they were fed and then fell immediately asleep. The Battle of the Imjin was over.

Although the Chinese offensive rolled to within five miles of Seoul, its back was broken on the river line. Later reports showed that the full weight of the attack had been directed on the British 29th Brigade. The 64th Chinese Army carried out the assault on this sector with three divisions in column. This attack was held for three days by the four battalions of the Brigade. While the Glosters were virtually destroyed, and heavy casualties were suffered by the other battalions and by the 8th Hussars, in the final withdrawal the enemy's losses from April 22-25 were so heavy the 64th Army was rendered virtually ineffective for some time afterwards. Above all, the three days during which the Spring Offensive was held up on this sector allowed the remainder of I Corps to withdraw and to secure the line of the Han river, including the capital city of Seoul, the prize for which the Chinese had gambled and lost.

The Ulsters lost ten officers and 176 other ranks, a large number of whom were missing, including thirty-one killed. Since the beginning of the year almost half the battalion had become casualties. The 8th Hussars lost two men killed, both troopers attached from the Royal Armoured Corps, and six Centurion tanks. Four Centurions shed their tracks and two were abandoned because of mechanical failure. They were to be destroyed to prevent them falling into enemy hands and US planes attacked them with napalm and rockets. Despite being pounded by armour-piercing shot from a range of fifty metres the two tanks abandoned because of mechanical defects - one had tipped over a bank nose first into a deep trench and got stuck, while the other had its gears stuck in reverse - did not catch fire and both were subsequently recovered and repaired.

Although the Glosters were the heroes, both the Ulsters and Irish Hussars won great distinction in the Imjin battle. Major Rickord, acting CO of the Ulsters, said, "I believed we had lost the battle, had suffered a disaster. But I was afterwards reassured that it was by no means a disaster. The morning after we came out, the soldiers were singing Irish songs, playing a banjo. I told the quartermaster to get them a bath and their green tropical uniforms. He said: 'It's much too cold for that.' But I said - 'No, go on, do it. It'll make all the differnce in the world to them to get a change of clothes.' And forty-eight hours later they were fit to fight again, which was a wonderful feeling. I think they felt very proud of the fight they had put up. We felt no particular animosity towards the Chinese. Indeed, I think we felt great respect, even liking for them. But the regiment's old motto - *Quis Separabit* - was something we felt very strongly about."[13]

9

Duty First

Australia was the second country to come to the aid of South Korea sending a fighter squadron to escort US bombers on an attack on a North Korean airfield near Hamhung on July 2. The first Australian - and Commonwealth - casualty was on July 7 when a 77th Squadron commander was lost over Samchok railway. When the war broke out in June 1950 the 3rd Battalion, The Australian Regiment, was stationed at Hiro, on the Japanese island of Honshu, preparing to return to Australia. As part of the British Commonwealth Occupation Force Japan (BCOFJ) the 67th Battalion had arrived with 34th Australian Infantry Brigade in Japan in February 1946 to help in the Allied occupation of the Japanese home islands. As conscription had ended in 1945 the 34th Brigade was an all-volunteer force. On November 23 the 67th Battalion was renamed 3rd Battalion, The Australian Regiment. The following year King George VI granted the prefix "Royal" to the Regiment. With the outbreak of the Korean War, and Britain's commitment to the United Nations cause, Australia mobilised the 3rd Battalion for duty in Korea. The Battalion underwent ten weeks intensive training at the former Imperial Japanese Army jungle-training centre at Haramura. On September 27, the Battalion augmented by two drafts from Australia and 960 strong, embarked in the USNS *Aiken Victory* at Tokyo. They landed at Pusan the following day and joined 27th Commonwealth Brigade at Taegu.[1] John Hawkins, from Enniscorthy, County Wexford, was serving with the 3rd Australian Battalion. (His younger brother, Paddy, later served in Korea with 2nd RAR.)

John Hawkins was born in 1926 in Drumgoold, Enniscorthy, in the shadow of

Vinegar Hill, one of Ireland's most famous battle sites. He served three years in the Irish Army before going to England to find work after WWII. (At the end of WWII, or the Emergency as it was known in Ireland, the Irish Army was scaled down and many veterans of the period, unable to find work in a flagging economy, decided to emigrate.) From England John emigrated to Australia in 1948 on the "ten pound system". An estimated one million British people, including many Irish resident in the UK, left struggling post-war Britain to seek a new life in Australia.

The British and Australian governments arranged their transportation by ship upon payment of a ten pound fare, hence the name. Australians referred to the newcomers as "ten pound poms." John arrived in Sydney and after working at various odd jobs decided to join the Australian Army. There were many emigrants in the 3rd Australians, John Hawkins, D Company, recalled. "Captain Ryan's (his company second-in-command) people were from County Kildare. There were a couple of Tipperary men, and Tommy Sinnett, from Blackwater, Wexford. There was an Irishman, a Scotsman and a Welshman in my section." John also met William Kevin Murphy from Ennis, Co. Clare, serving with B Company, who was later killed in action at Kapyong, "at the staging area in Pusan and a couple of other times." Like all Irish soldiers, or civilians, abroad they would reminisce about home, usually over a beer or two. He also met "an O'Brien, (Private R. G. O'Brien, or Pte. T. W. O'Brien) from Tipperary around the winter of 1950. He was in a different company, but we would speak a little Irish on the two-way radio to confuse anyone listening in."[2]

Five days after arriving in Korea the 3rd Australians suffered their first casualties, when two men were killed in action near Waegwon. Soon after its arrival in Korea 3rd RAR was attached to the 27th Commonwealth Brigade, which in turn was attached to the US 1st Cavalry Division. On October 5 the Battalion deployed to take part in the Eighth Army offensive. "The worst part of the war was the first year," John Hawkins said. "You were never two nights in the one place. The three battalions (of 27th Commonwealth) leapfrogged each other all the way to the Yalu. We were the Americans spearhead and when they 'bugged out' we were still their spearhead. We were shoved aside as the 1st Cavalry came up to take the glory. But there was no glory in Korea. The Chinese poured in and we had to clear everything out of the way to get the Americans out. The Chinese were good fighters. The North Koreans were good, too. Ruthless, very cruel, but they didn't balk. They had no problem sending refugees through minefields."[3]

The Chongchon river, forty-five air miles north of Pyongyang, was the preliminary objective of Eighth Army preparatory to the final drive to the Yalu. The 4,000 strong US 187th Airborne were dropped ahead at two separate points, Sokchon and Sunchon, in the hope of capturing North Korean officials, blocking the main body of the retreating NKPA, or rescuing a trainload of US POWs. However, the 187th failed to catch any North Korean officials, the main body of the army or the train carrying the POWs. The force making the Sukchon drop, however, landed behind the rearguard of the NKPA. The paratroopers attacked the NK regiment from the north while the 27th Commonwealth Brigade closed up on the south side. There the 3rd Australian Battalion distinguished itself with a spectacular bayonet charge. Just north of Yongu the Australians acting as the advance point and riding on medium tanks of the attached US 89th Tank Battalion, came under fire from an apple orchard on both sides of the road. Lieutenant Colonel C.H. Green, the Battalion commander, ordered Company C to flush out the North Koreans in the orchard.

The American tankers had orders not to fire because the paratroopers were believed to be nearby, so C Company fixed bayonets and charged into the orchard. John Hawkins was serving with D Company and when they fixed bayonets, in this, his first action, he could feel a shiver run up his spine. Soon Col. Green ordered D Company to clear the area to the west of the road. The North Koreans had been forming up for their final breakout attempt against the American paratroopers and were caught by surprise by the sudden appearance of the Australians on their flank. In this bloody hand-to-hand battle the North Koreans lost 150 men killed and 200 captured. The Australians, incredibly only suffered seven wounded. The Australians linked up with the Americans, who were overjoyed to be relieved, but momentarily suspicious of the Aussies.

Because of their strange garb and heavy overcoats some of the Americans thought the Aussies were Russians![4]

The following day Col. Green was mortally wounded by a shell fragment. The Aussies second major action was on October 25 at Pakchon, called the "Battle of the Broken Bridge." Using the element of surprise 3rd RAR thrust across a half-destroyed bridge, over the Taenyong River, in the dark to rout the North Korean defenders. In the ensuing battle eight Australians were killed and twenty-two wounded. An Australian combat photographer snapped John Hawkins, and his comrades Ted Mosley and Snowey Amey, "relax after fierce fighting for Pakchon", with the broken bridge in the background. On October 31 the 3rd RAR relieved the Argyll and Sutherland Highlanders and for the first time the Royal Australian Air Force 77th Squadron supported the battalion with air strikes on enemy held hills. "We were watching a Corsair napalm a hill," John Hawkins said. " It was a big plateau, but we would have to climb straight up. The Corsair would napalm the hill then rocket and strafe anyone that tried to escape. As he did two of his rockets kissed and he went straight into the hill. He was killed by the blast, probably killed outright, but we saw him go straight into that hill."

On November 1 5th and 8th Cavalry Regiments of the US 1st Cavalry Division were attacked by Chinese troops. The month of November was spent retracing the steps of the earlier advance as the Chinese attacked behind them. On December 4 the North Korean capital was abandoned, and a week later the Australians were in reserve at Uijongbu, 24 kilometres north of Seoul. The Chinese pushed on relentlessly and by January 4 Seoul had been abandoned. Through February and early March 1951 bitter fighting continued on steep and narrow ridges, given the names according to their height in metres, Hill 614, 410, 532 and 703. Conditions were terrible in the middle of the harsh Korean winter. The wounded were forced to slide down the snow-covered hills to safety. "You had two bitter enemies in Korea. One was the cold." John Hawkins recalled. "We were fighting in snow, in 30 and 40 degrees below. We were not equipped for the weather. None of the army's were. But the Yanks came good with the winter clothes. We didn't mind the fighting, that's what we were paid for, we were all volunteers, but the cold was so bad. We (the Irish) were used to a bit of snow, but some of the Australians had never seen snow - they were from the desert. We had get them up and walk them around to get their circulation going. We got these long woollen gloves, which we wore on our feet. " Living and fighting in numbing cold also posed a number of problems when it came to weapons, transport, supplies and a soldier's physical and mental well being. Weapons were meant to be Arctic-tested to keep any moving part moving, no matter how cold it was. Most just froze anyway and moving parts had to be kept moving all night in case they were needed in a night attack - a favourite tactic of the Chinese. The Australian's equipment was the same as that of WWII. Infantry were armed with the SMLE Mark III and the Owen, an Aussie-made 9mm sub-machine carbine. Steel helmets were issued, but these, John Hawkins said, were "a nuisance, only good for a direct hit downward, though they were handy for boiling water and shaving in."

At Cham-ni, between February 13 and 14, a US Armoured Reconnaissance Patrol was ambushed. When the troops of 3rd RAR and 1st Middlesex came upon the scene they saw only dead bodies and the abandoned jeeps and tanks. About sixty US soldiers were killed in the ambush. "I wore one of their boots for six months afterwards," John Hawkins said, "as mine were wore out. We rescued about thirty taken prisoner. The rest were lying dead in the snow. It was a slaughter." On February 25 12 Platoon, D Company, 3rd RAR, captured Hill 614, an important piece of high ground at the second attempt, enabling the UN forces northward advance to the Albany Line to continue. Hill 614 was the key to the whole area and the pass from Sokkong Valley for a brigade attack. An earlier attempt had failed and 12 Platoon waited until the air and artillery softening up barrage was just over and stormed up the hill. "We were lucky. The Chinese were half dead coming out of their holes. Eleven of us took Hill 614. We used every weapon we had… tommy gun, Owen, Garand rifle, M1 carbine. Everyone in our section was wounded, mostly minor, but some seriously. Charley Thorburn was the most serious. He was shot through the shoulders." John Hawkins received minor burns when his uniform caught fire while he was "lying behind a dead gook who was napalmed."[5]

The continuous fighting and horrendous casualties finally slowed down the Chinese New Year Offensive and the UN forces switched to offensive action. Seoul was retaken again on March 14. The Australians went into reserve where they remained until March 25 and then took part in the advance to the 38th Parallel. After a month of hard fighting in which they lost 55 killed, 205 wounded and five taken prisoner, the Aussies withdrew to the south-east into corps reserve near the village of Charidae, seven kilometres north-west of Kapyong. The Brigade, however, was on three hours' notice to move in support of any of the three divisions on the IX Corps front. The British Government hoped to relieve the 27th Brigade, which had been at war for over seven months, during its period in reserve. The two British battalions of the brigade, the Argylls and the Middlesex, were to be replaced by the 1st Battalion, The King's Own Scottish Borderers and the 1st Battalion, The King's Shropshire Light Infantry.

The Australian battalion and the New Zealand field regiment were not to be withdrawn as units, but individual members were to be relieved after approximately one year's operational service. Therefore 3rd RAR and the 16th New Zealand Field Regiment were constituent members of the Commonwealth Brigade throughout the war. The Canadian battalion was scheduled to become part of a full Canadian brigade in May. Brigadier Burke and the headquarters of the 27th Brigade were to be relieved in late April by Brigadier G. Taylor and the headquarters of the 28th Brigade. The formation was then to change its designation to become the 28th British Commonwealth Infantry Brigade. Advance parties of 27th Brigade Headquarters and the Argylls departed for Seoul en route to Hong Kong on April 19. With the front ominously quiet the Australians made plans to celebrate Anzac Day, April 25, with the New Zealanders. The Turkish Brigade, who were encamped four kilometres away, were invited to send a detachment to a service on Anzac Day. Australian soldiers gathered the wild azaleas in bloom on the hillsides to brighten their commemorative wreaths which were to be laid at the service.

The Australian Battalion looked forward to a well-earned rest with a full ROK division between it and the enemy. Conditions in the reserve area, known as

"Sherwood Forest," were spartan; the men were living in small, two-man shelters, with only one or two larger tents per company. Some films were screened for entertainment, one of which was enlivened when a soldier dropped a lighted cigarette by a small drum of petrol which was supporting a plank seat in the outdoor cinema.[6] Fortunately no one was injured in the ensuing explosion. John Hawkins recalled this as one of the funniest moments of the war. "They were showing a movie for the Brigade. Everyone was there, all types of uniforms and regimental caps about. The screen was on the back of a lorry. Lads were sitting on stumps of trees, and up in trees, when suddenly there was a mighty explosion, flash and flames. Men ran every way. I dropped down between two tree stumps and was hit by boots running in every direction. I got up and shook myself and saw I wasn't injured. One lad was found in a paddy-field with a roll of film around his neck. He went through the screen. What happened was someone dropped a cigarette into a jerrycan of petrol being used as a seat. We thought we were under attack.

"We decided to have a 'do' for Anzac Day," John Hawkins recalled. "We saved up our beer ration, but the next minute the balloon went up. The South Koreans threw away their weapons and uniforms. Company B, 4.2 inch Mortars, a chemical warfare group, also bugged out." Just before midnight on April 22 the Chinese launched their Spring Offensive and the 6th ROK division withdrew in disorder through the Australians positions. The next day 27th Brigade was ordered north where they deployed to defend the Kapyong Valley. That evening, the main Chinese force reached 3rd RARs perimeter. The battalion was positioned with A, C and D Companies on high ground to the east of Chuktun ni, and B Company positioned on the left flank on a long scrub covered rise between the road and a small stream. They were to cover the ford across the river and to guard the road from the north-east. "If the high ground was taken the door to Seoul was open," John Hawkins said. "Then you would have had another Dunkirk. Seven-hundred Australians were trapped on Kapyong. We had only taken up our positions. Some of the Argylls were already on board ship in Inchon harbour. We heard about the others (Ulsters) on the Imjin while they (the Chinese) were giving it to us at Kapyong."[7] D Company's position was the most vital. The men of D Company had a long and difficult climb to the summit, carrying their weapons, ammunition, food and communications equipment. Hill 504 is crowned by a steep-sided, narrow, U-shaped ridge, the two arms of which lead down via spurs running to the north-west. Captain Gravener positioned 12 Platoon with a section of medium machine-guns at the northern end of the ridge. 11 Platoon were placed centrally on the ridge on a knoll separated by a small saddle from 12 Platoon's position and l0 Platoon on the summit of Hill 504, which was at the south-western edge of the ridge. D Company Headquarters was with 11 Platoon. Although the steep, convex slope in front of 12 Platoon prevented it from seeing far to its immediate front, it had an excellent field of fire across the ground leading up to A Company's position on the western flank.

They were 50 kilometres behind the frontline so felt relatively secure. However, as the daylight began to fade small groups of South Korean soldiers were noticed moving back along the road towards Kapyong. The CCF 'First-Step, Fifth Offensive' demanded a massive assault by well-trained and well-equipped Chinese forces in the western and central sectors culminating in the capture of Seoul; while two Field Armies would advance on the east-central and eastern fronts and take Chungju and Taegu. The hope was that UN troops would be left in disarray with no alternative but to evacuate the peninsula. Initial attacks by three Chinese divisions led to the Battle of the Imjin, forcing the retreat of the 29th Brigade to Tokchon. While this battle raged the Chinese attacked the 6th ROK Division at the sharp end in the Kapyong Valley, the customary route followed by invaders from the north.

After dark the flow of South Koreans towards Kapyong increased to a torrent. They withdrew in disorder, indicating a serious collapse on their front. Groups of soldiers milled about without direction from their officers and NCOs. Overladen vehicles clogged the road. Drivers and occupants impatiently abandoned any that stalled and sought places on other vehicles, even ox-carts, or joined the less fortunate mass of troops walking southwards. Some of the South Koreans were moaning with fear and exhaustion, and dumped their equipment as they passed. In this column were the 16th New Zealand Field Regiment and the 1st Middlesex.

They took up positions to the rear of the 3 RAR headquarters. Chinese forward troops mingled with the fleeing South Koreans and began probing attacks on Australian positions. Soon after nightfall, a nearly full moon rose over the battlefield, illuminating both defenders and attackers. The first Chinese attack fell on the outpost platoon of American tanks and was beaten back. An hour later a much heavier attack was made on the tanks, mortally wounding the platoon commander, and seriously wounding three other tank commanders. The tankers fought with their hatches open so that they could observe enemy infiltrators attempting to close with their tanks, but without protecting infantry they were highly vulnerable and began a fighting withdrawal. The Chinese launched probing attacks on A and C Companies, inflicting over fifty casualties. Headquarters and C Company were under constant pressure during the night. D Company, on the summit of Hill 504, spent a quieter night. It was not probed until 1600 on 24 April when some six Chinese approached their perimeter. About an hour later, Company Headquarters personnel shot one enemy soldier and 10 Platoon captured another. The Chinese then ceased their efforts against D Company for two hours.[8]

Col. Ferguson was particularly concerned about the safety of the Regimental Aid Post which, located in a paddy field across the road from his headquarters, was under fire all night. Some wounded men had reached the aid post during the night, where the Medical Officer, Captain Beard, gave attention from his limited resources in the darkness, assisted by Chaplains Laing and Phillips and the Salvation Army representative, Major Robertson. Although the Chinese fired on the aid post, they did not attack it directly; nor did they fire on men when they were loading casualties aboard the battalion's ambulance, which prominently displayed the Red Cross. Ferguson's caravan, a converted 2.5 tonne truck nicknamed "Pandora's Box," (because, John Hawkins said, you would never know what might appear from it) was not so lucky. The caravan became bogged in a ditch during the withdrawal and Ferguson, with great reluctance, ordered his batman to destroy it. Before setting it on fire the batman saved his Commanding Officer's Zenith radio, battle maps and wife's photograph. John Hawkins had great praise for the battalion chaplains and Mr. Robertson of the Salvation Army.[9]

"You could be lying there with bullets whizzing all around you when you could get a tap on the shoulder and turn around to find Mr. Robertson with a cup of tea. They (the chaplains) deserved medals for the way they looked after us." He also had great praise for the Red Cross who were always on hand with tea, or cigarettes, when they came off the line.[10]

The coming of daylight had improved the situation of the four forward companies but the battalion's position was nonetheless serious. The rifle companies were cut off, and were over four kilometres behind the enemy front. They had fought hard all night and A Company had suffered nearly fifty casualties who could not be evacuated. Col. Ferguson decided to withdraw B Company from its exposed hill on the western flank to a new position behind C Company. Before departing, B Company men counted 173 Chinese dead on their perimeter and in the valley. A clearing patrol had captured thirty-nine prisoners and they also had to be taken to the new position. During preparations for the withdrawal, which included the laying of a smokescreen by the New Zealanders, enemy pressure increased on the western flank and B Company suffered its first casualty of the battle when one man was wounded in the arm. The whole withdrawal was covered by the platoon of American tanks, which was still with the company. The company vehicles, onto which eight seriously wounded Chinese had been loaded, were escorted back to the Middlesex position by the tanks, which then occupied the ground immediately below C Company.

Throughout the withdrawal B Company exchanged shots with Chinese who were hiding in broken ground, on small rises and in the river-bed. The prisoners were divided into groups and dispersed amongst the rifle sections for easier control. The company passed some horrifying sights as it crossed the body strewn valley. The prisoners repeatedly pointed at the bodies of their comrades who had been blown to pieces. Shortly after Col. Ferguson ordered his troops to reoccupy the hill from which B Company had just moved. It now appeared that the 27th Brigade would be reinforced by American troops and their move forward would be facilitated if the Chinese were cleared off the small hill which commanded the road. The retention of the hill would also have made impossible any Chinese attempt to attack Hill 504 from the western flank. 5 Platoon made a spirited attack on a knoll between C Company and the old B Company position but were forced to withdraw after suffering seven casualties.

Lieutenant Montgomerie, commander of 4 Platoon, was then ordered to take over the attack. Just before his men moved into another assault some American tanks arrived from the rear and gave support. Montgomerie led his men across the open ground in a right-flanking attack. They came under fire and suffered a few casualties in the opening phase. When they were within thirty metres of the forward Chinese trench, the weight of enemy fire increased. Montgomerie then led a desperate bayonet charge against the nearest line of trenches. Corporal Davie, commanding 1 Section on the right flank of the platoon, led his men into the first trenches. In fierce hand-to-hand fighting they cleared the Chinese from these trenches at a cost of three casualties. Davie's section then came under heavy machine-gun fire from the rear trenches. He gathered together his remaining men and they hurled themselves at the defenders. Montgomerie quickly reorganised the whole platoon and they fought their way forward from trench to trench with grenade and bayonet. The Chinese defended the position bravely but were unable to hold the Australians.

The leading members of the platoon then saw that they were under fire from another knoll in front of them. Leaving his rear sections to continue clearing the first position, Montgomerie and Davie's section quickly pressed on to the second knoll. Their aggressiveness was too much for the Chinese and some climbed out of their trenches and fled across the open ground. The majority fought to the death. When the whole position had been captured fifty-seven dead Chinese were counted in the first position and twenty-four in the second. The whole operation had cost B Company three killed and nine wounded. Among those killed was Corporal William Murphy, from Ennis, Co. Clare. (Lt. Montgomerie was awarded a Military Cross for his outstanding leadership, while Cpl. Davie was awarded a Military Medal.) Once the knolls had been occupied by 4 Platoon, the men of B Company could see that their former hill position was held in strength by the Chinese and a major attack would be required to dislodge them. Before any plans could be prepared for this next move the men were ordered by Col. Ferguson to withdraw. Brigadier Burke had decided during the morning to move the Australian battalion back to the Middlesex area, believing correctly that it would not be able to survive another night of heavy attacks in its exposed, isolated position.

During the morning of 24 April, D Company, which was on the summit, was under constant and increasingly heavy attack. For over three hours 12 Platoon, at the forward edge of the company's position, was continuously attacked. The security of D Company's position was vital to the whole battalion. Not only did it occupy the commanding heights of Hill 504 but it also protected the battalion's open right flank. 12 Platoon repulsed all attacks, which were made up a very steep slope on a narrow front of four to five men supported by many others in depth and by mortar and grenade bombardments. In the first six attacks the Chinese lost some thirty men killed and the defenders suffered seven wounded.[11] "Every man on that hill knew fear," John Hawkins said. "I thought I would never make it out alive. You could hear the sound of the Chinese bugles and whistles and then they came over the ridges. The Chinese had to attack up steep slopes and took massive casualties." 12 Platoon, under the command of Lieutenant Johnny Ward, were on point on the high ground on the right flank. "The Chinese came in waves. The American Forward Observer was killed in hand-to-hand combat." All through the night the Chinese attacked again and again. Each time they were repulsed, they regrouped, and attacked again. Their casualties were horrendous, but they continued attacking, charging over the bodies of their dead comrades.[12]

The New Zealand gunners played a notable part in D Company's defence right through the day. The artillery observer parties with each of the forward companies were doubled to control accurate fire which was brought in to within fifty metres of the Australian positions. Each enemy attack was met with a devastating 25 pounder barrage and with intelligent employment of artillery and the aggressive defence 12 Platoon broke up the Chinese assaults. The Chinese failed to break through, though the Australians had little knowledge of the casualties the Chinese were suffering because the steepness of the slope afforded concealment of the enemy evacuation movements. There was a lull in the attacks for an hour and a half, although D Company was continuously fired on by mortars, machine-guns and rifles Captain Norm Gravener decided to move 12 Platoon back to the centre of the company position, believing that if the battle continued into the night, the forward platoon would be overrun. He hoped that with a tighter perimeter his company could continue to maintain its hold on the summit, although the withdrawal of the forward platoon gave the Chinese a more protected line of approach and assembly area for attacks on the ridgeline. Chinese machine-gunners continued to fire on the Australians as they moved, but news of the evacuation did not reach a new wave of Chinese infantry about to attack and D Company had the satisfaction of seeing a full-scale assault go in on 12 Platoon's old defences. The Australians then subjected the area to intense machine-gun and rifle fire. The artillery also struck the Chinese hard as they tried to establish themselves on the northern end of the ridge.

Capt. Gravener then called for air attacks to dislodge the surviving Chinese from the old 12 Platoon area. Unfortunately the spotter aircraft directing the airstrike dropped a spigot flare onto the position occupied by Lieutenant Mannett's 10 Platoon and the Company Headquarters. The two attacking Corsair aircraft then dropped their napalm right into the heart of the D Company defences. The Chinese had already started some fires in the dry scrub on the hill. The napalm set off many more and the flames raced across the summit, adding to the distress and confusion caused by the accidental attack. The napalm attack was quickly halted by Captain Mick Ryan, the company Second-in-Command, who ran out under enemy fire waving the marker panel, which had been placed on the ground to identify the Australian position to the pilots. The napalm killed two Australians, wounded several and destroyed weapons and ammunition which were of great importance to the defence of D Company's position. Seeing this confusion, the Chinese made a frontal attack on 11 Platoon, which was repulsed with heavy casualties. The enemy did not abandon their efforts, however, and continued to attempt to infiltrate D Company's eastern flank throughout late after-noon.

Soon after the airstrike, at approximately 2330, the battalion's withdrawal began. B Company moved back first, closely followed by C, A and D Companies. Major Ben O'Dowd decided to move carefully so that the four companies could give as much support to each other as possible. He moved A, B and C Companies onto the high ground behind D Company then despatched B Company along the ridge to locate enemy positions and dislodge them. The other three companies then withdrew in a leap-frog fashion, with one in a blocking position, one preparing the next blocking position through which the former would withdraw, and one company moving back to the next stage. D Company continued to bear the weight of the enemy attacks and was prevented from moving at the scheduled time by a particularly determined assault. Heavy machine-gun and mortar fire preceded the attack. The Chinese infantry then ran headlong at the company's forward weapon pits in an attempt to overrun the position.

Once again they were hurled back by vigorous defensive action and Capt. Gravener decided to begin thinning out his position before the situation deteriorated. 10 Platoon covered the evacuation of the area, closely engaged by the enemy. In the gathering darkness the Chinese vigorously pursued D and A Companies along the ridge. The battalion completed its difficult and brilliantly executed withdrawal from Hill 504 aided by the New Zealand artillery who played a vital role in keeping the Chinese at bay. They delivered highly accurate fire, with shells falling only fifty metres behind the rearguard.

By 0130 all elements of the Battalion had reported in. Col. Ferguson checked them through, waiting at a pass on the road into the new position. The battle had cost the Australians dearly. Thirty-two men were killed, fifty-nine were wounded and three captured. Among the dead was Corporal William Kevin Murphy, from Ennis, Co. Clare. The Battalion had withstood a continuous attack by far greater numbers of Chinese for over twenty-four hours. Although they did not know it when they reached the Middlesex area, the men of 3rd RAR had halted the Chinese advance in their sector and no further attempts were made to break through on the eastern flank of the 27th Brigade. When the 6th ROK Division had fled on April 23 it gave the Chinese Army Commander what he hoped was an open road to Seoul. At Kapyong his ambition was frustrated by 3rd RAR who delayed the CCF for twenty-four hours permitting the UN theatre commander to reposition a force in the path of the Chinese forces, thus securing the road to Seoul. (In recognition of this battle the President of the United States awarded 3rd RAR his Distinguished Unit Citation.)

The next day there was very little activity on the front and the Australians went forward to the former battalion headquarters area and reclaimed abandoned equipment. The Chinese, exhausted by the fighting, had withdrawn and had made no attempt to destroy it. The men were giving food, ammunition and a bottle of beer. They knew then that the battle was over. For many of the men who had crossed from Japan to Korea with the Battalion in September 1950, Kapyong was to be their last major action before completing their operational tour. They had fought hard, admidst chaos and confusion, in appalling weather, in operations which had ranged far over the Korean peninsula. During this period the 3rd RAR had suffered 87 killed, 291 wounded and 5 captured.[13]

John Hawkins operational tour was now over, but like many of the men he decided to stay with the Battalion. Later he had a very lucky escape when a mortar shell landed in front of him and failed to go off. At times, particularly at Kapyong, he thought he would never make it out alive, but he had no fear of dying, that was for some other guy. "We were volunteers. We didn't mind the fighting. That was what we were paid for. We could not blame anyone for sending us there. We were like brothers. We weren't brave. We all knew fear, but you had to control it." John Hawkins returned from overseas duty to Australia in 1954. In the 1980s John returned to his native Enniscorthy, where he still resides.[14]

10

To the Trenches

While the 29th Brigade stood on the Imjin General Van Fleet organised the UN forces along the No Name Line, a reserve position north of Seoul. By April 29 the Chinese were halted all along the line. During the first week of May the UN forces moved forward about ten miles. Uijongbu, which had been abandoned at the height of the offensive, was recaptured, and the Kimpo peninsula was cleared of enemy troops. On May 15 the Chinese and North Koreans launched another offensive. But, by May 20 that offensive was spent. On May 22 Van Fleet opened his own counteroffensive, designed to exploit the exhaustion of the Chinese. The Chinese and North Koreans retreated as fast as possible, but the retreat was more like a rout. As the weather cleared the UN air forces bombed and strafed everything that moved. There was little doubt that, had the political will existed, the communist front now lay open. The morale of the Chinese army in Korea was shattered. But Washington had decreed that the objective was to bring "an end to the fighting and a return to the status quo; the mission of Eighth Army was to inflict enough attrition on the foe to induce him to settle on these terms." The war had reached a stalemate. On the new front, give or take a few miles at various points, the UN forces would hold their ground for the remainder of the war.[1]

Michael Cyril (Mike) Kelly arrived in Korea in mid-April 1951 and was attached as a medic to Company E, 8th Cavalry Regiment. Born in 1928 in Uhran, Eyeries, Castletownbere, Co. Cork, Mike had emigrated in 1949 to San Salinas. He had two aunts in California, one in San Francisco and one in Santa Rosa. He arrived on December 23 after a five-day train journey from New York and began work in January 1950 as a railway engineer, or train driver. He was drafted that year and was inducted into the US Army on September 8. Mike took basic training as an infantryman at Fort Ord and left San Francisco on March 28 1951. After a seventeen-day sea journey he arrived in Japan and five days later, Korea. On April 22 twenty-one Chinese and nine North Korean divisions slammed into Line Kansas in an attempt to capture Seoul. The 1st Cavalry Division joined in the defense line and the bitter battle to keep the communists from the South Korean capital. The communist advance was halted on May 15 and the Eighth Army pushed them back to the Kansas Line. The 1st Cavalry moved deeper into North Korea reaching the base of the "Iron Triangle" an enemy supply area encompassing three small towns. After taking medical aid training near Inchon Mike Kelly was assigned to the Medical Company attached to Company E, 1st Battalion, and "as a medic on patrol I carried a .45 automatic and a carbine and did my share of fighting, you had to. There was an awful lot of night fighting, over-running of positions; heavy fighting all the time. There was a terrible amount of casualties. It was terrible to see them all stretched out." Mike met several Irishmen, including one from "Sligo, who was captured and went missing."[2]

The UN had begun to construct a strong defence line along the hills (known as the Kansas Line) overlooking the river, and this line was to be made completely secure before any further advance took place. In June UN forces continued the advance to the Wyoming Line, running just south of Chorwon and Kumwha at the Iron Triangle. Here the Chinese and North Koreans began constructing their own defensive lines. They had seen their Spring Offensive bleed to death on the interconnecting artillery and machine-gun sites of the No Name Line and now began to construct their own version of such an entrenched line. Advancing UN forces soon encountered stiff opposition. Serving with the 35th Cacti Regiment, 25th Infantry Division, was an Irish-born native, Private E2 Daniel "Donal" Harrington. Born in 1926 Donal Harrington lived in Ardnacluggan, Eyeries, Co. Cork. He was a friend of Mike Kelly, also from Eyeries, and the two had attend-ed school together. Donal emigrated to America and settled in Brooklyn. He was a very accomplished and adept gaelic football player and captained the 1950

Cork senior football team in New York. He was drafted into the US Army in 1950 and assigned to the Cacti Regiment, which by now was a solid veteran unit and had been in Korea since June 1950. He was seriously wounded in action on April 25 1951 and returned to duty on May 14.[3]

"One day as these guys were laying telephone wires," Mike Kelly recalled, "this guy overheard me talking and asked did I know another Irish guy, Donal Harrington. I said I did that he was a friend of mine. He said 'I'll try and hook you up.' These telephone wires stretched the whole width of Korea. About two hours later he came back and said, 'I have him on the line do you want to talk to him?' I spoke to Donal and had a good chat. But a big push came on and Donal was shot and wounded. He died in Japan."

As General Ridgway had predicted, the Chinese were determined to hold the Iron Triangle and adjacent ground as long as possible. Drenching rains during the last two days of May began to turn roads into boggy tracks and, along with low clouds and fog, limited close air support and both air and ground observation. "During the monsoon season," Mike Kelly said, "the roads became the rivers." After two clear days the full attacks got under way on June 3 but rainstorms returned to hamper operations throughout the next two days. Aided by the bad weather, Chinese delaying forces fighting doggedly from dug-in regimental positions, arranged in depth, held the advance to a crawl. Donal Harrington was killed in action in the fighting on June 6. "Donal was (mortally) wounded," his friend Mike Kelly, recalled.[5] Donal Harrington's body was brought home for burial and he was laid to rest in Castletownbere Cemetery on February 2 1952, coincidentally the same day as a Memorial Day Mass in St. Patrick's Cathedral for nine, then-known, Irish casualties of the war. The Chinese finally gave way under the pressure and began a phased withdrawal, moving north. As the battle lines solidified the 25th Division secured the high ground overlooking Kumwha.

Another Irishman, Pvt William (Billy) Collins, was killed in action on May 18 1951. He was twenty-two and a native of Tullig South, Co. Limerick. Billy Collins emigrated to America in 1947 in search of a better life. His mother had died a year earlier and he settled in Astoria, Queens, New York, where his Uncle Martin had an apartment. His brother, Mossie, followed him over in 1948. Billy Roche, a neighbour from Ireland, also came over to join them. All three stayed in the apartment and Billy and Mossie worked at the Manhattan branch of A&P - a well-known New York supermarket chain. Billy looked forward to the day when he would become an American citizen and with this in mind he declared his citizenship papers. In November 1950 Billy was called up for army training and in February 1951 he arrived in Korea. There, he was assigned to a heavy mortar company in the 23rd Infantry Regiment, 2nd Infantry Division.[6] The division saw some hard fighting in the Second Chinese Spring Offensive when they bore the brunt of a Chinese attack on the center of the No Name Line. The Chinese attack began on the afternoon and night of May 16.

More than 137,000 Chinese and 38,000 North Korean troops were hurled against the front manned by the 2nd Division and the ROK 5th and 7th Divisions on the right. On their success depended the course of the war for it was an all-out effort on the part of the communists to smash and destroy the Indianhead Division, thrust through the ROKs and outflank the entire Eighth Army line. The dead piled up in front of the Americans who refused to yield against the tremendous odds. The following night the Chinese attacked again driving some elements of the division out of their hilltop positions. Their attacks were temporarily successful as the ROK 5th and 7th Divisions fell back leaving the 2nd Division virtually surrounded. But the US 9th Infantry drove north and the 23rd and 38th Infantry regiments pushed south wiping out the Chinese threat. As nightfall approached Division artillery reported every available piece firing into the gap in the lines while, overhead, B-26 bombers unleashed tons of bombs onto the masses of troops streaming through the break.

Meanwhile, the 23rd Infantry Regiment was under attack all along its front. Communist troops streamed through the abandoned ROK positions threatening the entire Division right flank. Aware of the danger this posed, General Ruffner tried to modify the right flank of the No Name Line so the 23rd Infantry could deny its flank to the enemy. After fierce fighting the 2nd and 3rd Battalions of the 23rd Infantry were joined by the 1st Battalion at Hangye and immediately the regiment set up its new defensive line tying in with the 9th Infantry Regiment. The French Battalion went into blocking positions on the MSR and by midnight the line was secure, the adjustment complete and the enemy thwarted in their efforts to outflank the Division. Thousands of dead littered the battlefield in what became known as the "May Massacre". It was a major defeat for the communists, but it was not without its cost in Allied lives.[7] Billy Collins was killed in action in the fighting on May 18. His death was a bitter blow for his brother Mossie. It came as a huge shock to his family in Ireland, as Billy had concealed the news that he had been drafted into the army and sent to Korea. In New York a newspaper reported: Astoria Soldier Dies For Nation Not His Own. Billy Collins' remains were interred at Long Island National Cemetery, Pinelawn, Farmingdale, NY. In a poignant graveside ceremony, the folded US flag was handed over to Mossie Collins in the presence of his Uncle Martin. Billy Roche also served in Korea. He survived and settled in America.[8]

Medical Sergeant Mike Kelly was wounded in the head and knee while on night patrol, for which he received the Purple Heart. (He also suffered frostbite on his left ear.) Mike was also awarded a Bronze Star for "bravery in action" when he saved two wounded men on another patrol. "We knew the enemy was in the hills and forest and went there on patrol. We weren't in there very long - a half hour - when we got slaughtered; five or seven dead, eleven wounded. Going out through a valley up a hill these two Irish-American fellas, were left behind. It happened so quickly. We were disorganised when we had to withdraw. I heard two voices calling my name. I said to the company commander, 'I'm going down to get these two fellas.' He said I was out of my head, but I said, 'That's my job.' I went down the hill. They were shot in the legs. I don't know where I got the strength, but I carried one in each arm. I just got to the top of the hill when some other soldiers came to help me." Both soldiers were evacuated and survived. This incident and the loss of his wallet on the battlefield led to a false report that Mike Kelly was missing in action, and these details were printed in the *Cork Examiner*. It took twenty-one days before the truth emerged and for that time

Mike's parents were unaware of his fate. Sgt. Mike Kelly left Korea at the end of the year as the 1st Cavalry Division, after spending 549 days of continuous combat began rotating back to Hokkaido, Japan.

The 8th Cavalry Regiment was the last unit to leave. Mike Kelly spent three months in Japan before the USS *Breckinridge*, the vessel which brought him to Japan, brought him back to San Francisco. "It was very sad going back, part of the ship had bodies of those killed (in Korea). That was the saddest part." He was transferred to the Army Reserve in September 1952 and then returned to Ireland for a three-month stay. "The best thing I done was to come back to Ireland... back to my roots. It helped me to settle down. I was a complete nervous wreck. War ruin's your whole life, but thank God I got over it. It's hard on the women, too." After three months in Ireland Mike Kelly went back to the US and back to work as a train driver. He settled in Connecticut for a time and returned to Ireland in 1971 "for good".[9]

When the 1st Ulster Rifles went back into the line again the UN advance had carried the line very nearly up to the Imjin river. The Ulsters had been reinforced with a draft of about one-hundred men from the Royal Irish Fusiliers and were nearly back up to strength. They took over from the US 1st Cavalry Division in the same hills where the battle of the previous month had been fought. The Battalion were to relieve the Greek Battalion who had just occupied the heights against only moderate resistance and were patrolling forward to the Imjin itself. Here they met the men of the Greek Battalion, "a tough-looking lot of dark, bushy-moustachioed men in American uniform and equipment". Capt. Hamill wrote: "It was puzzling, however, to find in the midst of this Hellenic atmosphere, that the Greek Battalion's Command Post sign featured prominently the name "Garry Owen," together with the 1st Cavalry Division's crest.

"It transpired that the 7th U.S Regiment, to whom the Greeks were permanently attached, is the oldest American Cavalry Regiment, having fought, in fact, under the famous General Custer at the Battle of the Little Big Horn in the Indian War of 1876. The Regiment had originally, been recruited from Irish emigrants, and for many years now had used the tune of "Garry Owen" as their Regimental March. The 7th Cavalry, we found, were still proud of their Irish origin, and in fact still celebrate St. Patrick's Day as a Regimental holiday. The most amusing touch of all was to find that the Greeks, through their association with the 7th Cavalry, here in Korea, had adopted the "Garry Owen" sign (and a considerable respect for its traditions), as much as they had their American equipment, clothing, and transport."[10] Capt. Robin Charley spent the summer training reinforcements "in the hills of japan overlooking Hiroshima. I stood on the steps of the demolished Osaka Bank which was ground zero of the atomic bomb and I looked at the utter devastation of about a mile in all directions from that point."[11]

On June 23 the Soviet Union suggested truce talks in Korea and on July 10 UN and communist delegations met for the first time in the town of Kaesong to open ceasefire negotiations. Many in the West thought the war would soon be over. Yet, it would take two years of argument, threat and counter-threat and much recrimination before the armistice was finally signed. On the frontline the situation seemed almost to resemble the trench warfare of World War I. Battles of considerable size were initiated by both sides. They had the aim of weakening the resolve of the enemy, seizing ground in order to improve the local tactical situation or acquiring a bargaining counter to be used in the ceasefire talks. More men would die after the negotiations began than before.

Pat O'Connor, from Ballydavid, Dingle, Co. Kerry, arrived in Korea "about a year after the war started". He had emigrated to America in 1947 and was living in Chicago, when he was drafted in January 1951. After basic training in Fort Leonard, Missouri, he went on to Fort Stoneman, California, and then to Yokohama, Japan, where he spent several weeks. Posted to the US 2nd Infantry Division he was assigned as a machine gunner on an M3 half-track. (The M3 was an armoured personnel carrier with wheels in front and a tank-like track system in the rear. Able to carry up to twelve men, the M3 could also tow artillery and was equipped with a .50 calibre Browning machine gun. The M3 was also used in a support role for US infantry on the MLR. Its great range and striking power made it deadly against troops staging for assault or against massed infantry attacks.) "Ours was a very remote area. Going up through Seoul there was nothing there; the buildings were very dilapidated. I never saw a cow, hens, nothing." Pat O'Connor "hated every bit of it (the war). Nothing bothers you when you are young, but I would not do it again. When you get older looking back you wonder how you did it." He served a year and one month in Korea and returned to Ireland in 1954.[12] Pat Kelly, from Millstreet, Cork, also arrived in Korea in 1951. He had emigrated to New York in 1948 and was drafted two years later. He was stationed in Hyundai when there were "no cars there, only an ox" for transport. Assigned to the 445th Ordinance Ammunition Company, Pat Kelly's job, as an ammunition carrier, was to supply the frontline troops with all makes of ammunition from large calibre shells to rifle bullets. It was a "twenty-four hour a day, seven days a week job". When he returned to New York after his tour of duty Pat could find little work and was employed as a bartender working a ten-and-a-half hour shift. He stayed in America for another twenty years and then returned to Ireland.[13]

In April 1951 the 28th Commonwealth Brigade Group had replaced the 27th, and then the 25th Canadian Infantry Brigade Group. In July these units were organized into the 1st Commonwealth Division. On July 28 in a simple ceremony at Tokchon the flags of Britain Canada, Australia, New Zealand and India were broken together, proclaiming the formation of the 1st Commonwealth Division. The Division was allotted a key sector. It was placed astride the Invasion Valley, leading to Seoul, a route which had already been used by the enemy in his advance southward. The Division, while under US/UN operational control, was administered by Commander-in-Chief, Commonwealth Forces headquartered in Japan. The first Canadian aid to Korea came on July 12 1950 from three Canadian destroyers. Canadian troops had first arrived in Korea on December 14 1950 and by the war's end 26,791 had served with the United Nations, with 516 dying on active service. Kevin O'Shaughnessy from Ballinrobe, Co. Mayo, served with the Canadian army in Korea. He was a psychiatrist living in Canada at that time and volunteered for service when as the Korean crisis deepened, the Government authorized the recruitment of the Canadian Army Special Force. It was to be specially trained and equipped to carry out Canada's obligations under the United Nations charter or the North Atlantic Pact. Instead most of the unit's were destined for Korea.[14]

The first days of August found the US 2nd Infantry Division adjusting its positions and preparing defences along the Kansas Line. Hill 1179, firmly in the control of the Americans, had eliminated enemy observation of the Kansas Line activities in the east. However, three hills overlooking the western portion of the line - Hills 983, 940 and 773 - were now being used by the enemy as observation posts. Patrols from all the divisions three regiments on the line, ranged out to determine the extent of this new threat. Information gathered on the enemy defences on these three hills pointed to an increasing urgency that these heights be captured as they posed a serious threat to the Kansas Line and also served as observation posts from which the enemy called down increasing amounts of artillery fire. On August 18 the 2nd Division, along with the Republic of Korea (ROK) 36th Regiment began an assault on Hill 983. Known as the Battle of Bloody Ridge, the battle would last almost two and a half weeks. Two Irishmen serving in the same regiment, 23rd Infantry, would die in the bloody battle; Michael Fitzpatrick, from Mayo, and Philip Lynch, from Galway.

Michael Fitzpatrick was born in 1928 and lived in Cappagh, Claremorris, Co. Mayo. The second youngest of five children Michael's mother died when he was five years old. He emigrated to Chicago in May 1947 when he was eighteen and settled in Whiting, Indiana, where he worked with a steel company. In his spare time he played the accordion and gained a reputation for his prowess on the instrument in the Chicago Irish community. The first songs Michael learned were "the old Galway Bay and the Boys from the Co. Mayo". In December 1950 Michael Fitzpatrick was drafted into the US army. He was trained as a medic and was shipped to Korea in May 1951 where he was assigned to the Medical Company, 23rd Infantry Regiment. On August 18 the ROK attack on the enemy-held hill-mass began.

An estimated two North Korean battalions were entrenched on the hills in well-bunkered positions and they hotly resisted the advance. The 23rd Infantry, making a diversionary attack in the east, met heavy resistance and, although G Company succeeded in securing the heights of Hill 1059, E Company was forced to pull back after being subjected to an intense artillery barrage. It took the ROKs another two days to capture Bloody Ridge and Hill 940. Three days later two North Korean battalions counterattacked on Bloody Ridge, and surrounded the ROK 36th Regiment, forcing it to surrender. Michael Fitzpatrick wrote to his sister, Mary "Mae" Doody, on July 15, before moving up to the frontline.

"Dear Mae,

"Just a few lines to say hello. I don't know If I should write this letter or not but its something to kill time. The Lord only knows when I will get to mail it. I have about nine letters in my pack and no place to mail them. As soon as I get to some mail box I will drop them all in. We are completely cut off from civilization. Well Mae we departed Japan on June 1st from Sasebo. Its about one hundred miles from Korea. We got to Pusan the following morning. We didn't even get to stay in Japan one week. While we were there we were restricted to our area.. We got to see quite a bit of Japan. It took us about thirty-six hours from Tokyo to Sasebo.

"I thought I was going to see something when I got to Pusan, but its no more or no better than a filthy sewer. We got a train from Pusan and travelled up the east coast. I never did find out what place it was. We left there again by truck and moved on about fifty miles to Wangu. I don't know how long we will be left here. Its not a bad place. We had our first country bath since we left the old sod. There is a kind of a creek or a river right beside me. It feels good for a change. We had to take a bath today. I was never as black or as dirty before in all my life than I was last night. The roads are newly made roads and they are made from dirt. By the time we got to Wangu we were white from dust. We had to take our clothes off and go out and dust them.

"We sleep in big tents. About thirty guys to each tent. Our beds are one blanket, rain coat and the bare ground. The weather is pretty tough. I got all sunburnt today. It has been raining quite a bit this last while. Anyhow this is supposed to be the rainy season in Korea. Well, Mae we have seen some of the ruins after the war. Mostly all the houses are completely demolished. Nothing left only a pile of burnt cinders. Its pretty easy for a Korean house because they are no more than four posts stuck in the ground and a kind of grass or straw roof. It's a pitiful sight.

"Well Mae we are assigned to the second Division and the 23 Inf. Regt. Right now the second Division is in the reserve. I don't know how long that will last but some guys say it might be in the reserve for several weeks and maybe only one day. Its hard to tell. The darn army changes its mind so often you can't believe a thing till it actually happens.

"Did you get any mail from John Culligan. I was going to write to him but I thought he might be in the same boat as myself, no permanent address. I will mail this as soon as I get my permanent address and not till then. From the time I mail a letter till I get a response it will take at least thirty days. So when I write don't just leave it till tomorrow to mail it. Answer it right now and don't forget. I better bring this to an end and see if we got any movies tonight. By the way we get movies here. Our theatre is a white sheet hanging on a few high posts at the bottom of a hill. We get a lot of big logs to sit on. The only thing we lack here is news. We don't hear a darn thing.

"Well Mae I will call this off for now, hoping it finds you and hoping to hear from you soon. Bye bye and good luck and good wishes from your loving brother Mike.

"P.S. We are just after moving. I don't know where we are at but we are mighty close to the real thing. I'll write again as soon as I find out where I am at."[15]

Mary Doody received her last letter from her youngest brother on August 16 1951. Two days later, Michael was listed as missing in action. Just after writing this letter the 23rd Regiment was moved up to the front line. While moving up a hill the 23rd Regiment lost several men killed and wounded in an enemy minefield. Another medic, Pfc Vernon Fields, from Bluefield, West Virginia, stepped on a mine, which blew off his left leg. He recalled seeing Mike Fitzpatrick moving towards wounded comrades on his right. It was the last he saw of him. Vernon Fields said Mike Fitzpatrick was a brave and likeable young man with a great smile. Mike Fitzpatrick was killed in an ensuing firefight. His body was recovered and sent back a few weeks later to the US for burial in Chicago. However, because he was not a citizen, he could not receive a military funeral. A lone officer represented the army at the funeral.[16]

The UN forces made immediate plans to retake Hill 983 and the 9th Infantry Regiment was given responsibility for securing, occupying and defending the 983-940 hill mass. In a double-envelopment plan the 23rd and 38th Regiments attacked on the morning of August 27 as the 9th Infantry continued the direct assault on the ridge. Fierce fighting throughout the day failed to net any gain and by nightfall, Hill 983 was still firmly held by the North Koreans. Private E2 Philip Columba Lynch, a machine gunner, was killed in action that day attacking enemy positions on Bloody Ridge. Born in Kilconly, Co. Galway, Philip Lynch had emigrated to America, settling in San Francisco. His family heard of his death on the radio while in their home near Tuam, Co. Galway. Philip Lynch's body was brought back to Ireland for burial.[17] It took another week of fighting before Bloody Ridge fell into American hands. On September 4 and 5, the North Koreans evacuated Bloody Ridge, leaving the bodies of 500 of their troops behind. In nearly three weeks of fighting the Americans and South Koreans had suffered more than 2,700 casualties, while the communists had sustained an estimated 15,000.[18]

J.T. Jennings, a native of Mayo and Kildare, arrived in Korea in August 1951 as a medic assigned to the 32nd Infantry Regiment, 7th Infantry Division. The 7th Infantry Division had been in the frontline since landing at Inchon in September 1950. The end of June brought the 7th Division a welcome assignment to the rear, the first relief from frontline duty since the Division had reached Korea. There was the inevitable reshuffling of assignments, and Colonel Charles McNamara Mount, Jr., took over the 32nd Infantry. After a brief rest in Pusan the Division was ordered into defensive positions north of Hwachon. Toward the end of August, a number of limited objective attacks were ordered to take key terrain features and improve the front lines. In ten days the Division captured five important hills, in what one division historian has described as "the best fighting in the entire Division's history." When the Division returned to the lines after another assignment in reserve, it was to the Heartbreak Ridge sector recently vacated by the 2nd Division. The 7th Division also took in the northern end of the "Punchbowl."

As J.T. Jennings was arriving in Korea another Irishman, Charles Dennehy, was leaving. Charles had been wounded while the 32nd Infantry fought their way out of the Chinese trap at the Fusan reservoir. He had spent a month in the naval hospital at Kove, Japan, recovering from shrapnel wounds to his arm and leg. Originally going to Korea in September 1950 he thought of it as an experience and an adventure. On his return to his unit Charles Dennehy was more pessimistic as he knew what to expect. Although he liked the Korean people Charles Dennehy was glad to be leaving Korea. He had seen many atrocities committed by the North Koreans, but one of the worst things he had to witness was while fighting North Korean guerrillas behind American lines. "The North Koreans put families out of their houses so they could sleep there. Regretfully, we had to burn down their houses. This was very sad."

After its evacuation from North Korea the 7th Division had been refilled with replacements and assigned to IX Corps, taking part in the attack on the Hwachon reservoir in a rocky volcanic crater known as the "Punchbowl". As part of the attack the 32nd Infantry Regiment captured Chechon and Chunchon on their push north. Eventually the attack resulted in 17,000 Chinese dead and another 10,000 captured, resulting in the inability of the CCF to launch any further campaigns against the UN forces. Charles Dennehy left Korea in August 1951 and was discharged in September 1952. He had taken part in four major and three minor engagements and was awarded a Purple Heart (for wounds received) and a Bronze Star (for sixty days in combat). He returned to Ireland in October, stayed for a year, and then returned to the US. He now lives in Co. Kildare.[19]

J.T. Jennings arrived in Korea courtesy of the Pipeline. He was among 3,100 replacements who arrived by troopship, first in Japan, and then to Inchon. "... with a full 60lb pack and rifle strapped on my back I was climbing down a rope ladder into an open top LST (Land & Sea Transport vehicle). Inside the transport we were packed, NYC subway style, shoulder to shoulder and backs to bellies. This was as far away from life in Ireland as you could ever imagine. When the LST hit the beach an army bulldozer pushed earth under the flap and off we marched into waist high sea water. We collected on the beach, marched to windowless trains with boards for seats.

"Sometime during the night," Jennings wrote, "we arrived at the 7th Infantry Division Headquarters in Chunchon, South Korea, approximately 12 miles from the front line. The Commanding General welcomed us to, what he said, was 'The best fighting army unit in the world.' He said we had nothing to fear for our safety - this mountainous terrain would be well combed with air strikes and artillery fire prior to our taking additional ground! I was then assigned to Combat Medics, 32nd Regiment, 7th Infantry Division and told it was time to move out. It didn't take long to find the General's statement, about our safety, wasn't totally true! We moved forward to the front line by trucks to the area known now as Heartbreak Ridge. When our convoy reached base camp, camouflaged with branches stuck in them, two men from our truck became so scared they jumped from the truck and refused to go another inch. What they faced was a court martial and its consequences, what we faced God only knew.

"My first night at camp I was assigned guard duty. I was given the password, shown my post and told our long distance 155mm howitzers would be firing eight-inch shells from eight miles back, over our heads, towards the front line area ... Dungeon-darkness is the only way to describe that night. Every so often, a red ball of flame would appear in the sky and seconds later the shell would explode a few hundred yards ahead. In addition, but not routinely, the artillery men would make 'Screaming Mimi's.' They would attach the lids from 'C' ration cans onto the howitzer shells and once launched they'd go Zing, Zing, Zing ... as they hurdled overhead towards the enemy in the distance. In the darkness and fearful, I heard a noise. I shouted 'Halt, advance and be recognised.' I aimed my rifle at the object. Fortunately, he gave the password and walked toward me. It was the Lieutenant who had assigned me guard duty earlier that night. He asked me if I had a round in the chamber of my weapon. I smartly answered 'Yes, sir.' He immediately gave me 'Holy Hell' for having my rifle ready to fire. The next day I moved forward to a front line platoon. As a Combat Medic my job was to take care of the wounded as follows: Stop the bleeding, kill the pain (with Morphine), prevent shock, then get the wounded man to the nearest stand-by vehicle, an ambulance or jeep. For wounded with missing limbs, I had to call in helicopters so they could be transported to a MASH (Mobile Army Surgical Hospital) Unit.

"Fatalities and injuries were constant." Jennings continued. "To retrieve the wounded it was necessary to move forward by foot or crawl under intense fire cover. Many times bullets from both sides ripped into the ground, just inches from me. At night, because of the mountainous terrain, the enemy used mortar fire or 'Mail' as their weapons of choice. On the front lines these barrages were steady. The continuous casualties and destruction of equipment necessitated a stand-by regiment being at the ready. This was the only way we could return to Division headquarters to get replacements for those killed or wounded. We would then return to another front in the 'Iron Triangle' and relieve another hard-hit company. It would all happen within a matter of days. Day and night the front line was hell on earth. Air strikes were called in by 'FO's' - Forwards Observers or 'Suicide Sams' - as they were known. One of them was my brother, Tom. He was in the 1st Calvary Division and we never met in all our time in Korea. The FO's job was to observe enemy movement from a concealed or camouflaged post, place a specific color banner as a marking point on the ground in the area. He would then communicate a clock position - relative to the target - back to the command and the pilots would fly over and drop their bombs. The FO's would follow the same procedure for artillery fire.

"We lived, slept and ate in foxholes, bunkers and trenches. We received two hot meals a week, otherwise breakfast, lunch and dinner was 'C' rations." In a rare phenomenon in war often the best food was served in the front lines where conditions were worse, while service units in the rear, where conditions were better, frequently endured indifferent food. "After eight months in the front lines," J.T. Jennings wrote, "I was brought back to a supply assignment and, interestingly, in all of that time I seldom felt isolated. The army had a points system - four points a month for front line duty. When we accumulated 36 points we were eligible to rotate back to the United States. I was lucky enough to leave company headquarters inside ten months. The extra month was spent waiting for a replacement. On my way out of Korea I would see troops in new companies running for cover during warnings or drills. I would just stand there and watch in amazement and realise that military discipline was still around. Up front, we respected our superiors. We did our job, protected ourselves and those around us. We were in the thick of it, all together as one." Sgt. Jennings left Korea in July 1952 after ten months at the front. He arrived back in the US the following month and was discharged in November 1952.[20]

When the North Koreans withdrew from Bloody Ridge they fell back to another ridge just north, which would rank with its neighbour in the chronicle of the costliest ridgeline battles in Korea. This ridge was known as Heartbreak Ridge and was every bit as well defended with bunkers, trenches and gun positions as Bloody Ridge. The 2nd Infantry Division was again given the task of capturing Heartbreak Ridge. Another 3,700 American and French troops became casualties, while the communists suffered an estimated 25,000. One of the American dead was Irish-born Michael Herlihy from Ballydesmond, Co. Cork. Living in San Francisco Michael Herlihy was drafted into the US Army and sent to the 38th Infantry Regiment, 2nd Infantry Division. Pfc Herlihy was killed in action on September 12 as the 38th Infantry captured Hill 868 after three days of hard fighting. His remains were brought back to Ballydesmond for burial.[21]

Another Irishman, Michael Conroy, who emigrated from the Claremorris or Crossboyne area, Co. Mayo, was killed in action on September 19. He was drafted while living in Cook's County, Illinois, and as a Pfc was assigned to the 9th Infantry Regiment, 2nd Infantry Division. [22] The 2nd Division had borne the brunt of the fighting and bore a higher casualty rate than any other unit in the

Eighth Army. One of many Irishmen fighting on the "Bloody Ridges" Kerry native Sergeant John Leahy was recognised for his bravery in the fighting on Heartbreak Ridge. Born in Lixnaw, Co. Kerry, John Leahy emigrated to America in August 1949 and was drafted into the US Army on September 1 1950. He served as a sergeant with distinction on the frontlines in Korea, where he was attached to the 82nd AAA (Anti-Aircraft Artillery) Battalion, 2nd Infantry Division, and was giving a citation for capturing a North Korean spy behind American lines.[23] Brian Coyne, Williamstown, Tuam, Co. Galway, was also involved in the fighting around Heartbreak Ridge. Serving with the 1st Cavalry Division he was badly wounded in the head. Brian Coyne was drafted in New York in August 1950. At the time he was engaged to be married. However, he did not return to America until July 1953. His brother John was also drafted and served in England with the USAF.[24] Heartbreak Ridge was finally taken on October 13 after thirty days of vicious combat.

There were many other engagements along the front during the autumn of 1951. In September a series of local attacks, counterattacks and patrols occupied both I and IX Corps. This led into a general UN movement in October to a new front on the west known as the Jamestown Line. On October 3 in Operation Commando, five I Corps divisions - 1st Republic of Korea (ROK), the British Commonwealth and the US 1st Cavalry, 3rd Infantry and 25th Infantry Division - began their advance to the Jamestown Line, ten miles into enemy territory. The campaign cost 4,000 casualties. The 24th Infantry Division completed its reserve training and occupied the Kumsong Valley, replacing the 7th Division. The 1st Cavalry Division caught the brunt of the communist resistance in its move north-west from the Yonchon area and suffered 2,900 casualties in a seventeen-day operation that pushed the line about five miles westward. Maurice Angland was serving with Company D, 8th Engineer Combat Battalion, 1st Cavalry Division. He was a native of Rockchapel, Co. Cork and lived in Chicago. On October 4 Pfc Maurice Angland was killed by mortar fragments while attacking enemy positions near Saemal. On October 5 the 8th Cavalry Regiment captured Hill 418 against sporadic enemy resistance while the 7th Cavalry Regiment captured Hill 313. Pfc Thomas Quinn, 5th Cavalry Regiment, was killed in action near Old

Baldy on the Jamestown Line on October 6. He was a native of Ballinlough, Co. Roscommon and lived in Toledo, Ohio.[25]

The 3rd Infantry Division fought a costly engagement known as the Battle of the Bloody Angle (September 28-October 6) just west of Chorwon. The division sustained more than five hundred casualties in securing ridgelines flanking the Chorwon-Seoul railway, which was reopened to supply the front. Corporal Patrick Sheahan, from Newtown Sandes, Co. Kerry was killed in the fighting on October 4. He had emigrated to New York in 1948 and was called into the US Army in 1950. He was serving with the 7th Infantry Regiment, 3rd Infantry Division. Pat Sheahan had been in Korea since April and was due for discharge in June 1952. He was planning to return home for a visit then. In September he wrote to a school-teacher friend, Frank O'Connor, who received the last letter on the day Pat died. The letter was published in the *Irish Echo*.

"You said that you would send me the Irish Echo or anything I need, but there isn't anything I need, or at least there is nothing I could use over here now. My sister has been sending me the Irish Echo since I came here, but a good many times I never get to read it, especially if we are attacking, but still I have been keeping up with all the news in New York even if it's a bit late before I get to hear it. None of the GI's are a bit pleased with what Truman, the Government, or the U.N. are doing for us. I think they could do a lot better and a lot of us think that the U.N. didn't want peace at all, it certainly looks like it over here. We are near Chonwon now and it is quite here, but we have a lot of patrols. I got hit with a little shrapnel some time ago, but it wasn't much. I was back with my outfit again in a few days. It is easy to get stripes over here but as you know, rank doesn't mean much here. I am an Assistant Squad Leader in a rifle squad and I was made a corporal a couple of weeks ago. There is no other Irish man in my company - in fact there hardly any Irish in this Battalion but there is a whole lot of Irish scattered in different outfits. The weather is pretty good now but the nights are cold already; they will surely be bad a couple of months from now. I hope to hear from you soon again and hope the crowd continues to attend your classes and get their High School Diplomas."

Cpl. Pat Sheahan was a particularly brave soldier and was awarded the Bronze Star and Silver Star. On June 8 he saved the lives of two of his comrades, while on October 4 he killed all the members of a machine gun crew who had his platoon pinned down. His citation for the Bronze Star read: "On June 8, 1951, near Sam Ywie, Korea, Company "A" was engaged in the assault upon Hill 736 when it was suddenly subjected to heavy enemy machine gun fire which cut off four men from their unit, wounding two of them before they could reach a place of cover. Private Sheahan, seeing his comrades fall, stopped to carry them, one at a time, to a position of safety and then remained with them while another went to locate a medical aid man. At this point a large enemy force commenced to assault his position, but he stood fast, firing into the attack with his rifle until his platoon broke through to rout the foe. Private Sheehan's unwavering heroism and determination were instrumental in saving the lives of two fellow soldiers and reflect great credit upon himself and the military service."

His citation (posthumous) for the Silver Star read: "On October 4, 1951, Company "A" with the First Platoon serving as assistant unit, attacked Hill 282, near Chungse-ri, Korea. Stiff enemy opposition prevailed and the sweeping fire of a hostile machine gun soon pinned down the platoon and halted its advance up the hill. Corporal Sheahan, realising the gravity of the situation and aware that the enemy weapon must be neautralised, courageously crawled forward under the lethal hail of fire and completely destroyed the emplacement with accurately thrown hand grenades. Uncertain as to whether all the enemy soldiers had been killed by the explosion, he rose to his feet and, rushing forward, fired a long burst into the smashed entrenchment, eliminating all possible opposition. It was thus revealed to the enemy, as he carried out his singlehandedly brave action, that Corporal Sheahan fell, mortally wounded by the savage fire of an adjacent automatic weapon. Corporal Sheahan's aggressive gallantry and selfless devotion to duty were instrumental in the successful completion of his unit's mission and reflect the highest credit upon himself and the military service."[26]

Patrick White, a native of Dundalk, Co. Louth, and living in Moline, Illinois, was killed in action on October 6. He was serving as a Pfc with the 14th Infantry

Regiment. On August 1 1951 the 14th Infantry, fresh from the US, was assigned to the 25th Infantry Division, then fighting in Korea. The 14th Infantry moved to the Kumwha valley area where it replaced the 24th Infantry Regiment, which was being inactivated as part of the integration of the Army. Patrick White emigrated to the Chicago area shortly before the outbreak of the Korean War. His brother, Corporal Michael White, was serving with the 1st Cavalry Division in Japan at time of Patrick's death. The circumstances of Patrick White's death are vague but word in his home community was that he died when he threw his body to cover a hand grenade that had been thrown by the enemy among his comrades. Pfc White's posthumous Purple Heart is dated November 19 1951. His body was brought back to his native Dundalk for burial.[27]

Despite all the hopes for peace that had blossomed when the ceasefire talks commenced in July, the period from their start until November, when stalemate had settled over the front, was one of the bloodiest and most costly in the entire war for both sides. During this period UN forces had suffered 60,000 casualties, over a third of them American while communist losses were 234,000. By the end of the fighting in October it had become clear that any further UN advances against the enemy main line of resistance would require unconscionable losses. It also became clear to the communists that the war would not be won on the bat-tlefield so they made their way back to the negotiating table. In a prelude to a plan to achieve victory through strength the communists had claimed the UN had tried to murder their negotiating team and so had earlier withdrawn from the talks. With the military tide turned once more against the communists they proposed a resumption of negotiations. Talks began once more on October 25 at the neutral site of Panmunjom, in the no-man's land between the two armies. One of the conditions for the ceasefire negotiations agreed to both sides was that hostilities would be continued until a truce was signed. This policy condemned thousands of men to their deaths as the talking stopped and re-started.

11

Over There

Within minutes of arriving on the Korean peninsula UN soldiers were hit by the stark contrast of their previous civilian existence, or regular army life, to the nightmare world of a country decimated by war. William Harry O'Mara arrived in Korea in August 1951. He had emigrated from Cong, Ballinrobe, Co. Mayo, in 1949 and was drafted the following November while living and working in Brooklyn, New York. He takes up the narrative of his arrival in Japan and Korea. "The journey to Japan was reasonably pleasant, we passed close to the Aleutian Islands, watched the flying fish and huge jelly-fish, probably ten feet in width, and then the Yellow Sea which is really yellow I suppose from the silt washed out from China. We slowly made our way to Yokohama harbour, which still had huge chains across the entrance protecting it from submarines, since the Pacific war. Having docked beside a huge grain ship we watched the diminutive Japanese carrying large sacks of rice on their backs, up from the holds, down the gangplank, past the tallyman and on to the waiting freight-train. They did not walk, they ran like ants, round and round.

"Our next destination was a camp outside Tokyo, issued M-1 rifles with large bayonets and taken to the range for rapid fire exercises. No sparing of ammo. Next morning we had five hours of continuous bayonet practice and anyone who has handled the M-1 rifle will appreciate how our arms felt after that. I wondered what sort of war we were preparing for, would it be a repeat of the Crimea? It was just probably to get us in shape again after the journey. This was followed by an address from a bellicose officer who, with other gruesome predictions, told us that in all probability thirty percent of us would be either killed or wounded and those who might survive are the men who heeded their training officers. I thought it a bit late for this revelation. That night we boarded a train to travel to Sasebo in southern Japan. This was a spotless train, run by the Japanese, with sleeping bunks, starched sheets and pillow cases. Before we got under way an American officer, accompanied by Japanese stewards, came through the cars on inspection. He discovered a tiny cigarette burn on my pillow, castigated the stewards and had them rush me a replacement. Such luxury, perhaps this war won't be so bad after all.

"It was a three day journey, Mount Fuji in evidence for much of the early part, higher than I thought. It was a narrow-gauge rail and we made many stops. The Japanese ignored us, perhaps due to the outcome of the war. We pulled into one elevated station and, while walking the platform, I noticed there were no substantial buildings in the city. I then discovered that we were in Hiroshima, destroyed by the atom bomb and on informing my companions, they displayed no interest, which seemed peculiar. We reached Sasebo at night and marched from the train to the docks where an army brass band waited to play us on board. This was the last bit of civilised culture we were to experience for many a day. They played 'Over the Waves'. The ship was huge, a very old Japanese luxury liner and we were only about two hundred men. I went down into the engine room which was, for me, spectacular and somewhat frightening. Everything was huge, steam escaping, oil spurting out, the old pistons were enormous and the grease-covered Japanese in loin-cloths were wielding large wrenches and hammers to keep things running. They kept bowing to me making me feel like a V.I.P., probably thought I was another inspector.

"My moment of importance did not last long. When I came topside a lieutenant ordered me to stand watch on an upper deck for the rest of the journey through the Korean straits. I was not too pleased with this as there was a heavy mist and I had no idea what I was guarding or watching for. I settled into a corner to pass the time. Below me four officers were having a conversation concerning the best method of getting the most out of the peons, as they referred to us soldiers. In America the term peon had a particular connotation associated with the slave trade and penal servitude and, as I was one of those referred to, it interested me. The discussion went along the lines that as we were usually of low intelligence and used to privation and hard knocks the best method was to kick arse hard and often. What wonders a couple of years in college and a brass bar can do for some men. For a moment I relished the thought of blowing their heads off, indeed I discovered later that what was termed 'Fragging' did occur but with a bit more finesse. Fortunately I discovered later that few of the line officers espoused those sentiments, most were genuinely caring men who worried about the welfare of those under their command.

"We arrived in Pusan early next morning and it was pouring straight down rain. We disembarked and lined up for chow. It was for what is gastronomically referred to in the army as shit on a shingle a good description of boiled minced meat dumped on a slice of hard toast. Our mess dishes filled up with rain water before we could eat it, so it was just dumped. We marched to a waiting train with leaking freight cars. Some contrast to the Japanese luxury. It eventually got noisily moving but halted on the outskirts of Pusan, as there was only one line for two-way traffic. On our left was a hill on which a new military cemetery had been established with neat rows of white crosses. While we waited, that days burials was taking place with the last post sounding and volleys fired. What a comforting introduction. On the right-hand side was a shanty-town where hundreds of refugees had crowded under sheets of tin and cardboard which were crumbling in the rain. A depressing sight but, to some, a bit of paradise. When the train stopped, from under the sodden coverings, females appeared and, standing in the mud offered their wares to the soldiers. This must have been a regular occurrence, catching the troop trains on their way up as they halted for the line to clear. The women were aged from about ten to fifty, bare-footed, wet and filthy. They lifted their rags as an inducement and quite a few men jumped off, slithered down the embankment and followed them into the ramshackle shelters.

"A train slowly moved past us with open flatcars occupied by natives, mostly old men and women, all lying down in the rain, apparently too weak to move. They had survived the winter, had been rounded up and sent back. The younger people were either killed or, if male, conscripted, or female, taken away. Politicians and militarists who advocate conflict do not consider these consequences. Here we were going up to an uncertain future, on our left soldiers being interred in water-logged graves and on the right a few having their last fling. I was friendly with a lad called Leonard, we used surnames mostly in the army, and we were together on the train. He had finished teacher training and was drafted before the Korean War. They sent him to Korea with the U.S. occupation army. He was there for six months and returned to the States. He was now back for the second time but to a different situation. Watching the men jumping from the train I said "How could they do that, such filth and squalor, soldiers being buried beside us and that could be their fate shortly." He said that he did a course in psychology during his teacher training and he figured that it was primeval motivation to perpetuate the species before coming to a sticky end. He went on to show that even plants and trees, when in jeopardy, will produce extra seeds and shoots to ensure survival of the species. My comment was that the quality of the participants in this situation left a lot to be desired. Shortly afterward we were separated and I never saw him again. With his unlucky army history perhaps he did not make it home the second time.

"I was at this time seeking motivation to help give me some enthusiasm for what we were about to get involved in. Democracy, as opposed to communism of which the Americans were paranoid, did not excite me, certainly not worth dying for twelve thousand miles away from home. The recent, overheard, attitude of some officers to soldiers did not encourage loyalty and dedication. I felt as Sarsfield did when dying of his wounds far from home "Would this were for Ireland." Self-preservation was not sufficient or satisfactory, anyway we were told that it would be over in a few months. What an elastic little word 'few' can be. "From the train we transferred to trucks and a very bumpy ride through some scenes of recent conflict and destruction. Tanks, trucks, guns and equipment were strewn everywhere, mostly ours, which was not comforting. Up ahead we witness our first air-strike, it looked so pretty in the distance. The planes were like toys, circling then diving, coming round and diving again. There was now constant explosive noise which we would become immune to and heedless of. That night we arrived at 3rd Battalion, 31st Regiment of the 7th Infantry Division and in the dark a lieutenant assigned us to replace casualties in the companies. We would go up with the gook train in the morning. Three of us were going to the same company and we went under some trees near the remains of a village and rolled out our sleeping bags. But sleep would not come easily. There was a heavy stench in the air and I remarked that Korea was one stinking country and, if we had to take territory, why this hole. A sentiment often expressed in the following months.

"In addition to the bad air there was a battery of heavy mortars nearby and they fired constantly, every thirty seconds. Mortars, particularly heavies, make a tremendous cracking sound and as yet we had not become accustomed to constant noise. The fact that so much short range artillery was pouring out indicated to us that there must be a concentration of enemy nearby, which was not sleep inducing. At daybreak we were half asleep and one lad went to the ditch to urinate. He quickly returned and said "Let's get the hell out of here, look what we have been sleeping beside." In the ditch behind us the earth was loose and body parts were protruding from it. They were probably murdered villagers or Chinese soldiers but we did not wait to investigate. That morning the gook* train, consisting of native bearers loaded with ammo, and supplies on A frames, led us to the companies. The company commander looked haggard. He welcomed the three of us and assigned me to a machine-gun crew. There were no choices. The troops were dug-in around some low hills with the Chinese on higher ground ahead. The gun was in a hole, covered with some logs and after the recent rain it was a mess, boxes of ammo and grenades everywhere and little room. The two residents were rough looking characters and my first obser-vation was that, no matter how bad things got I would not let my appearance and condition deteriorate to that extent. Their first query was "Had I brought a bottle?" and their disappointment was evident."[1]

*Gook is a Korean word which means person.

Harry O'Mara remained a machine-gunner for three weeks, then a demolition man for several months and finally was assigned to a "recovery" unit for the remaining seven months of his tour. "If a patrol came in and a man was missing we went out looking to see was he killed or captured, or still alive. We were on recovery, even if a man was missing for several months and made some bad discoveries. So many men were missing that politicians were under pressure to do something about it and it (the recovery unit) started from a little coterie to rectify the problem of missing men." After eleven months and fourteen days on the frontline Harry left Korea in July 1952. He left the Army in September 1952 with the Korean Service Medal with two Bronze service stars, one overseas bar, Combat Infantryman's Badge, UN Service Medal, and the Bronze Star Medal. Harry O'Mara spent several years in the US before returning to Ireland in 1961.[2]

With no prospect of employment in Limerick City in 1948 Paddy Sheehy left 1 Keeper View Terrace in St. Mary's Parish to live and work in New York. Soon after his arrival he took up work with the Pennsylvania Railroad Company, while also continuing his education. In 1950 he was drafted into the US Army and like many Irishmen he was destined for frontline duty in Korea. (The powers that be had decided that Irishmen made better infantrymen and most of the Irish draftees were destined for the army rather than the air force or navy.) After special training in Louisiana Paddy Sheehy was made part of a tank crew and assigned to the 7th Infantry Division. His unit took part in the Inchon landings and the advance into North Korea. Paddy's abiding memory of the war was the cold of the Korean winter. "The bitter east winds from Siberia used sweep down and the temperature often reached minus twenty five below freezing. With the wind this would reach minus forty chill factor. If you left your gloves off by some chance, your hands would immediately freeze and stick to the barrel of your gun ... One was lucky to get a couple of hot meals brought up during the week. Our rations used freeze and we had to light fires to try to thaw out the tins. On one occasion there was great excitement as we were about to be served with steak from the mobile canteen. Sadly, the Chinese intervened and the meal had to be abandoned as had the several crates of beer.

"We were well decked out for the conditions, but the Chinese, who had at that stage become embroiled in the war, suffered greatly. Their padded jackets, which weren't waterproof, became frozen stiff in the snow. While we had our strong boots, all they had was a kind of sneaker with rubber soles. It will never be known how many of them died of frostbite." One of the most chilling sights of the war was the hordes of Chinese troops, all expendable to their superiors, coming over the hills. "There was so many of them that they would come in waves. The first lot would have the grenades, the second sub machine guns, the third rifles and the fourth would be unarmed ... they were there literally to pick up their fallen comrades weapons as they were mowed down and take their place in the charge ... The Chinese used literally shovel their dead into large holes and in the spring thaw there would be thousands of rats devouring the corpses. After the war I met a Chinese professor who had defected to New York who said that the hospitals were overflowing with victims of the bubonic plague that ensued."

Fighting in a tank in the depths of winter was almost as tough as living in a foxhole. The tank's air intake sucked a constant icy blast into the turret, causing the commander and gunner to suffer a special misery. Periscopes frosted and condensation turned into icicles inside the hull. Starting up the engine was often a major problem. Though Paddy Sheehy was one of the lucky ones and survived the war unscathed, he was within seconds of death on one occasion. "It happened when we came under severe mortar fire from the Chinese. Our tank, which contained 180 gallons of petrol and several boxes of ammunition, was hit and caught fire. As tank commander, I had to get out and beat out the flames with my jacket while I received covering fire from my crew. Luckily, I put out the fire and we survived. My Platoon leader was not so lucky ... he was shot through the neck and killed. "Looking back, I consider myself very lucky to have survived Korea. Ten of my platoon, including our leader, were killed and eleven wounded. I didn't get a scratch. There was a Limerickman who was killed in the war: Foncy O'Connell from Garryowen ..." After he left the army in 1952 Paddy Sheehy returned to his employment with the railway company. On retirement he returned to Ireland in 1989, back to Keeper Terrace in St. Mary's Parish, Limerick. Paddy Sheehy died in 2004.[3]

12

The Hills of Korea

As talk of peace circulated once more around the hills of Korea men whiled away the weeks in their trenches and bunkers and continued to fight and die in small local actions. On October 3 five UN Divisions, including the British Commonwealth Division, attacked elements of four CCF Armies, to correct a sag along I Corps and X Corps' boundaries. In the successful, but savage fighting, I Corps estimated 21,000 Chinese casualties to over 4,000 UN casualties. On October 4 the 3rd RAR helped capture Hill 355 after heavy fighting. The following day the 3rd RAR gained the summit of Hill 317 (Maryang San). On October 7 the 3rd RAR drove towards "The Hinge" on Hill 317, and beat off strong counter attacks. Here Lance Corporal Richard Boyle, from Dublin, serving with the Royal Australian Army Medical Corps (RAAMC), was wounded.[1]

On October 19 the 1st Cavalry Division captured the last of its objectives on the Jamestown Line, completing Operation Commando. Fighting since the beginning of the month, the division inflicted almost 16,000 enemy casualties and reduced the crack Chinese 47th Army to half its strength. Aphonsus "Foncy" O'Connell was with the cavalry since they had first arrived in Korea. He had emigrated to New York in 1947 and stayed with an uncle in Brooklyn while he worked as a carpenter, a family tradition. He was drafted into the army and sent to the 8th Engineer Combat Battalion, 1st Cavalry Division. At the outbreak of the war, the 8th Battalion was quickly ordered to Korea and landed at Pusan in July 1950 where the 8th Engineers were pressed into immediate action demolishing bridges in order to halt the advance of the NKPA. In addition to demolition and construction duties the combat engineers also cleared enemy minefields and obstacles and often acted as infantrymen on the front lines. In September 1950 Foncy O'Connell was with the 8th Engineers when they took part in the amphibious landing at Inchon. The hazardous task of clearing mines was one of the main duties of the 1st Cavalry Division engineers and on October 29 1951 Alphonsus O'Connell was killed as he was engaged in clearing mines left behind by retreating Chinese forces. Only weeks later, his battalion was withdrawn from Korea after over 500 days in combat. Alphonsus O'Connell was from Sarsfield Avenue, Garryowen, Limerick, an area synonymous with the 1st Cavalry as the division had adopted the rousing Garryowen as its marching tune. Word of Foncy's death reached his uncle in New York who called the parish priest, Fr. O'Grady, back in Garryown. Fr. O'Grady was given the sad task of informing the O'Connell family of their son's death in Korea. Foncy had been expected home for Christmas that year. His remains were buried instead in a military cemetery in New York.[2]

Another Irishman serving with the 1st Cavalry was killed on November 5. John Mills, born in 1929 in Enniskillen Street, Belfast, lived in Jersey City. He was serving as a Private E2 with the famed 7th Cavalry Regiment. In their positions on Hill 200 the 7th Cavalry were under constant night attack. On one night alone 135 Chinese were killed as they tried to infiltrate the American lines. After an action on November 5 John Mills was posted as missing in action. No body was recovered and on December 31 1953 he was declared officially dead. Another Irish native, Patrick McEnery, from Glin, Co. Limerick, was also posted as missing in action a week later on November 13. He was serving as a Pfc with Company I, 3rd Battalion, 19th Infantry Regiment, 24th Infantry Division. Pat McEnery's body was never recovered.[3]

On November 12 Gen. Ridgway ordered Gen. Van Fleet to desist from major offensive action and assume an active defence of the existing front. Local attacks were still permissible, meaning that Eighth Army could still seize terrain suitable for defensive positioning, but all offensives could only be to obtain outpost positions not requiring more than one division. No operation in greater than battalion strength could be mounted without the authorisation of Ridgway. It was a policy designed to speed up the negotiations and show the communists and the rest of the world that the UN had no interest in further territorial gains in Korea. While the talks went on the communists dug in, creating almost impregnable defensive positions along the 155-mile front. They were well aware of the war-weariness in the UN countries and wanted to further humiliate the Western democracies. As the negotiations dragged on in the winter months of 1951-52 the fighting continued, although it was now what was called "warfare of position," - small patrol and company sized actions.

In the winter of 1951 the US Army finally integrated the military forces fighting in Korea. At the beginning of the war the US 24th Division, an all-African-American unit, had performed badly, not because the troops were bad, but because the whole US military system had for years militated against Africans being able to perform properly. During the hardest days of the war incoming African-American troops had been integrated in other units because there was no other option, as the units needed replacements quickly. These soldiers performed better than the ones in all-African units, and the US Army finally began to learn. Another success was the retraining and proper use of ROK units. From the beginning the ROKs had been poorly trained and poorly led. Now Gen. Ridgway provided the ROK units with their own artillery, retrained most of the officers, and gave the ROKs the confidence they needed to hold and their own sectors. On the eastern side of the peninsula the South Koreans had total responsibility for their sector, with three divisions in the line.

Armoured vests, or "flak-jackets," were another one of the great successes' of the Korean War. Introduced to UN forces in early 1952, the flak jacket became the most important piece of equipment an infantryman had, next to his weapons. The Marine vest was sleeveless, had nylon padding around the upper chest and shoulders, and plates of fibreglass bonded with resin that covered the lower chest, back, and abdomen. The Army vest used layers of basket-weave nylon. Neither vest could stop a rifle bullet at close range, but both could reduce casualties by mortar and artillery fire and hand grenade fragments. In addition, the pistol ammunition used by CCF burp guns could also frequently be stopped. USMC statistics showed that flak jackets prevented sixty to seventy per cent of all abdominal and chest wounds. Helicopters also came into their own. Developed too late for effective use in World War II the US Marines discovered the versatility of the rotary wing machines as early as August 1950 when they began to use helicopters for reconnaissance, rescue, casualty evacuation, liaison between units and laying communication wires. A year later the marines were using helicopters to ferry troops to the battlefields.

The leading jet ace of the Korean War was Irish-American Capt. Joseph McConnell Jr., who scored his first victory on January 14 1953. In a little more than a month, he gained his fifth MiG victory, thereby becoming an ace. On the day McConnell shot down his eight MiG, his F-86 was hit by ground fire over enemy-controlled waters of the Yellow Sea west of Korea. After only two minutes in the freezing water, he was rescued by a helicopter. The following day he was back in combat and shot down his ninth MiG. By the end of April 1953, he had scored his tenth victory to become a "double ace." On the morning of May 18 1953, McConnell shot down two MiGs in a furious air battle and became a "triple ace." On another mission that afternoon, he shot down his sixteenth and last MiG-15. McConnell, was the first triple jet ace in history and is still the top-scoring American jet ace. A native of New Hampshire, Capt McConnell shot down a total of sixteen MiG15s while flying a F-86 Sabrejet, named Beauteous Butch (after the nickname of his wife). McConnell was a B-24 navigator during World War II and remained in the Air Force after the war becoming a pilot in 1948. He was assigned to the 39th Fighter-Interceptor Squadron in Korea in late 1952 and scored all of his kills from January to June 1953. On August 25 1954, while testing an F-86H at Edwards Air Force Base, California, Capt. McConnell crashed to his death.

Private Michael McCormick, from Cahercrea West, Loughrea, Co. Galway, arrived in Korea in November 1951. "There was snow on the ground when I got there," Michael McCormack said. "It was below zero, nowhere to sleep, only a hole in the ground." Mickey McCormick was born in 1930 and emigrated to San Francisco in May 1950. He had an uncle in San Francisco who was a building contractor. He came to New York to meet him and employed him as an apprentice carpenter. His sister, Maureen, also emigrated to San Francisco. "There was seven in the family, someone had to go. I was not there twelve months to the day when I was drafted." He was inducted into the US Army on May 9 1951 and completed his basic training with the 6th Infantry Division before been sent to Korea.

"Not one Irish, all Americans, (in his unit)" Michael McCormick recalled, "but they all called me 'Irish.' Only one or two buddies that trained with me, went over with me. The first day, (in Korea) we dropped our bags, waiting for a jeep to go to my unit, there was five or six bodies lying there, their coats over them. That was my first day. There was an awful lot of killing there, God help us. My first day on the line they put us in this big bunker. The river was to the left. We were very high up. The next minute these shells came in on us. We ran like hell into the bunker." Michael McCormick was assigned to the 25th Infantry Division to Battery A, 21st Anti-Aircraft-Artillery (AAA) Automatic Weapons Battalion (SP), as a munitions handler on an M16 halftrack armed with four Browning machine guns. Designed as an anti-aircraft weapon the army used the M16 in a ground support role. "We were firing indirect; got our co-ordinates from a forward observer. We could be firing for three or four hours, tracers everything. It was nuts. We had many an escape; mortars, artillery. The Chinese were deadly accurate with mortars, (could) put them in your hip pocket. They were very near getting us, but they didn't succeed. We were very lucky, I suppose.

"We were never really up in the frontline. The infantry would be a few hundred yards ahead of us. We used to see the poor devils coming back on stretchers. Helicopters coming in to take out the wounded. Artillery pounding all day and night. No matter how many Chinese you killed they still kept coming." Michael saw action at the Kumwha river, the Punchbowl, and "fired up on Heartbreak Ridge... I only had one shower in twelve months. The dust and dirt was terrible... There was nothing to be seen where we were. Driving up (to the front) you saw an odd house, plenty of rice paddies. " Michael McCormick served a year on the frontline, before returning to San Francisco in December 1952. He suffered stomach and hearing problems as a direct consequence of his time in Korea.[4]

The 1st Battalion, the Welch Regiment arrived in Korea in November 1951 to serve a year's tour with the Commonwealth Division. Lt. Col. H.H. "Dixie" Deane, an Irishman and career soldier, commanded the 1st Welch. He was not the only Irishman in this traditional Welch regiment. Jack "Nobby" Clarke, from Cabra, Dublin was among many Irish natives serving with the The Welch Regiment. In November 1950 Jack decided to follow in his father's footsteps and join the British Army. He quit his job, travelled to Belfast, and joined the Royal Ulster Rifles. He completed his training in Ballykinlar Camp, but then transferred to the Border Regiment in the hope of becoming a glider pilot. Jack planned on going to see his brother, who was also in the Borderers, and was wounded in Palestine, "but that didn't work out" and he found himself stationed in Norfolk, where the Welch Regiment was trying to make up the numbers to send a battalion to Korea.

The battalion strength was made up of English, Scottish and Irish reinforcements from the Gloucesters, Highland Light Infantry, King's Own Scottish Borderers, Inniskillings and Ulster Rifles. As one Welsh soldier said there could not have been a better combination. Private Jack Clarke volunteered for the Welch Regiment and was soon on board the troopship H.M.T. *Empire Fowey* destined for Korea. Travel on the *Empire Fowey* took six weeks from Southampton to Pusan, with continuous training on board ship, including the firing of 25 pounders and the normal troopship routine of life-boat drills.[5] The advance party of the 5th Royal Inniskilling Dragoons was also on board and Sergeant J. Bertrand described the voyage "as like a scene from of Kipling".[6] After calling at Aden, Colombo, Singapore and Hong Kong the *Empire Fowey* docked at Pusan on November 10. From Pusan the Welch Battalion travelled north to Britannia Camp, in the Commonwealth Division area. "We marched around Pusan as the locals came out to give us a wave," Jack said, "and then took a train for two nights to the front. The first thing we met were trains with open carriages, carrying empty shell cases, all coming back from the front to be filled."[7]

On November 12/13, in heavy rain, the 1st Welch moved up to Chongdong-Ni and relieved the Gloucesters, who were positioned just north of the confluence of the Imjin and Samichon Rivers. They were arriving along with the Korean winter, with temperatures falling as low as thirty-nine degrees. "The cold was out of this world," Jack Clarke said. "It was very, very cold and the conditions terrible. A pair of pigskin boots lasted about two weeks, then you went and got another pair. You had to put Vaseline on your lips when taking a sip out of your mug to stop them sticking to it." On November 24 the Welch moved across the Samichion River and took over a section of the line from the 1st ROK Regiment, overlooking the Samichon Valley. This area was known as The Hook, the name denoting its protrusion of the line into what would normally be enemy territory, or no-man's-land. These positions faced an unoccupied feature slightly higher than the surrounding area, namely Hill 169, or, taking its code name, Top Hat. There, facing Hill 169, the Battalion was to experience its first clash with an enemy who had the advantage of being better acclimatised and more familiar with the ground.[8]

Life in the dug-outs was in many ways similar to the trench warfare of WWI. Pte. Jack Clark was assigned to the Machine Gun Platoon. They were armed with the water-cooled Vickers machine gun, which also dated back to the Great War. "They were good for making tea and having a shave," Jack joked. The Vickers machine gun, first adopted in 1912, was water-cooled - via a jacket around the barrel, which held about a gallon of water. The gun used standard rifle .303 ammunition and fired some 450 rounds per minute. "You went up to the front, did what you had to do. Went off and found a few poles, got some telephone wire to make a bed spring out of it and lived like rats in the trenches. The first time a few shells were lobbed over. I said to myself 'What am I doing here? I should be back home in Dublin.' The place was just a mass of bunkers, no trees, everything blown out of it. And when the Chinese came at you, it was bugles and whistles. Some would have no weapons, they were just waiting for mates to 'get' it. All you did was open up and hope they'd go back. There were hordes and hordes of them. The other side of the hill was just a mass of people. Once two came running into the bunker. Red stars on their hats, we didn't know whether they were Chinese, or North Korean, and didn't ask. We just shot them." Devastating UN automatic weapons fire would sweep the Chinese ranks, and was usually accompanied by heavy shellfire. In attacks like these the Chinese lost heavily, but to the CCF leaders they were an acceptable loss if they gained their objective.[9]

The period from November to the end of the year was reasonably quiet along the Commonwealth Division front, though positions were subjected to regular bouts of shelling, while activities were confined to extensive patrolling, strengthening positions and improving communications. On November 30 the Battalion suffered its first fatal casualty when Private J. Corcoran was killed by a landmine while on patrol. Three days earlier the UN and Communist delegates meeting at Panmunjom finally agreed that in event of an Armistice, the existing front line would become the Line of Demarcation. In anticipation of an early Ceasefire the UN Command had ordered that its forces confine its activities to Active Defence. No further aggressive operations were permitted, except for such local attacks which might be required to strengthen the main line, or establish posts to its front. The effect of these orders was to produce a stalemate along the front until July 1953.

Meanwhile, the Ulster Rifles were participating in their last action in Korea. Private William May, from Dublin, arrived as a replacement to the Ulsters in June. "We took over positions from the Turks. Most of the time was spent observing, going out on patrols and watch, of course. We had to keep watch twewnty-four hours a day. On guard four hours on and four hours off." Billy May was assigned to Support Company attached to A Company. There were two (Vickers) machine guns attached to each company and there was three men in each machine gun section. To the Americans we were known as 'Brodie's Flying Assholes' probably because we were seen to be everywhere."

Billy May had been conscripted in 1950 while working at an advertising agency in London. He was sent to the Royal Irish Fusiliers in Ballykinlar, Co. Down, and after basic training was sent to Germany. After the heavy casualties suffered in the Chinese New Year and Spring offensives the Royal Ulsters were badly depleted and needed a reinforcement draft. About 100 men came from the Irish Fusiliers and the Inniskillings. Billy May was one of them. They went by boat, the *Empire Fowey*, from Portsmouth to Kuala Lumpur and from there by Dakota airplane to "get there quicker". However, a hurricane over the Philipines forced them to land at the American airbase, Clark Airfield. "We were there for five days. It was like a holiday, like an American city. Best time we ever had. It was an enclosed area; cinemas, ice cream parlours, theatres. From there we went by plane to Pusan, where we lost everything in another storm. Tents, the lot, went up in the air."

Billy May served the last four months of the Royal Ulsters tour as a machine gunner. However, he deemed himself very lucky as the main fighting for the Irish regiment was practically over. His tour consisted of patrols, stand-to and thankfully, he said, very little action. "Once on patrol I saw the results of napalm, a horrible weapon. We were on patrol and came across this tunnel, about 100 feet long. Don't know what it was for. A napalm bomb was dropped at the entrance and it rolled in. These Chinese troops were sitting there holding their rifles, along with their transport mules. They were incinerated just sitting there as they were, mules and all." Billy May spent a further eight months in Hong Kong before he was demobbed. He now lives in Dublin.[10]

On October 4 during Operation Commando the 1st RUR were covering the left flank of the Canadian Brigade attack on Hill 187. However, the Chinese withdrew refusing to meet a prepared attack and the operation went without any casualties. As darkness fell, the Battalion marched for the last time out of the line and back to an area beside the Paekhak reservoir, three miles to the south-west, where the following day the 1st Royal Norfolks began to take over. Over the next couple of days the Ulsters moved south in transport, across the Imjin and down the dusty road to Britannia Camp, five miles north of Uijongbu. Three "very cheerful days" were spent in the transit camp, where the Ulsters said farewell to Brigadier Tom Brodie.

On October 11 the 1st Royal Ulsters left for Pusan, entraining, fittingly enough, at Uijongbu, where twelve months before they had first entered the campaign. On arrival in Pusan the Commanding Officer received the following, message from General Steele, which he read out to all ranks at their last parade in Korea: "I, as Colonel of the Regiment, send all ranks a personal message of thanks on the occasion of the Battalion leaving Korea on completion of its tour of duty on active service there. It is just about a year ago that the Unit embarked at Liverpool on the beginning of a foreign tour. The experiences of that year have been momentous for the Battalion and for everyone who has served in it of whatever rank. You have had to contend with very severe and variable climatic conditions and to adjust your training and operational methods to overcome novel types of opposition. I have been much impressed and gratified by the personal reports of senior visiting Officers who have seen you either in action or at rest. Your doings will be read with pride both now, and in the future you have written another glorious chapter in the annals of the Regiment. To those who have been with the Battalion throughout, I send a special word of thanks. To all others present on leaving Korea, I send my sincere thanks. I think particularly of those who have laid down their lives serving with you. I greatly appreciate the memorial which has been raised to them in Korea. To you, Colonel Carson, and to your whole Command, I send best wishes for the future, and may you have a happy service in Hong Kong."

Eleven days later, the Troopship *Empire Halladale* sailed for Hong Kong. Capt. Hamill wrote: "as the mountainous coastline faded into the distance, the Riflemen lining the rails watched it go with a curious mixture of feelings. In this last momentous year the Regiment had lost and won so much. Many who had gone out from England were left behind, and many would never come back. But, although it might often be difficult through the fog which surrounds the conference table at Panmunjom to see what has been achieved, there was, and there is, a feeling of pride that we, first in the 29th British Independent Brigade Group and then under the 1st Commonwealth Division, had played our part in proving to the world that the Free Nations would fight if need be for the principles in which they believed; and this being so, would fight well."

The Ulster Rifles lost 102 men killed in action, or died of wounds, in their year in Korea. The Regiment had performed superbly winning the acclaim and respect of their allies. (In July 1951 a memorial stone was unveiled near Happy Valley dedicated to the men of Ulster Rifles who lost their lives in Korea. All possible steps were taken to safeguard the memorial, but as time passed, the urban sprawl of Seoul spread northwards, eventually threatening the site. In late 1962 the memorial was removed and taken home by HMS *Belfast* to St Patrick's Barracks, Ballymena, the new North Irish Brigade Depot, which was then under reconstruction. In 1964, with the Depot established the memorial was placed in its new position on the south side of the parade square. A ceremony is held there every year to commemorate those who lost their lives in the Land of the Morning Calm.)[11]

On December 2 the 5th Inniskilling Dragoon Guards, arrived in Korea to replace the 8th King's Royal Irish Hussars. It was the third Irish regiment in the British Army to see service in Korea.* The 5th IDG, under the command of Lieutenant Colonel Arthur Carr, left Liverpool on October 29 on board the troopship *Georgic*. (Col. Carr was with the regiment since the days of the BEF in 1940 France.) Shipboard games and fancy dress parties accompanied the military training to alleviate the boredom of the long journey. Sgt. J. Bertrand wrote, "Some of the Skins, veterans of previous campaigns, started on their card marathons, which commenced in the English Channel and finished in Chinese seas." After calling at Hong Kong the *Georgic* pounded its way through the tail of a typhoon in the South China Sea to arrive in Pusan on December 2 in clear sunny weather.[12]

The regimental historian described the port city thus: "Pusan, a sprawling port of shanty towns, was hideously overcrowded with thousands of refugees, while vast

---

*The 5th Royal Inniskilling Dragoon Guards were the descendants of the 5th Dragoon Guards and the 6th Inniskilling Dragoons. These two regiments were amalgamated in 1922 to form the 5/6th Dragoons, a title which was changed to 5th Inniskilling Dragoon Guards in 1928. The regiment attracted many Irish recruits and was usually about sixty per cent Irish, with the majority coming from Northern Ireland.

dumps of military stores and supplies lay on every side, through which large six-wheeled U.S. Army trucks sped raising clouds of dust. The anchorage was crowded with shipping, and palls of smoke from Pusan's industry and power station hung in the still cold air over squalor, dust and an impression of disorganised chaos minged with Eastern odours." From Pusan the Skins headed north to take over from the 8th Hussars as the Divisional Armoured Regiment.[13]

By December 6 the last of the 8th Hussars had been relieved. Traditionally units of the British Army have many affiliations with units of other armies worldwide. The 8th Hussars had fought side by side with the 3rd Royal Australians and had supported them during Operation Commando and the Battle for Maryang San. On December 4 1951, prior to leaving Korea, the CO of the 8th Hussars entered the 3rd RAR Officers Mess and drove a lance into the floor, declaring, "We are now affiliated!" The 8th King's Royal Irish Hussars left Korea in the middle of December, leaving behind seventeen members killed in action, or died accidently - four officers and thirteen men.[14]

The 5th Inniskillings were equipped with the Centurion battle tank, which took some manoeuvring up the steep slopes, a feat much admired by neighbouring American tank crews. From the hill top positions they had excellent fields of fire reaching deep into the enemy positions. Tanks were deployed within infantry company localities on the tops of hills. During the day the crews cooked meals and carried out maintenance tasks in addition to shooting at any targets they could reach. During the winter months, the hills being frozen as well as steep, the tanks could not easily change positions, and there were some problems about rotating tank crews in the more unpleasant company positions even when the infantry reliefs took place every two weeks. The cold was a particular problem and Sergeant Williamson's "hand stuck to the tank when I forgot to put my gloves on before a squadron net at Stand To". The tanks had to be started up every two hours at night but even so there was a constant demand for new batteries. The squadrons were soon accustomed to the operational routine of a month in the forward areas followed by a month in reserve.[15]

The 1st Welch Battalion spent Christmas 1951 in the line and festivities were understandably curtailed, but each man had a Christmas dinner of turkey, vegetables, Christmas pudding and cake, and a ration of beer. In the line British troops lived on American C rations, but also received cans of 50 English cigarettes and, during the winter months, a daily tot of rum. (The Camels and Lucky Strikes from the C rations were given to their Korean helpers.). Like the Irish regiments the Welch celebrated their patron saint, St. David, (March 1) and every effort was made to spend the occasion in as near as possible in the traditional style. Leeks were flown in from Japan, and accompanied a special dinner - pudding, chocolate, cigarettes and a ration of beer. On March 10 the 29th Brigade was relieved by the Canadian Brigade and withdrew to reserve, with the Princess Patricia's Own Light Infantry relieving the 1st Welch. They returned to the line on April 18 taking over Hill 355 from troops of the US 2/15th Regiment. In the summer the men were given a spell of rest and relaxation in Tokyo in relays of small groups. They were trucked to Seoul and flown by US transports to Tachikawa airfield near Tokyo. "After six months back to the rear where we were deloused, given clean clothes and given five days R and R in Japan, then back to the front for another six months." Jack Clark was impressed with Tokyo, which despite being bombed severely during WWII was much more exciting than Dublin. Downtown Tokyo during the Korean War was a mecca for Allied servicemen with its wide streets and good sidewalks, theatres, bars, and open-air markets selling jewellery, watches, china, perfumes and clothing from the most exclusive houses in Europe and the US.

During May and June, as casualties slowly mounted, it was just more of the same; patrols, brief, violent fire-fights or shelling. They spent much of the time digging, wiring and trying to locate and mark minefields. "You just got on with it and hoped to get out of it." Jack Clark said. "It was a kip of a war; dirty, filthy conditions. I often wondered why I was there. I should have been back in Dublin." At twenty years of age Jack Clark, like many of the young soldiers in Korea, had no political leanings or interests. He just wanted to finish his stint in Korea in one piece. After over two years of service in Korea he was amazed at the naivety of some American troops. To the northeast of the Welch was the US 3rd Division.

1. Michael McCormick poses with a captured Chinese burp gun, 1952.
(Photo M. McCormick)

2. James B. Dunwoody, Ulster Rifles, outside his dug-out.
(Photo J. Dunwoody)

John Hawkins (left), Tommy Sinnott and Kiwi Stewart, who was killed at Kapyong, pictured in Pusan as they arrived in Korea 1950. (Photo J. Hawkins)

1. Group of Ulster Rifles (left) Rfn Maher, and (right) Rfn. Con Gouldsborough, killed in action April 25 1951. (Photo T. McConaghy) 2. POWs celebrating their release. Henry O'Kane, RUR, (second left) and Gerry Hassett, RUR (extreme right). (Photo H. O'Kane)

1. Michael McCormick in Pusan, 1952
2. J. T. Jennings in the Iron Triangle,
May 1952. 3. Sean Taheny (left)
Korea 1952.

Michael McCormick's half-track in position Korea 1952. (Photo M. McCormick)

1. Mike Kelly (right), Korea 1951. (Photo M. Kelly) 2. Tony Blake, taken in 1941 (Photo R. Leach) 3. Paddy Sheehy tank commander, Korea 1951. (Photo D.O'Shaughnessy).

1. Happy Valley 1951. Unveiling of memorial to men of the Ulster Rifles lost in battle.
(Photo W. May)

2. UN graveyard Pusan, 1952. (Photo J. Clarke)

Charles Dennehy, Staigue, Cahirdaniel, Co. Kerry, served with the US 32nd Infantry in Korea, 1950-51. (Photo C. Dennehy)

"It was a terrible wasteful war. Raw American troops would go out on patrol with yellow cravats and shiny helmets. You would see them on the skyline," he said. There were frequent air strikes conducted by the US Air Force on enemy positions across the valley. After an incident when an American jet shot up a Welch trench as American planes passed over on bombing raids the British troops put out huge coloured markers with arrows pointing "keep going." Huge American artillery pieces fired shells over the British positions at targets in the valley. The British troops could hear the shells whistling over and sometimes could see a small cloud of debris from the strikes far away in the distance. "The American artillery would come in behind you with massive artillery pieces, with what we used to call 'persuaders'. God help them on the other end. They would just fire them. No targets! Then drive off to another hill." The British, always envious of the wealth of American material were amazed at the casual wastage of their Allies. "If one of their trucks broke down, they would just throw a grenade under the engine and get another one. The poor British guys would be there forever with a big screwdriver."

On October 25 the Battalion completed its last stint on the front line, being relieved by the 1st Battalion, Royal Australian Regiment. In the United Nations Military Cemetery overlooking Pusan harbour, on November 6 1952, the 1st Welch gathered to honour and say farewell to the thirty members of the Battalion who had been killed in Korea. "It never leaves you. It (war) leaves its mark," Jack Clark said. He lost many friends in Korea and still has flashbacks of his period there, and suffers from Post Traumatic Stress. On November 9 the Battalion embarked for Hong Kong, and when the 1st Welch sailed back to Britain, Jack Clark volunteered for service in Malaya. Jack Clark left the British Army in 1955 after five years service. When offered £100 to re-enlist for a further five years, Jack had had enough of soldiering, he said, "I practically ran down the road." He worked in England and Scotland for some time then returned home to an Ireland that was much the same as when he left.[16]

In January 1952 the 3rd Royal Australian Regiment occupied positions on hills in the sector of the divisional line near 227, on 159 and 210. While 1st

Commonwealth Division became renowned for its defensive patrolling in Korea, no other battalion patrolled in such numbers, or as effectively, as the 3rd RAR. Every night they had about 200 men on patrols forward of their position, in two or three man listening patrols, in standing patrols, or in ambush or fighting patrols, each up to about eighteen men in strength. On January 26-27 the Battalion tried unsuccessfully to capture Hill 227. A Squadron, 5th Inniskillings, provided close fire support and the value of the tank fire was particularly evident during the tricky withdrawal as the Chinese reacted very vigorously with drenching mortar and artillery fire and an infantry counterattack. The Inniskillings lost their first man here, Trooper D. Veasey. On February 29 Corporal Dennis Grahame, from Cork, was wounded in action, while serving with the 3rd RAR.[17]

On St. Patrick's Day all squadrons of the 5th Inniskillings were busy, except A Squadron, which alone celebrated the day with a fun fair and a basketball competition. As April brought warmer weather the operational tempo was heightening. Larger fighting patrols on both sides sought to dominate no man's land and the troops in forward positions spent longer times in their tanks. 1st Troop, B Squadron, positioned on Point 355, which was known as "High Hell" or "Little Gibraltar" because of its shape, were repeatedly shelled and mortared.[18]

On June 17 the Inniskillings took part in Operation Jehu, a raid on Point 156 designed to inflict maximum damage on enemy positions and capture some prisoners for intelligence. The day before the raid some of A Squadron troop leaders and crew commanders were carrying out a reconnaissance of their special fire positions when an anti-personnel mine wounded Second-Lieutenant Sutherland and his other 2nd Troop tank commanders. Lt. Sutherland lost a foot, while the others were less seriously wounded. The next day the attack began as 1st Troop, C Squadron, crossed the start line and according to the Regimental journal, "Led by Lieutenant Taylor, fresh from an infantry patrol over this area, the troop went at a fine gallop and soon established itself on the first objective, a 100 metre high ridge half way to the main objective." Behind them heavy artillery fire poured down on the troops of A Squadron. "The passage of 1st Troop across the paddy had broken the 'bunds', and now the area rapidly turned into a quagmire."

Three tanks became bogged down, but the remainder reached their first objective. Lt. Taylor's tank was hit by a rocket, which started a small fire. Lt. Taylor jumped out of the tank and successfully put out the fire. For the offensive spirit he displayed throughout the attack Lt. C. Taylor was awarded the Military Cross.

1st Troop were soon within 100 yards of the final objective, but the tanks were unable to surmount the rocky spur on the crest. However, the Centurions were able to fire at a series of bunkers not visible from their own lines. After blasting away at the bunkers the order to withdraw was given, which meant, according to Sergeant Bertrand, a "perilous return to our own lines. The route out through the minefield had unfortunately being blocked by a tank minus its tracks, thus necessitating a return over the face of Point 159 at a speed of about 3 mph and through another of our own minefields; this of course delighted the enemy guns, who for what seemed like hours to the tank crews involved, had good targets to engage." The Chinese infantry now emerged out of their bunkers and opened up with small arms, while their artillery fired dozens of rounds at the retreating tanks. Sergeant Major Clayton's tank was hit four times and according to the regimental journal "all marvelled at his debonair unconcern in leaving his lid open; only the exercise of considerable restraint kept him from going over personally to 'inspect' the opposition." Sgt. Clayton was later Mentioned in Dispatches.

Within an hour the raiding force were safely back in their own lines, except for the three tanks bogged down in the valley below. Two recovery vehicles were damaged by mines and artillery trying to rescue the tanks, but by the end of the day two tanks and one ARV were recovered. The recovery of the remaining ARV and Centurion became an operation in itself. It took another two days to recover the ARV, but as it was being towed over Point 159 the Chinese artillery, seeing a covering smoke screen began to clear, opened up again. On Point 159, Second-Lieutenant A. Albrecht, 4th Troop, A Squadron, was killed, his tank set on fire, and both Captain Manning and the New Zealand FOO were wounded. It took another week to recover the remaining tank.[19]

Throughout the summer months the Chinese tried to drive the Skins off the crest of Point 159. On September 5 a high explosive shell entered the turret of a tank and killed the entire crew. In early November the 1st Black Watch with 4th Troop, B Squadron, relieved the US Marines on the Hook and from the middle of the month increased shelling, mortaring and enemy patrol activity forewarned them of an imminent attack. It came on November 18. The Black Watch, having stoutly defended their positions were forced back by the overwhelming Chinese attack. The Black Watch launched a counterattack that involved B Squadron and the Canadians. Fighting raged on into the early hours of November 19 but as dawn broke the Chinese retreated, unable to consolidate their situation on the Hook. The Hook was finally secured by the British counterattack and the tanks of 4th Troop withdrew to their harbour positions. The Scottish and Canadians suffered more than 100 casualties in the fighting. Minor affrays involved the regiment throughout the rest of the month and until December 8-9 when the 1st Royal Tank Regiment took over the Inniskillings section of the line.[20]

On December 12 1952 the regimental chaplain, Reverand D. S. Coey, conducted a moving memorial service for those from the 5th Royal Inniskilling Dragoon Guards who had lost their lives in Korea at the UN Cemetery in Pusan. One officer and eight NCOs and men were killed in action, and four soldiers died on active service. A further twenty-seven officers and men were wounded in action. Two days later the Inniskillings left Korea on board the *Empire Halladale* bound for duty in the Suez Canal Zone.[21]

Christmas on the frontline was always a time for reflection and thoughts of home and families. Private Harry O'Mara was serving with the 31st Infantry Regiment, who were in positions around the Old Baldy and Pork Chop Hill sector. Harry O'Mara wrote in *Recollection from Christmas Eve 1951 Front Line Position, US Infantry, Korea*: "It was a very still, star-lit night and unbelievably cold. We were on red alert as our officers expected some mischief from the Chinese who might expect us to be off-guard at Christmas. Their positions were uncomfortably close to ours.

"Across the snow from the Chinese lines came the plaintive and unmistakable sound of a flute. I immediately recognised the tune and it was not a Christmas carol, but the Irish strains of 'Danny Boy', the Derry Air. I thought that perhaps it was my imagination and I checked with my companions who confirmed the fact and the tune. Two days later we took the Chinese positions and, though I searched, I did not find the flautist or the flute."[22]

In New York, on February 3 1952, more than 3,000 people attended a Requiem Mass in St Patrick's Cathedral, New York, in tribute to the nine, then known, Irish-born servicemen recently killed in Korea. The remains of the nine young Irishmen were about to be shipped back to their families in Ireland for interment. In *The Irish Echo* report on the Requiem Mass in St. Patrick's, Frank O'Connor described how, in June 1951, Donal Harrington from Cork died in a hard-fought engagement on Korea's Hill 1046. "On the same hill", O'Connor revealed, "Patrick Maguire was machine gunned across the chest and right arm. He spent seven months in hospital and got out for the first time to attend the Mass for his comrades. He must go back again for another operation." In Eyeries, on Cork's Beara Peninsula, Eileen Harrington would clearly remember the exact date of the 1952 Mass in New York. By coincidence, February 2 was the day she buried her brother, Donal. Eileen also recalled how the Harrington family ended up comforting the man sent to console them. The escorting officer, who had just represented the US at another Irish funeral, was himself distraught. Following orders, he had turned down that grieving family's request for one last look inside their son's closed casket.[23]

Ron Price, Oxmanstown Road, Dublin, arrived in Korea at the end of March 1952. He had enlisted in the British Army in Belfast in December 1950 when he was twenty-one. His father was a WW1 veteran having served with the South Irish Horse on the Western Front. On seeing an advertisement for volunteers for Korea Ron put his name forward and was soon heading to Korea to H Squadron, 12th Field Squadron, Royal Engineers. The 12th Field Squadron (28th Field Engineer Regiment) were in Korea since June 1951 and were involved in bridge-building and repairs. Ron Price found, "It was cold. The winter months were bad.

There was a lot of action going on, but none near us. The Americans bombed our bridge on one occasion, but missed us, fortunately." Ron Price was eighteen months in Korea, which was the average tour for Royal Engineers, while the infantry had to serve twelve months.[24]

In May 1952 Matthew Ridgway was appointed NATO commander in Europe and was replaced by General Mark Clark as commander of US Far Eastern forces and the UN armies. Mark Clark was not of the same calibre as Ridgway. British commanders remembered him from the Italian campaign in World War II when he had squandered thousands of Allied servicemen's lives in his quest for personal glory. Clark immediately stepped up the bombing of North Korea, engendering the wrath of his allies and his foes. He wanted to win the war and chafed constantly under the political restrictions imposed on him from Washington. Clark even urged serious consideration be given to removing the restriction on employing atomic bombs to neutralise enemy air bases in Manchuria and North China. To the soldiers in the line he brought worry, doubts and confusion. The majority of them did not care about winning the war. Most were just content to survive their tour of duty. Many UN soldiers fought the war with little passion, save the desire to survive their tour and take up in civilian life where they left off. There was little hatred of the enemy - though maybe some for the North Koreans who were particularly brutal towards prisoners and civilians. An Irish-American youth from Boston, Billy Dickson, described the brutal nature of the hill fighting in his 1981 best-selling memoir, *Unit Pride* - a harrowing depiction of the war in Korea for the ordinary front-line soldier.

Pfc. Billy Dickson was a tough streetwise seventeen-year-old from Boston who arrived in Korea in June 1952. His mother was from Portlaoise, Co. Laois, while his father had abandoned the family when Billy was three. Raised in foster homes Billy Dickson had joined the Army when he was seventeen. After a brush with the law he was given a choice of the US Army or a reformatory. He picked the Army. When his unit was shipped to Korea Dickson said nothing about being underage for frontline duty because he did not want to be separated from Dewey Anthis, the only real friend he had ever known. On his first day on the line

Dickson witnessed American and South Korean soldiers interrogating a North Korean captive. After beating and shooting the prisoner in the leg the ROKs brought him into a thicket and shot the prisoner in the head. He vividly described the brutal nature of combat on one of his first experiences in action when Chinese troops attacked their positions at night: "I was in a sound sleep when something startled me awake. My first impulse was to stand up and take a look. Then I saw a head appear at the edge of the foxhole. I thought it must have been Dewey, coming to wake me. Then I saw the head was crowned with one of those gook hats. I moved my arm, which had been lying across my face, slowly toward the back of my head, and slid the forty-five from the holster. It was on half cock. I eased the hammer back all the way, afraid I'd make some noise that'd give me away. The head now was leaning more into the hole. A pair of hands appeared. One held a knife, the blade sheathed in the moonlight. The other just barely touched my chest, ever so gently. It glided toward my mouth, using my body as a guide. Then it clamped suddenly over my mouth and pinched off my nose. The forty-five had been pointed at the head ever since I'd caught the gleam of the knife. I pulled the trigger. The bullet caught him just right, shooting his head off his shoulders. I felt it drop on my stomach like an oversize squash. Blood pelted me, drenching me from head to foot. I grabbed my rifle and jumped up. Two more gooks were in front of the hole. I shot the first one with the burp gun, then the one with the long Russian rifle. They both fell in front of the hole. I snatched up the flare gun and fired it into the air. I looked in Dewey's direction and saw one going into his foxhole and shot him. The rifle firing and the flare woke up the whole company. The flare was going out when I fired another. It shot up casting a glare over the place like a klieg light. The Chinese, trying to kill the company without making a noise, had succeeded in infiltrating the area, but they'd been caught flatfooted. They were in the open now without a chance of retreating. They'd planned to do their work with knives, but now they switched to firepower. The staccato strum of burp guns began to vibrate through the area.

"The flare died but someone shot up another. I shifted my stance to get a better shot at a gook with a mortar. As I moved, a bayonet drove into the side of the foxhole, making its contact at the point where I'd been standing seconds before.

I spun back. The gook who'd thrust the bayonet down at me had lost his balance and was sprawling forward. I blasted him with the M-1 and when he landed his sense of balance had ceased to matter. His head, where the armor-piercing bullets had hit it, was gone.

"Using the two gooks in the hole with me for a footrest, I began to lob grenades down the side of the hill to turn back others trying to aid those gooks who'd made it to the top. Then one loomed up in the darkness, at the edge of the foxhole, and leaped in with me. He hit me on the side of the head with his rifle butt, knocking me backward. When I fell he lunged at me with his bayonet. I pulled the thirty-eight from the shoulder holster and squeezed the trigger. The shot caught him in the forehead and he crumpled. His rifle fell on top of him. I tried to find the forty-five but it was under the bodies somewhere. Right then I had no time to look for it. The ammo for the M-1 was gone, so I crawled out of the foxhole and picked up the burp gun from the gook I'd killed at the start. I looked over toward Dewey and saw a group of them swarming around his hole, like wasps outside a nest. A blast from the hole killed one of them. Before the others could use their numbers to advantage I ran over and swept them at chest level with fire from the burp gun. I put a bullet in each man's head to make sure they were done for the night. The burp gun was empty. I flung it down and jumped in the hole with Dewey.

"The gooks below explode up toward us like corn hot in the popper. We raked them with a steady fusillade, till at last silence settled over the slope. We crawled out of the hole, checking to see if any of the wounded still was alive. Those that were we shot. When they sneaked up the hill they expected no quarter. They got none." After several months on the frontline Billy Dickson was badly wounded and shipped home. His best friend, Dewey Anthis, was killed in the same incident. While serving time in Walpole State Penitenitary for armed robbery Dickson began collaborating on a book about his Korean War experiences with Professor John McAleer. A disgruntled employee stabbed Billy Dickson to death in 1974, and Professor McAleer finished the manuscript alone. *Unit Pride* became a best-seller on its release in 1981.[25]

On June 1 1st Battalion, The Royal Australian Regiment joined the 28th Commonwealth Brigade. The Battalion had left Sydney on March 18 sailing on the HMAS *Devonshire* for Japan. After training and preparation in Japan the Battalion moved to Korea arriving in Pusan on April 6. After further training at Mam-Myon and Sandok the Battalion moved into the line taking over from the 1st Royal Leicesters. Serving with 3rd RAR was Private William Fleming, from Letterkenny, Co. Donegal. On July 2 after vigorous patrolling 1st RAR raided Chinese positions on Hill 227. In this, their first action, they lost four dead and thirty-three wounded. A week later 1st RAR moved to Naeochon and were positioned alongside their fellow countrymen in 3rd RAR. Patrolling activity was maintained and throughout its stay in the line the Battalion was constantly shelled and mortared. Pte. William Fleming, was wounded in action on July 21, but made a full recovery.[26]

Medical Sergeant J.T. Jennings, US 32nd Infantry Regiment, left Korea in July 1952, after his tour of duty was over. He wrote, "Three thousand two hundred of us boarded the troopship General Collins in Inchon, South Korea on July 14, 1952. Two days later we arrived in Sasebo, Japan. That night, for the first time in 10 months, I slept in a bed. Also at this camp we were grouped according to U.S. Army area unit. In my case - the 1st Army from North East, USA. On July 23, 1950, units boarded the troop ship *General Black*. We arrived in San Francisco on August 6, 1952. Because of the international dateline we had no Tuesday going West to Korea and two Fridays in the same week returning to the U.S.

"The passage of time has taken a bit of a toll on my memory, but one moment I will never forget was when our ship sailed beneath the Golden Gate Bridge! With the cities of Oakland, San Francisco and Berkley in full view, I sudddenly could hear machine gun bursts, the mortar and howitzer fire and feel the impact they had on so many of my comrades who were counting the days to rotation ... yet never made it to this spot where I stood - to see America again. Tears began streaming down my face for them and for their families who had been praying for and counting on their safe return from the war in Korea.

"Despite what some publications and writers have reported, we were given a heroes welcome by the press, military dignitaries, USO and Red Cross. Page 37 of *The San Francisco Chronicle/News* shows a full page including nine photos on August 7, 1952 - under the headline Veterans of Korea Welcomed at Fort Mason. From there we were ferried to Camp Stoneman, California and three days later I was on my way, again via DC 3, to my army area - 1st Army Area, Camp Kilmer, New Jersey. Camp Kilmer is named after the famous WWI soldier-poet who was killed in action. I was based at Camp Kilmer until final separation. I was given credit for two years service even though I had served only 21 months. This was due to the 1st Echelon, four point, monthly system which made me eligible to rotate back to the U.S. in nine months. I would like to note that while we were separated from active service, we were transferred to active non-participating service reserves leaving us subject to 'active duty' recall within five years. I received an Honourable Discharge as a 'Sergeant First Class' on November 22, 1952.

"Serving our adopted country did not entitle us to U.S. citizenship. We could not become Commissioned Officers, nor did we qualify for civil service jobs until we had met the three years in service or five years in the country formula ... We risked our lives for our adopted country. However, the rewards have been fabulous. I have been blessed with a wonderful wife, a well-educated family, a good career and I am now enjoying retirement." J.T. Jennings returned to New York after his discharge and now lives in Long Island.[27]

As J.T. Jennings was leaving Korea in July 1952 another Irish emigrant, Sean Taheny, from Gurteen, Co. Sligo, arrived in Korea. Sean Taheny emigrated to New York in 1949 when he was eighteen. He went to live in the East Bronx with an aunt who claimed him over. Sean found that work in New York "was scare and the money bad". His first job was mowing lawns in St. Raymond's Cemetery, Bronx. Sean was working as a grocery clerk in November 1951 when he was drafted and while he was not overjoyed to go into the army, word was that if you refused you would be sent home and never allowed back into America. His dream, like thousands of other emigrants, was to start a new life in America. He began his basic training in Fort Dix, New Jersey. When he was finished his sixteen weeks basic training he was given six days leave then ordered to report to Far East Command for duty in Korea. He travelled alone to Seattle, Washington, which he found strange. In Seattle Sean Taheny boarded the troopship *Marine Adair* and spent the next nineteen days at sea. The first port of call was in Japan, where some men got off while Sean stayed on board for the journey to Pusan. In Pusan his name was called and he was sent northwards on a train "so slow you could walk beside it. I got off the train and got a truck to the 45th Infantry Division depot. In a matter of hours I was on another truck to the front. I volunteered to drive a jeep as I had driven a couple of times in New York. I had to follow a truck in front of me in the dark, with no lights on. A couple of lads hopped in and some said it would be a great job if we crashed as we would end up in hospital and not have to go to the front. I was hoping to get a job as a driver, but no such luck. I was sent to the Intelligence and Reconnaissance Patrol; always out front to tell where the enemy was. There were ten or twelve of us going out, but we always came back without three or four."

Sean Taheny - he was known as John in the army - was assigned to Headquarters Company, 179th Infantry Regiment, 45th Infantry Division. The 45th, known as the Thunderbirds, was a National Guard Division from Oklahoma, one of only two National Guard divisions to see combat in the Korean War; the other being the 40th of California. The division had shipped out to Japan in March 1951 and arrived in Korea in December 1951. The division was assigned to I US Corps in the Yonchon-Chorwon area, in positions fronting Old Baldy, Pork Chop Hill, Heartbreak Ridge, and Luke's Castle. The majority of the Oklahoma's Guardsmen began returning to the US in the spring of 1952, after their two-year terms ended and were replaced by active soldiers. Despite the fact that there were thousands of Irishmen in the US Armed Forces Sean said, "I never met one Irishman from the day I went into basic training to the day I left." He only found out in 2000, while attending a Thunderbirds reunion in Oklahoma City, that there was another Irishman in the regiment at the same time, but he was a cook. When Sean Taheny arrived on the line ambush and reconnaissance patrols were extremely active. Serving with Intelligence and Reconnaissance

Patrol he was "always out front," where the casualties were greater. Three major raids were conducted by elements of the 179th and its sister regiment, 180th Infantry, against strong enemy positions in the Hill 223 and Hill 290 areas. Despite tough resistance, the Americans succeeded in inflicting heavy casualties upon the enemy. The remainder of the combat activity centered about artillery fire placed on known and suspected enemy positions and personnel. From July 7-18 the action was the heaviest of the entire time the Thunderbirds spent on the line. The Chinese attacked in battalion size and patrol activity was aggressively conducted by both sides.[28]

In August 1952 the Chinese and North Koreans decided they would make another attempt to push the UN line farther south and soon the Western public were hearing and reading again about Heartbreak Ridge and the Punchbowl. The communist technique was to occupy the high ground at night, work on the bunkers and trenches, and then evacuate the area before dawn. When several nightly excursions had allowed them to complete a position, they moved in and occupied it. As military historian Edwin P. Hoyt wrote: "the Chinese were, in effect, trying to crawl their way to Seoul."[29]

13

POWs

The first minutes of captivity are always the most frightening, because it is then that the risk is greatest of being shot out of hand in the hot blood of battle. Some of the first American prisoners taken by the NKPA were eyewitnesses to the exceptional brutal treatment meted out by the ordinary communist soldier. Isolated and cut off from one another, many Americans surrendered in the first days before learning that the NKPA took few prisoners. More often the North Koreans tied their captive's hands behind their backs and bayoneted them. In the summer of 1950 the absence of a Prisoner of War policy by the NKPA became especially evident with the capture of Taejon. The NKPA killed several thousand South Korean civilians and summarily executed forty-two captured American soldiers. The North Koreans had not expected to fight the Americans and had no plan for dealing with American POWs. Additional executions of American soldiers occurred during this period, but there was no firm evidence that the North Korean High Command sanctioned this practice. The absence of an NKPA POW program coupled with the rash conduct of uncontrolled North Korean small units contributed to the atrocities. The majority of American prisoners died in the first winter of the war because the North Koreans were indifferent whether they lived or died. Wounded prisoners died from lack of medical attention because the North Koreans - and later the Chinese - were bereft of drugs and equipment, even for their own men, and not as direct policy. It was only when the communists realised the propaganda value of the UN POWs that conditions in the prison camps improved.

The first Irishmen killed in the conflict were missionaries from the Columban Fathers, taken captive and shot out of hand by the communists. Five Irish missionaries were killed by the NKPA in the first weeks of the war, while several more were sent to prison camps in North Korea, where another two died. Irish-born Columban Fathers, Monsignor Tom Quinlan and Fr. Frank Canavan, were taken into custody in the first days of the war and took part in the notorious "Tiger Death March" to the far north of Korea. Along with them were 750 US POWs and fifty-seven civilians, including a nine-month old baby and its mother. Many of the civilians were missionaries, and included Irish-born Sister Mary Clare and Bishop Patrick James Byrne, an Apostolic delegate to Korea from the USA. Sister Mary Clare was captured in Seoul on July 2. Byrne was born in 1883 in Washington, D.C. to Irish-immigrant parents from Co. Cork. He was captured in Seoul on July 11. The civilians and captured US troops were gathered together in Seoul and formed into a group for transportation to a prison camp in North Korea.

The group of foreign missionaries left Seoul on July 19 1950 for the North Korean capital, Pyongyang. On board the train Bishop Byrne took ill and was tended by three lay sisters in what Australian Columban, Fr.Philip Crosbie, described as "an unusual and touching version of the 'United Nations' - the American bishop nursed by a German, a Turk and a Polish-Korean, while representatives of France, Belgium, Ireland, America and Australia looked on."[1] They travelled only by night so the journey took two days. The missionaries were held in Pyongyang until the first week of September and then boarded a train for Sunchon. When the train journey was halted the missionaries were joined by a huge column of American POWs. On that first day Monsignor Quinlan recited the funeral service for one of the young American Catholic soldiers who had just died. After five days travelling the missionaries and the POWs reached their destination - Manpo, on the Yalu river. At Manpo the prisoners expected to be liberated by UN forces who were advancing steadily northwards, but on October 7 they were moved again, along with the American POWs to Jui-am-nee. On their travels they encountered Chinese troops who passed them heading south. The sight of thousands of Chinese quashed all hopes for rescue as the prisoners were marched back to Manpo.[2]

At Manpo a North Korean Army major referred to as "The Tiger" took command of the prisoner's and the march to Hajang-ni became known as the "Tiger March", or "Death March". When told their would be no transport and all the prisoners, old and sick, would have to march like soldiers, the prisoners' spokesman, Commissioner Herbert Lord, of the Salvation Army, protested, "But they will die if they have to march."

"Then let them march till they die!" The Tiger announced. "That is a military order."[3]

The American POWs took up the lead. Some of them were sick, and some were without shoes, few were adequately attired for what lay ahead. The weather during that autumn had been rather warm, so the soldiers had continued to wear their summer fatigues through their capture. Fr. Philip Crosbie attributes the appalling death rate from the pace of the march. "...it was this inhuman driving more than any other cause that made our march a march of death. Most of those who died were killed by the gruelling pace. The length of the journey, the lack of sleep, the bad and inadequate food, were all contributing causes; but many, perhaps all, could have endured these hardships if they had not been continually hurried along during the hours given to travel ... if they had been allowed to spread the journey over more hours of the day."[4]

When men began to fall out the Tiger personally shot one of the POWs officers as an example. The prisoners were marched for nine days over 120 miles of steep Korean terrain. During the march, the temperature had continued to drop. Sick and exhausted prisoners dropped rapidly, and their buddies were ordered to leave them for later execution. A night the prisoners were billeted in school houses or local villages. Here some prisoners died in their sleep. On the fourth day one of the elderly nuns fell back from exhaustion. An accompanying nun was forced onwards and the elderly nun was never heard of again. Later that day the same fate befell an elderly Russian widow. The death rate from the hardships of the march was appallingly high, but more was to come. On the morning of November 4 it began to snow and the pace of the march was increased to reach some mountain passes before they were blocked. When exhausted GIs began to fall by the wayside they were brutally, and coldly, shot where they lay.[5]

"We came upon an exhausted GI sitting by the roadside, then another." Fr. Philip Crosbie wrote. "beside each of them a guard was standing. We passed around a bend, and then two shots rang out behind us. We knew at once that they had been fired by the guards we had just passed… Our hearts ached with helpless pity as we came upon more and more men sitting or lying exhausted by the roadside, attended always by guards, who waited ominously till we stragglers passed. Then, each time, we listened in dumb anguish for the sound that always came - the sound of a shot behind us on the road." Twenty-two men fell out that morning and Fr. Crosbie had no doubt of their fate. "We passed them by as closely as we could and as slowly as we dared, and I spoke a few words about God's love and mercy."[6]

Through great courage, self-sacrifice and determination, Monsignor Quinlan saved the lives of many prisoners. He had replaced Commissioner Lord as one of the missionaries' spokesmen after Lord was appointed as interpreter for both the missionaries and the POWs. Together with Commissioner Lord he pleaded for transport for the weak and finally they were told vehicles would be found. That evening a truck and a bus carried off the women, children, old men and five very sick GIs. The pace of the march slowed as it was obvious many were nearing the end of their endurance.

Even though he knew it was a great risk to his own life, a young American soldier, Pfc Wayne "Johnnie" Johnson, was able to record the names of about 130 men who died during the nine-day death march. Many more died at a later stage of captivity and Johnnie Johnson secretly recorded the names of a total of 496 fellow prisoners who died. In August 1953 after the signing of the armistice only 262 prisoners from the original complement remained alive. The US Department of Defence debriefed all returning American POWs concerning their knowledge of those who did not return from the Communist prison system. Johnnie Johnson's painstakingly written record was a major contribution to this effort and helped determine or confirm the fate of many prisoners. In 1995 a Defence Prisoner of War/Missing Personnel Office (DPMO) analyst learned about Johnson's Tiger Survivors List while attending a Korean War Ex-POW reunion in Sacramento, California. DPMO analysts then located intelligence archives which contained Johnson's original debriefing report as well as other POW reports corroborating his information. Among these records was also found a debriefer's handwritten memorandum recommending that Private Johnson be recognised for his bravery. This information was forwarded to the Department of the Army, and in 1996, Johnny Johnson was awarded the Silver Star, America's third highest military combat decoration for valour.[7]

Tragically there are two Irish natives on the Johnson List: Sister Mary Clare and Father Pat Canavan. (Bishop Byrne is also on the list.) Sister Mary Clare (nee Clare Emma Witty) was captured in Seoul on July 2. She was Irish by birth, having being born in Enniskerry, Co. Wicklow in 1883, but was a nun in the Church of England. She had abandoned her profession as a schoolteacher to join an Anglican Sisterhood, and had begun her missionary career in Korea during WWI. Sr. Mary Clare trained the first novices and became the first Superior of the congregation. During World War II she was forced to leave Korea, but the congregation she had founded survived. After the war Sr. Mary Clare returned to Korea and she was Mother Superior in the Society of the Holy Cross, in the South Korean capital, when the Communists arrived. Near the end of the Death March, her strength ebbed away and she died quietly in her sleep on November 6 1950, in Chungkang-jin, where the transport had brought those too weak to walk. She was laid to rest in a simple grave on a hillside.[8]

Another nun who was present when Sr Mary Clare died, later wrote in the Catholic magazine *Missions*. "This morning we found our dear sister Mary Clare, dead on her bed of straw. A person of deep Christian charity, she helped us in times of distress. With her companions who helped her so much on the forced march, we prepared her body for burial. We carried her on an improvised bier to the top of a neighbouring hill, quite close to the camp. We ourselves dug her grave, only so deep as our failing strength allows, and we laid her down there."[9]

On November 8 the march ended, in the village called Chungkang-jin. Ninety-six American prisoners had died on the journey. Two nuns and a civilian had also died, and fourteen more missionaries and civilians were soon to follow. Once the survivors of the Death March reached the Yalu River prison camp at Hanjang-ni, even more died. Over 220 American soldiers lost their lives during their four-month stay there. The mild autumn led to one of the coldest winters in history. Bishop Patrick Byrne died at the camp on November 25. He was sixty-seven and the hardships of the march had taken its toll. A man of great charm and charisma, he became a catalyst in prison who united the very divergent groups of civilian prisoners from various nationalities. Fr. Crosbie wrote, "There was not a soul in camp who heard the news without a leaden sense of personal loss."[10]

Fr. Frank Canavan, whose health was never robust, died as a direct result of hardships experienced on the Death March, on December 6 1950, in Hanjang-ni. He contacted pneumonia on the march, seemed to get over the crisis, but then had a serious relapse. When someone tried to cheer him up with the hope that they might eat their Christmas dinner in freedom, he replied: "I'll have my Christmas dinner in Heaven." Fr. Canavan passed away on December 6.[11] His body was never recovered.

By the New Year the prisoners had given up all hope of being rescued. When the Tiger was transferred the beatings and ill-treatment of the POWs stopped and the prisoners felt a little bit safer. On March 17, St. Patrick's Day, the Sisters made shamrock and harp badges, out of some green material, for Monsignor Quinlan, and fathers Crosbie and Booth. Fr. Crosbie's badge was confiscated, but when the offending officer found Mgsr. Quinlan with a similar badge and was told the reasons of its existence, he returned Fr. Crosbie's emblem. Soon after the prisoners were moved to another camp at Ando and conditions began to improve.[12]

The Chinese could be unpredictable in their treatment of captured soldiers. Sometimes they were shot out of hand, other times they were returned to their own lines. A reconnaissance patrol of four men, under the command of Sgt. Nat

Kennedy, C Company, 1st Ulster Rifles, went out one morning to discover whether or not a small spur, known as "Slag-Heap Hill," was occupied by the enemy. This feature lay about 1,500 yards north of the Company position and just east of the main road. Sgt. Kennedy dropped off Rifleman Lyons, to lie up and watch the road, and to act as "getaway man" should things go wrong. Two hundred yards further on the patrol passed through a belt of trees and Kennedy stationed Rifleman Smith, with a Verey pistol. He was ordered to observe the movements of Sgt. Kennedy and Rifleman Pratt, the remaining member of the patrol, as they worked round the flank of Slag-Heap Hill itself. If he saw any sign of opposition he was to fire the pistol, which would bring down fire from the Battalion machine-guns and artillery on the area of the objective.

Kennedy and Pratt moved cautiously forward and were working round the west-ward flank of the hill when, behind them, Smith fired the Verey light. They looked back and saw ten or twelve soldiers, in Korean dress, surrounding Lyons, the getaway man. Before they could intervene, however, the pre-arranged artillery began to fall, between them and the road. The fire was heavy and Sgt. Kennedy, realising it was impossible to go back, decided to move forward a few hundred yards to a river-bed and lie up there until the excitement died down and they could work their way south again. After they had been lying in the river-bed some minutes, a spotter aircraft flew overhead. The two men took off their hats and waved, and were eventually seen by the pilot, who waggled his wings in recognition and flew off south. A few minutes later there was a splash in the shallow water beside them, and a grenade rolled into the riverbed. The two men jumped up and moved for cover, only to find themselves facing six armed North Koreans on the bank above. The grenade failed to go off and the two men were ordered to get up on to the bank and turn their backs to their captors.

"I took a deep breath," Sgt. Kennedy said, "because I thought I was going to be shot in the back." Instead of being shot out of hand, as they fully expected, the two were searched and then ordered to turn around. An officer, whom Sgt. Kennedy believed to be Chinese, then began to ask whether they were American. In spite of their denials, the officer was not convinced until the prisoners' weapons were produced and obviously recognised by him. Sgt. Kennedy then pulled out his paybook, which was greeted with pleasure by the officer, who shook them both by the hand and said, "American no good," at the same time making an unmistakable gesture with his finger across his throat! At this moment Allied jets began an air strike on to the hill above, and both captors and captives hastily got down into the riverbed. They remained there for some time until the jets flew away. The enemy then stood up to move off, and Sgt. Kennedy and Pratt prepared to follow them. However, to their surprise, the officer stopped them and, with a smile, pointed south-west in the direction of the hills on the far side of the road. Sgt. Kennedy realised that they were being released, and with little hesitation moved off towards the road, while the enemy party moved up the hill to the east. "These guys are going to shoot us," Kennedy said to Pratt as they continued walking. Eventually they reached a big hedge and just walked through it all the time expecting to be shot in the back. They came to a Korean house where the occupants gave them a drink of water.

After some difficulty in avoiding Allied artillery fire, the two men made their way back through the hills and eventually reached C Company's position as dusk fell. The following morning a South Korean peasant came up the hill to C Company, bringing a note from Rfn. Smith, which said that he was lying up, wounded in the leg, at the foot of the hill. A party was sent out to bring him in, and he was able to tell his part of the story. After firing the Verey light, he had opened fire on the patrol which captured Lyons. After killing two of the enemy, he was himself hit and taken prisoner. As he could not march, however, the enemy left him where he was and went off into the hills, taking Lyons with them. Smith was just able to crawl, and immediately started to make his way back towards the Battalion, until he was found next morning by the Korean villagers. Smith was evacuated to hospital, while both Sgt. Kennedy and Rfn. Pratt were sent back for a rest. Rfn. Edward Lyons died in a Chinese POW camp on August 31 1951 of heart trouble. He was twenty-six and a native of Belfast.[13]

Another group of Ulster's captured in January 1951 were made to kneel in the courtyard of a Korean house. A Chinese officer told them: "You have come here to murder the peace-loving people of Korea. But we shall treat you as students of the truth." The battalion welterweight champion, Corporal Massey, answered him in the unmistakable accent of the Belfast shipyards: "Listen, mister, will you go fuck yourself."[14] When an American patrol was captured in 1952 by Chinese troops and asked why they were in Korea, an officer cold-bloodedly executed the first two men when they said they were fighting communism. When it came to Pfc Billy Dickson's turn he told the truth saying he was only in Korea because he was given the choice of the Army or jail. The Chinese officer was happy with this answer and the rest of the patrol, taking their cue from Dickson, all gave similar answers. Content that there were no more enemies of communism among the American patrol - and after executing a South Korean guide - the Chinese let them go. However, the officer took one dog tag off from each soldier and told them if they were captured again they would not be so lucky.

Belfastman Corporal Joe Lavery, 1st RUR, was captured by the Chinese in the 1951 New Year Offensive. "I was taken prisoner with tops of boots and heel and no soles and I spent about two months marching through freezing cold. Where other people could sit down and have a rest, I had to keep moving about because I'd end up with frostbite. You can imagine (that) with inadequate clothing and probably at the most a tiny bowl of rice gruel or corn, millet, sorghum or beans about twice a day - (which) wasn't enough as a warmer-up meal, never mind a meal to keep you going and keep out cold conditions like that - people very quickly lost weight and started to ... die of starvation.

"I went blind for about three or four weeks. I found out later on it was through malnutrition, but luckily enough that came as summer was (approaching) and everybody was out, pulling all sorts of plants and leaves and boiling them up, and that, I think, was the thing that saved my eyesight because I started to get at least the greenery out of whatever was growing on the ground.

"In one camp we called the Bean Camp, because that's all we lived on, there were about 400 people (within) a month (who) died there, and there were only about fourteen or fifteen of us who walked out it alive. It wasn't necessarily all starvation. A lot of it was done by our side's planes coming over, machine gunning and rocketing us night and day, because the Chinese were using it as a staging-post. Later on, when we were being debriefed coming out, I mentioned the fact that, 'Surely to goodness, you must have known there were prisoners of war there', and I was told, 'Oh, yes, we did, but the important thing was to stop the staging of weapons from the Chinese down south.' They said, 'You were a prisoner of war then so you were really expendable.'

"I didn't, luckily enough, have anything to do with the North Koreans. Some other people were prisoners of war with them, and they were really vicious and cruel. It was the Chinese I was under. There's no guarding people who are sitting starving; you didn't really need to do a lot of guarding. If you had escaped, where would you go to with miles and miles and miles of frozen snow and no food and no chance of getting any?

"They were treating us as they would treat peasants ... so I think it was easy to resist the brainwashing, but it was the continuous, non-stop pushing at it, pushing at it, pushing at it (that) started to push their ideas over to some people who were influenced. But I would say there was no NCOs ever turned over to them and the vast majority had too much pride in their own regiment to allow them selves to be turned over to a communist ideology or anything like it."[15]

Corkman William Murphy was captured by Chinese troops near the Hoengsong/Wonju area on February 12 1951. Born in 1922 he emigrated fom Shandon Street, Cork City, to New York in 1948, to stay with an aunt. He enlisted in the US Army in 1950 expecting to be sent to Germany from where he hoped to visit home. Instead he was shipped to Korea in January 1951 and captured a few weeks later. About 400 prisoners were gathered together for a forced march to the Yalu river in North Korea. To avoid air strikes the column of prisoners and their Chinese guards marched by night in bitter cold weather. By day the prisoners were camped at small villages along the route north, receiving a single meal each day of rice, beans and millet. The only way to survive was to find friends. William Murphy teamed up with Henry Contreras, from Whittier,

California, and Billy Joe Harris, a farm boy from Missouri. A bond quickly developed between the three men on that long gruelling march north. When they were staying in huts along the route Murphy would go out and show a North Korean civilian his watch when the Chinese guards were not watching. Wrapping the watch in a rag, Murphy would offer to trade it for food or candy, but when the Koreans were not looking, he would swap the watch with a rock. The quick sleight-of-hand trick worked. The Koreans gave Murphy candy made from molasses, which he shared with his starving companions, Contreras and Harris. Murphy never completed the march. Just days before the prisoners arrived at their destination, on April 18 1951, the young Irishman died in his sleep of pneumonia, with Harris on one side of Murphy and Contreras on the other. As for the watch that helped keep the three friends alive, Harris took it and made sure the enemy soldiers could not find it. He also vowed to send the watch to William Murphy's parents, but he lost the address.

For years, the gold watch sat gathering dust, but Contreras never forgot the watch which helped save his life and the promise he had made to himself. Five decades later Contreras received a letter from William Murphy's nephew in Ireland. Stephen Murphy had contacted US military officials and learned that Contreras had provided the Army with details on how his uncle William Murphy died. Stephen Murphy wanted to know more about his uncle, who was among twenty-eight young Irish men recognised by President Bush in November 2003 for sacrificing their lives during the Korean conflict. William Murphy became a US citizen, posthumously, by order of the President. For Contreras, the letter from Stephen Murphy provided the perfect opportunity to keep Harris' promise to return the watch to the Irishman's family. Harris has sent the watch to Contreras, who sent it to the Murphy family. "I feel great about this, because Murphy was just a real good soldier," Henry Contreras told the Whittier Daily News in 2003.[16]

John Lee was also captured in the Hoengsong area on February 13 1951. Born in 1923 in the rural town land of Feothanach, Co. Kerry, John Lee emigrated to America in 1948 to stay with an aunt in Springfield. Just five months after arriving in the country John was drafted into the US Army. He completed his basic military training in Fort Dix, New Jersey. During his army training he met several others from his local area in Kerry, who had also being drafted. In December 1950 his unit, Company L, 38th Infantry Regiment, was flown to Anchorage in Alaska and went from there to Camp Drake, near Tokyo. On January 6 1951 Coy L arrived in the port city of Pusan. John Lee remembers vividly "the abject poverty and desperation of the thousands that lived there, the vast majority of whom were refugees fleeing the conflict further north." A little over a month later he was captured at Hoengsong when his company walked straight into an ambush and were annihilated. Taken from the battlefield the American prisoners were hidden in caves and dug-outs. Here everything was taken from them bar their clothes. They were told they would be freed in three days. Little did John Lee know that it would be nearly three years before he would again taste freedom.

The prisoners were not fed for five days and during that time they relied on snow for sustenance. They were marched north and to avoid being spotted by American planes they walked by night and slept by day crowded into Korean huts. One night, as they were marching a group of British prisoners passed by. John Lee shouted out and asked if there were any Irish among them. A voice with a Dublin accent answered and told them it was St. Patrick's Day. After many more days marching they reached a camp known as the Bean Camp, near Suan, which had been a Japanese mining camp. "Welcome to the Bean Camp. You are now in the hands of the Communist Volunteers," was the ominous greeting they got. Again, the POWs were told they would be released shortly.

This time few believed it. The Bean Camp was a staging area. It was known as the "Bean Camp" because prisoners were fed a ball of rice and soybeans rolled up into the shape of apples twice a day. It was already full with American, British, Australian and Turkish prisoners captured in the New Year offensives and many of them died due to hunger, disease, and no medical care. The Bean Camp had long buildings to house the prisoners on each side of the road. Twelve men had to share a hut of ten square foot, lying on a clay floor with no windows. They only had two meals a day of boiled barley, maize or millet. No bowls were provided and most men used their caps. John Lee had a bowl he found in a deserted Korean hut and later he managed to make a spoon out of a flat piece of stick. During his time in the Bean Camp John developed a close friendship with the Dubliner who had shouted out to him during the march to the camp. His arm was badly wounded and he was in urgent need of medical attention. John gave him his long sleeved jumper as his own was torn. They both made a pact that they would visit each other's parent's together, if, and when, they would be released. He also made friends with a group of prisoners who played cards in a hut at the end of one of the buildings. He usually played blackjack with them, but one day he called in and they were playing poker. John politely declined their invitation, as he did not know how to play poker and went back to his own hut. Suddenly, American fighter jets appeared overhead and began attacking the camp. The poker hut was hit and its occupants either killed or badly wounded.

On April 1 1951 the prisoners were told that they were to be moved to another permanent camp further north on the Yalu river. No mode of transport was to be provided, so the men would once again have to make the journey by foot. Due to his condition John's Dublin friend was unable to make the trip. John Lee later learned that he died from his wounds in the camp. Years later, when he was living and working in Dublin, John Lee called to see the young Dubliner's parents. Seven hundred Americans were divided into three groups for the journey northwards, while the POWs from other countries formed another group. Guides travelling on cows would direct the groups. Anyone attempting to escape was shot down and any prisoner who fell ill, or was incapable of carrying on, was left behind to die. John Lee remembers vividly many prisoners being beaten to death by their communist guards along the way. They walked by night to avoid UN aircraft who were unable to identify them, and slept by day cramped together in village huts or under trees on the mountainside. Many men died in their sleep and John recalled waking one morning to find a prisoner lying dead beside him, and another, across from him, rambling incoherently and crying out for his mother. He died shortly afterwards. Many days they got no water and very little food. What little food they received was cracked corn, barley, maize or millet seed. Many of the Americans refused to eat this and John Lee said that at one stage at least one prisoner was dying per day. Diarrhoea and dysentery also took its toll on the weakened men.

One day the column reached a bridge that had been badly damaged by bombing and was under repair. There was a large group of Communist troops waiting on the opposite bank. When the repairs were finished the prisoners crossed first, apparently to test the soundness of the work. As they climbed the hill on the opposite bank they were ordered to stop and rest. As they watched the Communist troops crossing the bridge American jets appeared above the brow of the hill and launched a rocket and machine gun attack that resulted in a huge loss of life. Soon after the prisoners were put on a train and the two hundred or so survivors were squashed into the carriages of a cattle truck. The train did not travel by day due to the fear of UN planes and John remembered that at one stage the train spent two days hiding in a rail tunnel. When the train reached its destination forty-two prisoners, including John Lee, were incapable of walking any further and were brought by truck to the camp in Chongsong, near the Yalu river, known as Communist Camp No. 1. After a three-night march the rest of the group reached the camp. It was May 20, John recalled. Only about 130 out of the original 700 reached Chongsong.

In Chongsong the prisoners were once again cramped into small shacks ten square foot in area with no windows. The food situation was as bad as ever and did not improve until towards the end of their captivity when they got steamed bread once a day. Boredom was the major bane of their lives but frost-bite, night blindness, forced labour, bad sanitation, air raids, and Communist propaganda and brain-washing ensured that conditions were far from humane. John Lee remembers that the dead were buried in their uniforms and without a coffin, at the foot of a hill they named Boot Hill. In 1951 they buried 500 prisoners in Boot Hill. He believes that the frugal conditions of the West Kerry of his formative years helped him to endure the horrors of captivity.

Many of the prisoners who came from large towns and cities would not eat the slop given to them by their captors, but if they wanted to live, they had no choice but to eat it. Many did not and died. John's Catholic faith was also a great source of inspiration to him. During his time in Chongsong he managed to make himself a set of rosary beads. He melted down empty metal toothpaste containers and poured them into a mould of a cross he made in hard mud. John then tied numerous knots in a piece of cord to represent the beads. He then tied these to his newly made cross. He still has the cross to this day.

In the summer of 1953 as tensions relaxed with the coming of the Armistice football teams were organised among the prisoners in Chongsong. John Lee was asked to play with an American team against a British team in a friendly soccer match. His American comrades assumed as an Irishman he would be familiar with soccer. He explained that the only football he ever played was Gaelic, so he lined out in goals where his football skills could be of use. Unfortunately, this reasoning did not pay off and the Americans were roundly defeated by the British. After the game one of the Americans noted the significance of the occasion. "Listen now, Irish," he said, "you will always remember that you played your first ever game of soccer for the Americans against the British, in a prisoner of war camp in Communist North Korea."

"Yes! My first game and my last one," John replied to the great amusement of all.

Back home in Kerry John Lee's mother Mary only found out a year later that her son was a prisoner in North Korea. The North Korean authorities sent a list of POWs to the American authorities who then notified John's aunt in Springfield. She sent a telegram to the Post Office in Baile na nGall in Corca Dhuibhne and the news was brought from there three miles away to Mary Lee in Feothanach. All other news regarding John Lee travelled the same twisted route. Mary Lee told her son years later that she always knew he was alive, and that it was her religion that gave her this unshakeable sense of hope. She travelled miles away to neighbours who had a wireless to listen in the hope that there would someday be good news about a war on the far side of the world. One day her wish came true as an armistice was signed in the summer of 1953, ending her son's two and a half years of captivity.[17]

Pat Quinn was also in Chongsong POW Camp. He was captured in February 1951 while serving with the 2nd Infantry Division. Born in Kilkeel, Co. Down Pat Quinn emigrated to the US in 1947. He was drafted two years later, discharged into the Reserve, but recalled to service on the outbreak of war in Korea. He arrived in Korea in November 1950. " Winters in Korea are bitter cold - 30 below with strong winds from Siberia," he said. "Summers are hot. Korea is a country of mountains and narrow roads; our tanks could not be utilized. After several encounters with the enemy, the Chinese Army made their big push in February of 1951. There were so many of them, they were like ants on a hill! We were surrounded, out of ammo and now suffered the humiliation of being taken a prisoner of war. The Chinese Army moved only at night. We were marched endlessly over hills and mountains by our captors. Days were spent on the side of a mountain. We were lucky to have food once a day. Food consisted of half cooked crushed field corn and beans. This caused extreme dysentery and diarrhoea and we had no control of our bowels. I hope you can picture what this is like when you have no change of clothes and it is bitter cold. The discomfort and smell never left you! We arrived exhausted and dehydrated to an area we called "Bean Camp" the early part of April. This was a row of mud-houses used as a staging area for prisoners. With no markings that this was a POW camp, we were subjected to bombing and strafing by our own planes."

" Sixteen of our officers were killed in one day! We complained that the camp was not marked and were told by the Chinese that they did not recognize the Geneva Convention nor the International Red Cross. We were moved further north arriving May 17, 1951 to Camp 1 which was a town near the Yalu River. The Korean civilians were moved out of their homes and this was now our POW camp. All of us had beards and long hair - not by choice but razors and scissors were not part of our world. Every seam in our clothing were infested with lice. Body lice suck the blood from their victims and we were the victims! We deloused every day; by this I mean squeezing the lice between your thumbnails and killing them. I saw toes of our men fall off from frostbite. All of us experienced frostbite. Young men with strong hearts begging God to take them due to high fevers, malnutrition and no medical or dental care. There were approximately 700

POW's in Bean Camp; out of that number approximately 130 came home. Every day our group buried four or five of our POW's on a hill. We named it "Boot Hill." It was now summer. There were millions of flies and wounds were full of maggots. We suffered from beriberi, night blindness, high fever and malnutrition. There were ten of us to a ten by ten room. We slept head to toe on the floor. In the winter, the walls were white with frost from our breath. A change of clothes was issued in July. Medical care - on limited basis - was started in late Fall of '51. We were subjected to Communist propaganda every day. We were not prepared for this indoctrination. A question that regularly comes up is - why didn't we escape? The answer is, we were too weak to climb the mountain and where would we go! Our features are different so we would be easily recognized. We were struggling to survive! We looked forward to the day we would be liberated. After the exchange of the sick and wounded in April of '53, our conditions improved." [18]

Another Irishman serving in the Royal Ulster Rifles also ended up in Chongsong. Rfn Henry O'Kane, of C Company, 1st Ulster Rifles, was captured as the 29th Commonwealth Brigade withdrew from the Imjin in April 1951. He was wounded in the head and leg by mortar fragments and collapsed into a ditch by the road-side. He unbuckled his equipment and limped down the road until he came to a group of men beside a Centurion tank. Here he lost consciousness and when he awoke the tank was disabled and Chinese troops were milling all around him as the British troops still able to move fled down the road. Another Ulsterman put a field dressing on his wound and gave him a swig of rum. The sound of gunfire receded as the Chinese pursued the British troops. At last a Chinese officer stopped and gazing down on the motionless huddle of wounded men, said in careful English: "I think it is a good fight." The British troops were wary, expecting to be shot at any moment. The walking wounded were gathered together and led away, hands on their heads. They never saw the stretcher cases again. The prisoners were given "safe-conduct passes", declaring that they had been "liberated by peace-loving peoples", then ordered to start marching.[19]

O'Kane's interrogation focused on how and why he was in Korea, rather than on military matters, as he said his interrogator probably knew more about the military situation than he did. After he gave his interrogator some details on his service with the RUR he had to draw a map of Europe to show the Chinese officer where Ireland was. He was told he was a tool of the American and British imperialists and with the help of "lenient policy" he would soon learn the "truth" and would be treated well. O'Kane pointed out that he had been refused medical attention since his capture and there was nothing lenient about that. He was taken to a primitive aid post where the shrapnel fragments were extracted from his head and leg without benefit of anaesthetic. Black ointment "such as we use for horses back home" was smeared on the wounds and then his original bandages were replaced. However, despite his pessimism, his wounds healed well.[20]

Henry O'Kane wrote of his experiences as a prisoner in *O'Kane's Korea*, a gripping testament to the brutality and plight of the United Nations POWs. He was in a column of about 200 Allied troops captured at the Imjim. Each day an NCO would count out their ration of soya beans - sixteen to a man. They were told they were to march to catch a train to safety, but as night followed night they realised there was no train. There was no temptation to straggle from the column and try to escape, for North Korean troops hung around constantly, begging to be given prisoners as hostages. "We were very glad of Chinese protection," Henry O'Kane wrote. "One night we doubled past a convoy that had been hit by the bombers. Knocked out trucks and mule teams lay on both sides of the road. Screams of wounded men and mules rent the night air. The Chinese drove us on, no one bothered with the wounded. This inhumanity was something we were to experience time and time again." They spent a week at a village on the delta of the Taedong river, being given daily political lectures. The prisoners were housed in a long school building.

"My memories of this school house, full of homesick, weary, hungry men lying on the wooden floor, are dominated by the sound of low soft Irish laments played on a harmonica. The player was a well known pugilist throughout the Irish Brigade,

Davey Crawford of Belfast."[21] After a week the prisoners began marching again, this time to their permanent home, Chongssong, Communist Camp 1, where they arrived in June 1951. Here, they joined some hundreds of Americans. The British were shocked at the pathetic state of the Americans. The appearance of hundreds of fresh British troops seemed the end to them. It seemed like the war would go on forever and many of them gave up hope. "These men had survived some of the worst conditions ever experienced by POW's; many had been captured in November in the north-east. The elite US First Marine Division, with the British 41 Marine Commando, fought a valiant battle at Tokyio Ri and Hamhung to win Battle Honours and Presidential Citations, but many were to lose the battle for life in the prison camps along the Yalu." O'Kane witnessed thirty-six prisoners buried in one day. That summer nearly 400 prisoners, mostly Americans, died.[22]

In late 1950 in the first Chinese offensive several thousand US soldiers and Marines were captured. Like the NKPA, the Chinese at that time had no established POW system. As an expedient, the CCF set up a temporary camp called the "Valley" located 10 miles south of Pyoktong, near the Yalu River. Primitive living conditions there resulted in the death of from 500 to 700 of the 1,000 POWs. American soldiers, most of them members of the 2nd Infantry Division captured at Kunu-ri in November 1950, were kept at a place called "Death Valley," thirty miles southeast of Pukchin. Forty percent of the camp's 2,000 inmates died within three months. The other internment point known as "Peaceful Valley," located near Kanggye, that held about 300 US POWs, had better living conditions than the other two camps and only a ten percent death rate. Overall, UN POWs died in large numbers during the first year of the war. Lack of food, shelter and medicine took its toll. During the first winter, some American POWs reported marching for days. Prisoners, weakened from battle, the cold and lack of food, who could not keep pace with their fellow prisoners were often left to die or executed by their captors. Prisoners carried and dragged one another through these marches. Some American POWs were young teenagers. One soldier captured during the Chosin fighting was sixteen years old.[23]

When Henry O'Kane reached Camp 1 he was in a bad way. He was suffering from beri-beri and dysentery, and his mouth was sore from lack of vitamins. Luckily, he was placed in a hut with some forty Filipinos and Puerto Ricans. They were simple peasants; men used to that kind of life who knew how to make medicine from herbs and thus keep themselves alive. That is what they did for O'Kane. He was lucky. Many more were not. Men used to living on a combat ration of 3,500 calories now found themselves depending on 1,200 calories of corn and millet. Their diet now had no vegetables and was almost devoid of proteins, minerals, or vitamins. Many prisoners, especially among the American contingent, just gave up living. Many Americans simply refused to eat the mess of rice and sorghum with which they were provided. They chose instead to starve. A man without friends had no hope. It was comradeship that kept most prisoners going. For the British prisoners this was easy, because they had their regimental tradition. Some had been in their respective regiments for years and many men had soldiered together for ages. The Americans, apart from the US Marines, did not have the same traditions. Many Americans were draftees; some had only arrived in Korea and had not even being familiar with their units when they were captured. Only about fifty British soldiers died in captivity out of around 1,100 captured while 2,730 out of 7,190 Americans died. The North Koreans murdered some hundreds of these in cold blood in the first months of the war. Many more died on the horrific journey to the camps, or in the first winter of the war. However, the majority died when they simply gave up hope. Most of the POW deaths were generally attributed to unchecked disease, untended wounds, malnutrition and extreme cold, rather than to organised physical abuse. Many of these deaths occurred prior to creation of the permanent camps.[24]

Through most of 1951, despite established camps, casualties continued to mount. Prisoners were fed what Korean peasants lived on and medical supplies were unavailable to the doctors. Finally the death rate, sometimes approaching forty percent, alarmed the Chinese. Soon food and medical supplies were provided and conditions improved for the rest of the war. By 1951 the communists decided that there was propaganda value in a POW system. The Chinese developed eight permanent POW camps that stretched over a fifty-mile sector in North Korea along the Yalu river. The communists segregated the POWs according to rank, race and nationality and created interrogation and indoctrination programs. With their indoctrination program, the communists tested each prisoner's faith in the democratic process, but the Chinese sought publicity more than converts to communism. Daily propaganda lectures and broadcasts that attacked capitalist society were conducted, and the communists persuaded some POWs to sign peace petitions and make pro-communist statements. Even though some UN POWs collaborated with their captors, most of them did so for personal convenience.

The exact number of British prisoners who died in captivity is uncertain, but it was probably around fifty, against a total of 1,036 repatriated by the Communists in 1953.   Only one British soldier refused repatriation. He was Royal Marine Andrew Condron - twenty-one Americans also refused repatriation, although like Condron they all eventually returned home. Among the British prisoners were 215 from the Royal Ulster Rifles - 120 captured at Happy Valley and 95 captured at the Imjin. Not all of them were Irish, but the majority were born in Ireland. Nine Irishmen serving in the Royal Ulster Rifles died while held as POWs. They were Rifleman Robert Craig, twenty-three, from Belfast, captured on January 4/5 1951, who died on or after June 25 1951; Corporal William Davidson, twenty-four, from Ballymoney, Co. Antrim, who was captured on January 5 1951, and died of beri-beri in a POW camp on June 1 1951; Sergeant Lawrence Kavanagh, thirty-three, from Pollerton, Co. Carlow, also captured at Happy Valley who died of "sickness" on September 4 1951 in a POW camp; Rfn Edward Lyons, twenty-six, from Belfast, who died of heart trouble on August 31 1951 in a POW camp; Rfn Daniel Maher, twenty-eight, from Tipperary, captured on the Imjin and died on or after September 28 1951, of causes unknown in a POW camp; Rfn Robert Martin, thirty-one, from Carrickfergus, Co. Antrim, who died on or after April 22 1951 as a POW; Rfn Willliam McWilliams, thirty, from Newry, Co. Down, who died on or after April 12 1951; Sgt Frank Nugent, twenty-eight, from Belfast, captured in Happy Valley and who died of causes unknown in a POW camp on April 18 1951; and Rfn Michael Reidy, thirty-one, a native of Ennistymona, Co. Clare, who died of pulmonary tuberculosis on August 2 1951 in a POW camp.

There were also other Irishman from various British units who became POWs: Michael Buckley, Monasterevin, Co. Kildare, captured in January 1951; and Diarmuid O'Sullivan Herlihy, known as Danny or Dermot, from Clontarf, Dublin. He was serving with the Royal Engineers on bomb disposal and "had a medal awarded to him for bravery, as he carried a friend who had been killed back to the base".[25]

Rifleman Albert Tyas, 1st Royal Ulster Rifles, was captured at the Imjin in April 1951. He was in Chongsong Camp 1 when the communist indoctrination began. He said, "They started indoctrination in about August/September 1951. Now indoctrination, it was political indoctrination what they did. They brought in educated Chinese people, very fluent in English. Each company had a good English-speaking instructor to instruct us and they would deliver a lecture on the feudal system, the capitalist system. We studied the Finnish war, the Russian Finnish war, the difference between Communism and Socialism and many subjects like that. They would break it down to economics every time; economics is the basis of everything in the Communist way of life. Then they would sit us in rings of ten men and we would have to discuss this question."[26]

"In the late summer the Chinese were to re-arrange the whole camp," Henry O'Kane wrote. "Men came in from various camps in North Korea. British Marines from American companies, RUR's from Hell Camps run by the North Koreans, legends of the Irish Brigade, Andy McNab, Paddy May, Jack Skin Kelly, Blind Jack Spence, Ray Fogarty and others who had survived since capture in January arrived. The Chinese also brought in to the British companies a number of Irishmen from various UN units. One whom I remember well was a large Tipperary man in the US Army who sported a Mohican haircut and was a camp cook in the British 5 Coy." The British companies were numbered 5, 6 and 7. The camp authorities had broken down the leadership of the prisoners by sending all officers, NCOs and potential leaders to different camps. 5 Company was made up of young soldiers; 6 Coy - reservists; 7 Coy - regulars; and K Force - volunteers. The prisoners were organised into platoons and squads. Each platoon had a Chinese commander and Chinese political instructor. They were in charge of discipline and political "re-education". Henry O'Kane was in 7 Company, 9 Platoon, 9 Squad. His platoon leader was an artilleryman, who had escaped from a POW camp in Italy during WWII, while his squad leader was Jeremy Hassett, RUR, from Cork. O'Kane's squad remained together until September 1953 when they were released in the POW exchange. For two years the prisoners endured political lectures and a general lack of the basic essentials. Food parcels were denied, as were visits from the International Red Cross. In the spring of 1952 new diseases began to appear, like twilight blindness, due to vitamin deficiency. "Our standard of food was never good," Henry O'Kane wrote, "it was governed by the way the truce talks kept going. When they were meeting things always improved... Despite all the tea in China all we ever had to drink was hot water. Tea did not appear until late in 1953."

It was not until December 1951 and then again in December 1952 that many relatives found out that their loved ones were still alive and held as prisoners of the communists when lists of prisoners were read out over the Communist radio at Christmas. By issuing the lists around Christmas the communists knew they would get maximum publicity. On January 26 1952 the director of the Columban's Foreign Missions was informed by the US Department of State of the names of "Fathers Thomas Quinlan and Philip J. Crosby. I regret to say that the list does not contain the names of Fathers Patrick Brennan, James F. Maginn, Francis Canavan, Thomas Cusack, or John O'Brien".[28] On December 30 1952 the *Irish Independent* reported "Irish prisoners in China: Messages from five Irishmen, members of the British Army, who had been captured by the Communists in North Korea are broadcast on Peking Radio. Among them are Rifleman John Shaw, who is not yet nineteen, but had been in Korea for more than two years." Rfn. Shaw had been captured on the Imjin in January 1951.[29]

On February 22 1953 Gen. Mark Clark proposed an exchange of sick and wounded prisoners. A week later the Chinese agreed and proposed that prisoners unwilling to be repatriated be transferred to a neutral state. (Eventually, one British and twenty-one Americans refused to go home, though over the years most actually did.) A month later the exchange of sick and wounded prisoners began at Panmunjom. By the end of May all the civilian prisoners were released. There were about fifty civilians, mostly captured at the beginning of the war, and included Bishops, Catholic, Anglican and Salvation Army missionaries, nuns of various orders, diplomats, business men, newspaper correspondents, men, women and children, Irish, English, American, French and White Russians. Ten had died in captivity, most of whom were elderly missionaries and nuns and included three Irish missionaries: Sister Mary Clare, Bishop Patrick Byrne and Father Frank Canavan. One of the British diplomats released was George Blake, who became a Russian spy. Fr. Phil Crosbie was released on May 25. He travelled unescorted for seven days by train from Pyongyang to Moscow, via Siberia. In the Russian capital Fr. Crosbie was met by staff of the Australian embassy at a Moscow train station. He was finally free.[30]

Tom Quinlan was held captive until March 21 1953. He was told that night he would be leaving in a half an hour. Following his release Father Tom Quinlan went back to Ireland where he received a "victorious welcome" in April 1953. President Sean Lemass greeted the returning hero at Dublin airport on behalf of the nation. Quinlan's niece, Carmel McHale, was among the first to greet him. "He was very emaciated, very thin and he wasn't able to drive," she recalled. "So I took a year off college to drive him around. He really was a hero. He was so strong, which, I suppose, came with being born on a farm. His spirit wasn't broken. He was determined to get back to work. He loved the Korean people, saying they were so gentle, so understanding." Tom Quinlan went back to Korea soon after and was made Apostolic Delegate from the Holy See in Rome to South Korea, a position he held until his death in 1970 in Sam Chok. He was reburied in Chunchon in 1972, the city where he had spent much of his life.[31]

In late July the UN POWs heard the news that they were finally to be released. In Chongsong as the Camp Commandant announced to the drawn up ranks of prisoners that the "peace-loving" CPVA and NKPA were allowing them "to return home" the news was greeted with silence by the 2,000 British and American prisoners, who were determined not to show their true feelings to their Chinese captors.[32] Almost immediately the POWs food increased and they were fed three times a day with fresh meat. Rice, bread, sweets, cigarettes, soap and toothpaste were also issued in great abundance, so by the time the International Red Cross visited the camp all the prisoners looked far healthier.

Pat Quinn said, "As we left to come home, I looked up at Boot Hill and with tears in my eyes I prayed for all that were not coming home with me. After thirty-one months in captivity I was released August 19 1953." In August the prisoners were brought to a small village near Panmunjom appropriately named "Freedom Village" where the exchange of POWs would take place.[33] John Lee remembers the words "Welcome Back to the Gate of Freedom" being on the large sign. "We had tears of joy in our eyes and some GI's broke down and cried. I felt sadness in my heart for those we had left behind dead but I am sure there was a better gate open for them in a better place." From Inchon it took seven days to reach San Francisco and John still remembers with pride the signs which read "Welcome Home" and "San Francisco is Honoured to Welcome You Back from the Battlefields of Korea," which were hung on the Golden Gate bridge. After spending a few days in hospital, all former POWs were entitled to a free flight home. John Lee was hoping to make it back to Ireland for Christmas but was unable to get a flight. "In early January," Brendan Fitzgerald wrote in *Duthaigh Duibhneach*, "he flew home to Ireland and made his way to Corca Dhuibhne and to Feothanach. It was a joyous return not only for Seainin's family, friends and neighbours but for the entire parish. The festivities lasted well into the night and many older local people still fondly remember the homecoming of Seainin Liam."[34]

Near the end of August Henry O'Kane finally began his journey home, as he boarded a truck to the railhead at Nampo, on the Manchurian border. From here the train took the POWs to Pyongyang and then on to Panmunjom and Freedom Village. After passing through the UN processing centre Henry O'Kane, and the rest of the British POWs, were brought to Britannia Camp, HQ of the 1st Commonwealth Division. At the NAAFI Club they were given a meal of their choice. Henry chose bacon and eggs and then, like the rest of his comrades, got "hopelessly drunk." Two weeks later he was on the cruise liner *Dunera* on the way back to Britain. The trip back home was marred by fighting as ex-prisoners settled old score. Some men classed as collaborators had to be taken off at various ports for their own protection.

After a long leave in Ireland Henry O'Kane returned to his unit but was then hospitalised for four months. After he was released from hospital he went before the Army Medical Board and was downgraded, which meant he could only be eligible for home service in the Army. Henry opted for his discharge and returned to civilian life. Henry O'Kane endured months of difficulty with twilight blindness caused by vitamin deficiency, and years of chronic insomnia. "In the camps in North Korea amid the privations and indoctrination I had begun to learn about myself," Henry wrote, "about people, along with the suffering, disease and death... As a fighting soldier in Korea in action I was scared most of the time, but it was war and one gets used to it. With comrades in arms I was aware that I had walked close to death. In the prison camps along the Yalu it was different. I was frightened, sometimes I was very frightened."[35]

14

Dying for Peace

In the autumn of 1952, as the peace talks dragged on, the US Marines were fighting and dying on Bunker Hill, on the Jamestown Line, southeast of Panmunjom. The war had turned into a nightmare with no end. There was no victory, just never-ending fighting, day after day. Irish-American Pfc. Alford McLaughlin was serving with Company L, 5th Marine Regiment. Born in Leeds, Alabama, in 1928, Alford McLaughlin enlisted in the Marine Corps in May 1945 and had served in the Pacific, Japan, and the Mediterranean before arriving in Korea in February 1952. He was awarded a Purple Heart for wounds received in August in the Bunker Hill area. On the night of September 4/5 Pfc. McLaughlin was again on duty in the Bunker Hill area when he stopped a Chinese attack dead in its tracks and was awarded America's highest decoration, the Congressional Medal of Honour*, and a Gold Star in lieu of his second Purple Heart for wounds received in that action.

Alford McLaughlin's citation reads: "For conspicuous gallantry and intrepidity at the risk of his life above and beyond the call of duty while serving as a machine gunner of Company L, in action against enemy aggressor forces on the night of 4-5 September 1952. Volunteering for his second continuous tour of duty on a strategic combat outpost far in advance of the main line of resistance, Pfc. McLaughlin, although operating under a barrage of enemy artillery and mortar fire, set up plans for the defense of his position which proved decisive in the successful defense of the outpost. When hostile forces attacked in battalion strength during the night, he maintained a constant flow of devastating fire upon the enemy, alternately employing two machineguns, a carbine, and hand grenades. Although painfully wounded, he bravely fired the machineguns from the hip until his hands became blistered by the extreme heat from the weapons and, placing the guns on the ground to allow them to cool, continued to defend the position with his carbine and grenades. Standing up in full view, he shouted words of encouragement to his comrades above the din of battle and, throughout a series of fanatical enemy attacks, sprayed the surrounding area with deadly fire, accounting for an estimated 150 enemy dead and 50 wounded. By his indomitable courage, superb leadership, and valiant fighting spirit in the face of overwhelming odds, Pfc. McLaughlin served to inspire his fellow marines in their gallant stand against the enemy and was directly instrumental in preventing the vital outpost from falling into the hands of a determined and numerically superior hostile force. His outstanding heroism and unwavering devotion to duty reflect the highest credit upon himself and enhance the finest traditions of the U.S. Naval Service." Alfrod McLaughlin left Korea in January 1953. He died in 1977.[1]

Pfc John White, from Caherdaniel, Co. Kerry, was serving with Company A, 1st Battalion, 7th Marine Regiment, when he was reported missing in action after an engagement with Chinese troops on September 24 in the Bunker Hill area. It was thought he was taken prisoner. His sister Maryanne heard the first news of her

---

*There were 131 Medals of Honour awarded to US servicemen for their actions during the Korean War. The Medal of Honour was instituted by Congress in 1861 and is awarded for gallantry and intrepidity beyond the call of duty without detriment to the mission. The grant is only made after a most searching inquiry. Eleven layers of military or naval authority have to approve the recommendation before it can proceed to the proper cabinet-level secretary (Army, Navy, or Air Force) who alone makes the final decision to award the medal. Originally only enlisted men were to be entitled to the award, but a few years after its introduction the Medal of Honour was made universal. Ireland lays claim to more Medal of Honour holders than any other country, with 258 recipients giving their birthplace as Ireland. (Germany/Prussia is second with 128 recipients.)

brother's fate when she was waiting on a ship in Cobh to travel to the US. He was first reported missing in action on September 24 1952. It was thought he was seriously wounded and died soon after been taken prisoner. However, his body was never found, so his family never gave up hope. In March 1954 a telegram arrived saying that he was dead. The telegram was dated on St. Patrick's Day. John was supposed to have been back by St. Patrick's Day 1953. According to his sister because he qualified as her legal guardian John could have avoided the draft, but he was intensely loyal to his new homeland and did not object when he was called up. John White was a neighbour of Charles Dennehy, who served with the 32nd Infantry Regiment in the Inchon landing and the advance to the Yalu. Both had taken their Communion and Confirmation together and had emigrated to the US around the same time.[2]

First Lieutenant Terence James McLarnon was killed in action on October 7. Terry McLarnon was brought to the United States in 1928 from Ireland by his mother and father. He was born in Belfast, but as his parents were from both sides of the sectarian divide life was not going to be easy. The young family emigrated to America and settled in Philadelphia. Terence graduated from Temple University High School and was commissioned in the field of artillery in March 1945. He served in the Philippines during World War II. After the war he was attending Yale University when he was recalled to active duty in November 1948 and served with the occupation forces in Germany until March 1952. The following May he was sent to Korea. He was battery commander of the 955th Field Artillery of the 45th Division on October 7 when the 155-mile front erupted in the fiercest fighting since early 1951. On that day 15,000 Chinese assaulted American and South Korean defenses guarding Chorwon and overran more than 100 hill positions. Terence McLarnon's body was brought back to Tampa, Florida for burial.[3]

On October 14 the IX Corps on authorisation from Gen. Clark launched Operation Showdown, designed to seize the hills of the Iron Triangle north of Kumwha. Van Fleet predicted he would capture the objective in five days at a cost of around 200 casualties. But the attack ground on for weeks against fierce enemy opposition and cost 9,000 US and 19,000 ROK casualties. At huge cost the UN had only achieved a slight improvement of its position. On November 4 Dwight D. Eisenhower was elected President of the United States and in the following month visited Korea for three days. The visit convinced him that further offensive action was useless and the struggle for the hills would only lead to more casualties. Ike decided to renew diplomatic efforts.

During December the US 45th Infantry Division continued an active defence of its assigned sector of Line Minnesota, with the 179th Infantry on the left beside elements of the US 40th Division. The 179th continued with aggressive patrols, periodic raids and the defence and improvement of their positions. Cpl. Sean Taheny recalled, "Sometimes we were on a hill, beaten off it, tried to take it back, loose it again, take it back again. We suffered a lot of losses this way. It was all down to luck. Boys beside you getting knocked off; just beside you. All good friends. You saw them wounded, killed, carried away. You heard later on they died." On Christmas Eve the Chinese broadcast Christmas songs and dropped propaganda leaflets on the 179th Infantry on Hill 812. Sean Taheny was not long back from five days R and R in Kukuru, Japan. After four months on the line, men qualified for R and R. He was flown straight from the frontline to Kukuru and after his five days and nights flown straight "back to the trenches." He collected some of the Chinese leaflets, which he still has today. One was a Christmas card, which stated:

"Merry Christmas and Happy New Year
From The Korean Peoples Army
The Chinese Peoples Volunteers
Where there is Peace there is blessing.
American soldiers: We are wishing you a Merry Christmas and Happy New Year. We also have something to talk to you about.

"Christmas day is a day of peace and happiness. A day for family reunions. But this Christmas, for you, there is no peace. You are far away from those you love, in Korea, a country you never heard of three years ago - hundreds of thousands of casualties ago. Your family longs for you across the wide Pacific. Will they ever see you again? Will you ever see them?"

On Christmas Eve night, despite all their talk of peace, the Chinese attacked Hill 812 in reinforced platoon size assaults. "They nearly wiped us out," Sean Taheny said. "They came into our trenches ten to one. The Chinese always came in great numbers, like a swarm of bees. We half expected them. There were more of us in the trenches then the bunkers. We had heavy losses. My platoon sergeant went out in front of me and was killed. I phoned for artillery, which stopped them. Most of the time our artillery saved us." Sean was awarded two Bronze Stars and the Combat Infantryman's Badge. (In total he received seven medals - two Bronze Stars, Combat Infantryman's Badge, Good Conduct Medal, National Defence Service Medal, UN Service Medal and Korean Service Medal.) He thought one of the Bronze stars was during this action when he took over after his platoon sergeant was killed. A lot of it he has blocked out of his mind. The violence and killing was just too much.

Because of the Chinese attack the planned Christmas Day dinner for the troops on the line was late. "What was supposed to be Christmas dinner was cold as a stone," Sean Taheny remembered. "I never got ten hot meals in Korea. C rations all the time and all the cigarettes you could smoke. We had heating tablets to heat the C rations, but the cold was so bad they were always cold. The weather you would never get used to it; monsoons, rain; frost and snow were the worst. It was desperate cold, a lot of frostbite. The cold was so bad you couldn't explain. We lived in bunkers and trenches the whole time. It was a month before you got a change of clothes and had to wash in a helmet. We slept in sleeping bags in the bunkers, but there was no comfort."[4]

On Christmas Day 1952 the Chinese attacked the 38th Infantry Regiment, 2nd Infantry Division, at outposts Eerie and Arsenal beginning the Battle of T-Bone Hill. They suffered an estimated 500 casualties during the intense battle, while the regiment only had 47 casualties, including six killed. On December 29 the 7th Infantry Division completed its relief of the 2nd Infantry Division in the I Corps section of the line. On February 7 1953 after a two-month tour of duty as a security force at Koje-do, the 17th Regiment rejoined the rest of the 7th Division in the Old Baldy and T-Bone sector. They immediately began intensive patrolling of the area. Two days later Private John Dillon was killed in action with the 32nd Infantry. John Francis Dillon was born in Hartford, Connecticut, on July 24 1930 to Patrick and Mary Dillon who had emigrated to America in 1929. When John was four, his Irish-born parents decided to return to Ireland. One of eleven children, John was raised in Coole, Kilteely, Co. Limerick. As a child, John was always immensely proud of his American status and used to tell everyone at school that he was an American and not Irish. It came as no great surprise when at the age of seventeen John announced that he wanted to return home to the US. He left Ireland in March 1948 and before sailing from Southampton he sent his last one pound note back home to his mother. Two years later, when he was nineteen, John Dillon volunteered for the army. He was sent to Korea where he served with Company L, 3rd Battalion, 32nd Infantry Regiment, 7th Infantry Division. On February 9, during a hard fought battle, in which he reportedly fought with great courage, Pvt. John Dillon was killed in action. John Dillon's remains were brought home to Ireland for burial at Coole cemetery on May 30 1953. At the graveside an officer of the US Army handed the Stars and Stripes, the flag for which John Dillon gave his young life, to his grieving mother. His broken-hearted mother cried every day for almost a year.[5]

On February 10 Gen. Maxwell D. Taylor, the famed commander of the 101st Airborne Division in World War II, replaced Gen. James Van Fleet as Eighth Army commander. Over a month later, after the death of Russian Premier Joseph Stalin, Georgi Malenkov, the top member of a collective leadership in the wake of Stalin's death, gave a speech voicing support for a cease-fire in Korea. The western press dubbed his speech the launching of a "peace offensive." Two days later, on March 17, Hill 355, also known as Little Gibraltar, held by the 9th Infantry Regiment, 2nd Infantry Division, was assaulted by Chinese infantry. Danny Keogh, an Irishman serving with the 9th Infantry, was killed in action that day. Daniel J. Keogh was born in 1928 and lived in Cartron Upper, a town land about a mile and a half outside the village of Drumlish, Co Longford. At over six foot tall he was a passionate sportsman and well liked by all who knew him. In April 1949, at the age of twenty, Danny Keogh emigrated to the US and sailed from Cobh to New York and from there made his way west to the home of his maternal aunt who lived in Sparks, just outside Reno, Nevada. Sparks and Reno had been a traditional destination for Irish emigrants especially from County Longford and many had found employment in the rail yards and railways of the Southern Pacific Railway Company. Danny quickly adapted to his new life in America and secured a job with the Sierra Power Company, spending a lot of his spare time involved in local sporting events. Three years after his arrival in America, in September 1952, Danny Keogh was drafted into the US Army. He was sent to Fort Ord, California, for sixteen weeks basic infantry training and returned to Sparks for some short leave in January 1953. Within the month Danny was on his way to Korea. His unit stopped off in Japan where they received further training and by early March Danny Keogh was preparing for his stint in the front lines in a rear training camp near Seoul. On the night of March 16 his company, which contained many new recruits like himself, were sent up the right hand side of a Hill 355. Hill 355 had been a Chinese stronghold taken by the 1st Commonwealth Division in fierce fighting in October 1951.

Since then the position had been held by various British, Commonwealth and American battalions, despite numerous attempts by the Chinese to retake it. As Danny Keogh and the rest of the infantry company came up the reverse slopes of the hill to relieve the company holding the position, a strong force of Chinese infantry launched a massive surprise attack and poured over the forward slope breaking through the American lines and attacking the relieving force. A fierce close quarter battle ensued as the American and Chinese troops fought in the trenches and bunkers on the left side of Hill 355. The battle raged all night with both sides showering each other with grenades and mortars. By dawn, on St. Patrick's Day, the Chinese attack had been driven off the hill with massive casualties to both forces. Chinese dead were estimated at about 500. Amongst the many American dead was Danny Keogh, killed by shell fragments from what may have been enemy mortar fire.

The American dead and wounded were taken back to their base camp, and the bodies prepared for evacuation back to Japan and from there onto the United States. The Keogh family were informed of Danny's death by a member of the American legation some weeks later. The chaplain of the 9th Infantry, James M. Johnson, wrote his aunt in Sparks a letter in which he said, "Memory of your nephew's heroic death will always be a source of inspiration to this regiment. He died bravely in defence of the principles we all hold dear and which will ultimately triumph in a peaceful world." Danny Keogh's remains went first to Nevada and then to Ireland where his flag draped coffin was carried by train from Dublin to Longford accompanied by an American soldier, Master Sergeant D. S. Shriver. On June 29 1953 the funeral cortege moved through the streets of Longford town and Danny Keogh made his final journey home to the Catholic Church in Drumlish where he remained overnight watched over by M/Sgt. Shriver. He was buried the following morning with full military honours in the old graveyard in Drumlish. Danny Keogh's name appears on the US Forces memorial to the fallen in Sparks, Nevada. There is also a Keogh Street named in his honour, also in Sparks.[6]

Between 1951 and the war's end, 3rd Battalion, the Royal Australian Regiment occupied trenches at the eastern extremity of the Commonwealth Division's position in hills north-east of the Imjin River. There they faced heavily fortified Chinese positions across a stretch of no man's land, which ranged from 300 metres to two kilometres in width. Serving with 3rd RAR was Private Peter White, who was born in Cahir, Co. Tipperary, in 1925. He emigrated to Australia after WWII and worked as a labourer around Maidstone, Victoria, before enlisting in the Australian Military Forces in 1951 for service in Korea. He arrived in Korea in 1952 and was sent to the 3rd Battalion, the Royal Australian Regiment. Positioned on Hill 355, or Little Gibraltar, accurate and current intelligence information on the enemy's activities to the Aussie's immediate front was badly needed. The most appropriate source was from a prisoner.

On the night of January 13-14 a fifteen-man patrol, which included Peter White, set out to capture a prisoner from the Chinese lines. As the patrol, led by

Lieutenant Brian Bousfield, approached the Chinese defences they suddenly came across a newly constructed trench system. Since aerial photographs had been taken two weeks before the Aussies were unaware of the existence of the new trench and nearly walked into it. The Chinese occupants opened fire with mortars and machine guns and launched an attack. The patrol beat off the attack and a small number entered the trench system in search of a prisoner.

Private Eric Donnelly, from Sydney, was the forward scout with the patrol. He said: "We were on patrol at night pursued by the enemy. Suddenly a flickering glow-worm type object arched its way through the velvety blackness of the Korean winter sky. It exploded with sickening finality between the snow-covered mountain called Hill 227 and the body of Private Peter White, our patrol's Bren Gunner. Peter was just lowering himself into position to cover the return of the prisoner "Snatch party", off to our left. It was the first grenade of what was to become a maelstrom of sparkling arcs that were flying over my head to the rest of the patrol below and behind me...The explosion lifted Peter two feet into the air before dropping him back to the snow. I could see that he was badly wounded but because of the intensity of the grenade barrage, I had my hands full trying to pin point the exact location of the throwers. I threw the two grenades I carried on my belt to where I thought the glow worm trails were originating, about 15 yards away up the hill. My first grenade exploded with a lot of noise. The second was muffled and I heard a lot of Chinese yelling and shouting. This makes me think that it landed in the enemy trench line. I let off a couple of bursts from my Owen Gun but could not see nor hear any results. The firefight with the rest of the patrol was really hoting up this time. I was leading a charmed life with all the grenades going over my head to the patrol below. Lieutenant Bousfield, in the thick of these exploding grenades, had to do something quickly to extricate us from this decidedly-tricky situation. His order rang out above the din: 'Down the hill - reform'.

"Until now, it was as if I were invisible. I was the closest to the enemy lines and no one was having a go at me. The only thing I can think of to explain this immunity is that I was invisible. I must have had a black rocky out-crop that was not covered by snow or a dark bush behind me that blended my battle-dress into the background. Although it was a dark night, after a couple of hours of traversing the valley, you could see quite a lot against the background of the thick, white snow. Another call from Lieutenant Bousfield to get 'Down the hill - regroup,'spurred me to cross the four yards to Peter White. I wanted to pull him down the slope like a sled. I only took two paces to my right when a bullet smashed into my right leg causing me to spin around like a ballet dancer pirouetting in the snow. I crashed to the ground alongside Peter, losing my grip on the Own Gun as I spun around. I called out, 'I've been hit,' and a mate of mine from Tasmania, Gordon Welles, yelled out 'Blue's been hit. I am going to get him.' Lieutenant Bousfield screamed out, 'Don't be a bloody fool - down the hill'. Gordon got to within two yards of me but then decided to obey Bousfield's command. He went down the hill as ordered. In the months to come I was to replay this scene many times in my mind's eye. At first I was bitter, thinking that I had been deserted by my comrades. Over time I came to realise that Brian (Bousfield) did the only thing possible, as he had the responsibility for getting us all out. If I had obeyed his order to get down the hill and regroup, instead of trying to get Peter White out, I may not have been shot. Who knows? The reality now was that the patrol had withdrawn down the hill and Peter and I were left to our fate. Peter mercifully died a few minutes later, so my attempt to get him out would not have succeeded anyhow."

The Chinese had accurately calculated the patrol's withdrawal route and positioned a thirty-man ambush party across it. Although seriously wounded Lt. Bousfield and a few others protected the rear of the withdrawing patrol with the Chinese in close pursuit. Lt. Bousfield then called in an artillery barrage to try and get both White and Donnelly out, but the patrol was surrounded by enemy troops and he had no choice but to abandon them to save the rest of his men. Eric Donnelly was picked up by the Chinese and brought back to their lines. He remained a POW until April when he was released with hundreds of other wounded UN prisoners. The patrol got back to their own lines but found four were wounded and three missing. The three missing were Peter White, who died of wounds, Ron Shennon, presumed killed in action, and Eric Donnelly, captured.[7]

In March the 2nd Battalion, the Royal Australian Regiment, arrived in Korea to replace the 1st Battalion, RAR. On May 5, after intensive training in the area during March and April, 2nd RAR went into the line with the Commonwealth Division assuming command of Hill 159. The Australian's began aggressive patrolling to wrest control of no man's land from the enemy. The US forces, who had taken over during the deep winter months, had failed to keep the enemy in check, and the communists moved with some impunity up to the allied defensive wire. Paddy Hawkins, from Drumgoold, Enniscorthy, arrived with 2nd RAR. He had emigrated from England where he worked as a coal-miner in Yorkshire. Paddy Hawkins' older brother, John, was serving with 3rd RAR, and had been in Korea since the beginning of the war. While on patrol in no man's land Paddy was wounded by an explosion and was found by US medics. They must have thought he was an American as he was sent to a US military hospital in Guam. He was sent back to Concord Hospital in Australia where he made a full recovery, but by then the Korean War was over.[8] The Battalion remained for the rest of the duration of the war, and finally returned to Australia on April 17 1954. 2nd RAR was in action right up until the end and won the Battle honour of "Samichon" in the Battle of the Hook, July 24-26, just before the armistice was declared.

A succession of bitter battles was conducted for the Hook and the British lost more casualties on its steep flanks than on any other single battlefield in Korea. The third battle of the Hook began in late May 1953 and the brunt of the fighting fell on the 1st Duke of Wellington's Regiment. On the night of May 28 the Chinese launched an all-out attack on the Duke's positions. Fighting continued all night. The next morning the British surveyed the area: positions that had been painstakingly hacked out of the earth over months were flattened or caved in. It took hours of digging to extricate men buried by shelling. The Chinese lost 250 dead and 800 wounded, while the Duke's suffered 149 casualties, including twenty-nine killed and sixteen taken prisoner. One of those killed was Private Michael Connor, a twenty year old from Clare.

In April one particular piece of Korean real estate became the centre of much attention and strenuous efforts by both sides. Named because of its shape, Pork

Chop Hill assumed an importance in tactical, political and even strategic terms that far outweighed its geographical significance. The hill stood in no-man's-land on the US I Corps front approximately 1.5km forward of the American positions on the MLR. The Chinese occupied Old Baldy which was roughly level with Pork Chop and could observe the American supply route from the MLR to Pork Chop Hill. On the night of April 16 two companies of Chinese infantry attacked Company L of the 31st Infantry Regiment, 7th Infantry Division at Pork Chop Hill. Before the alarm could be sounded the Chinese swamped the American positions. The next day attempts to relieve Pork Chop met little success. The relief forces were pinned down and by the evening the situation looked grim. The decision was made to counterattack and two companies of the 17th Infantry stormed the hill. Fighting continued all day until at last the Chinese yielded and withdrew. In the two days of fighting for Old Baldy and Pork Chop Hill, the UN forces suffered 300 killed, wounded and missing while the Chinese lost between 600 and 800 men. This marked the beginning of the Battle of Pork Chop Hill, which would last until July 11.

In the following weeks the men of the 7th Division gradually reconstructed the fortifications on Pork Chop Hill while the Chinese indicated their continuing interest by firing as many shells and mortar bombs at it as they fired on the rest of the divisional front. Patrick "Pat" Lavin was serving with the 17th Regiment as a medic. Pat, who grew up in the village of Arigna, in County Leitrim, had been fascinated by America all his young life. His mother, Nellie, had lived in the US for thirteen years and was always telling stories of her time there. An uncle living in New York promised the youngster he would take him over when he was fifteen. When he reached that age, Pat wrote his uncle, John Lavin, and reminded him of his promise. John Lavin warned Nellie that her son would face the military draft at eighteen, but that did not deter Pat. He moved to the Bronx, lived with his uncle and aunt, graduated from high school and, as his uncle had warned, was drafted into the army when he was eighteen.[9] J.T. Jennings was in Camp Kilmer when Pat Lavin, was drafted. They had both socialised together in the Bronx prior to J.T. being drafted and were good friends. "My last get together with him was in Camp Kilmer, N.J. in November 1952, " J.T. Jennings recalled. "At that time he was inducted and I was about to be discharged following my return from Korea." Pat Lavin opted for the Army Medical Corps and was posted to the Medical Company, 17th Infantry Regiment, 7th Infantry Division.[10]

On July 6 the Chinese launched their biggest attack on Pork Chop Hill. The Americans reinforced their defences until there were five battalions on the hill. The Chinese poured in more troops until they had up to a division in the field. After five days of savage fighting the 7th Division was ordered to evacuate as the CPVA's disregard for casualties and its intent on holding the hill outweighed its tactical value. The evacuation was conducted in daylight, using armoured personnel carriers that brought daily supplies to the front. It was nearly two days after the evacuation before the CPVA was aware of the withdrawal. On July 13 Chinese forces launched a six-division attack in the Battle of Kumsong River Salient. On July 19 Pat Lavin was killed by heavy enemy fire while trying to reach a wounded comrade on Pork Chop Hill. In a release from headquarters of the 7th Infantry Division it was stated that Private E2 Patrick J. Lavin, had "distinguished himself by heroic achievement" near Sokkogae, Korea, on July 19 1953. The report said, "Private Lavin, an aidman, was moving forward with his comrades when he noticed a casualty lying in the midst of intense fire and in dire need of immediate medical attention. Completely disregarding his own personal safety, Private Lavin voluntarily proceeded to the fire-swept area where his wounded comrade lay. As Private Lavin moved through the open terrain and neared the stricken man, he was caught in the burst of a hostile round and mortally wounded. The heroic actions of Private Lavin reflect great credit on himself and the military service." Pat Lavin was posthumously awarded the Bronze Star. He was buried in St. Raymond's Cemetery in the Bronx. J.T. Jennings recalled attending a memorial mass for his young friend and comrade.[11]

Not all casualties were from enemy action. Sergeant Mark Brennan died on June 18 1953 in the crash of a C-124A Globemaster cargo plane ferrying him back to his base in Korea after a week of R & R leave in Japan. He was twenty-three. Sgt. Brennan was serving with the 78th Anti-Aircraft Artillery (Automatic

Weapons) Battalion stationed at Suwon Air Force Base. Mark Brennan, from Kiltimagh, Co. Mayo, had emigrated to Greenwich, Connecticut, in 1949 to join his sister Helen, brother Martin and John (Gerry) Gannon, a neighbour from home. In August 1951, two and a half years after emigrating, Mark was drafted. He trained as an antiaircraft artillery gunner in Fort Bliss, Texas, and was then assigned to the 78th AAA Battalion stationed at Suwon Air Force Base.

Mark Brennan was one of four Irishmen serving with the US Army who died in accidents: Pfc. John Canty, from Lixnaw, Co. Kerry, serving with the 13th Engineer Combat Battalion, died of other causes on August 26 1951; Pfc. Owen Prior, Ballinamore, Co. Roscommon, a member of Company B, 772nd Military Police Battalion, drowned in a flash flood while crossing a stream near Samnang-jin on July 21 1952; Pfc. Michael McCormack, Taughmaconnell, Co. Roscommon, serving with the 658th Quartermaster Laundry Company, also drowned while crossing a flooded river near Chunchon on July 22 1952.[12]

On July 27 1953 the Armistice was signed by Lt. General Nam Il and Lt. General William Harrison at (1000) 10 a.m. at Panmunjom. Twelve hours later, the guns fell silent. Cpl. Sean Taheny was half way across the Pacific on a troopship returning to the US when the Truce was finally signed. "I did thirteen months altogether, while waiting to be replaced. I thought I'd never get out of there. A lot didn't make it."[13] In the last days of the war the communists sent in at least six armies along the Iron Triangle, the Punchbowl, and the Kumsong Bulge in a last ditch attempt to change the configuration of the frontline. It failed drastically with a horrendous loss of life. The final US ground combat was fought on July 24-26 as a heavy enemy attack was launched in the Berlin Complex (Boulder City) area held by the 7th and 1st Marine Regiments.

Officers and NCOs explained to the men the terms of the truce and the ultimate details of the cease-fire. There would be no celebrations, no firing, no fraternisation with the enemy. Weapons were to be left close at hand and men were to continue wearing helmets and flak jackets. No one was taking any chances. No one wanted to be the last casualty of the war. There were no celebrations, just relief. The armistice had been expected. Troops on the line were told that morning that the truce would start that night at 2200. The day passed slowly. In some areas Chinese troops policed their area, removing their dead and clearing minefields. Some came up to outposts and wanted to talk, others hung gift-bags on the wire. At 2200 on July 27 1953 it was all over.

The cost of the war was enormous: 1,250,000 men were killed, wounded or captured, a million of those were from China and North Korea. 33,629 Americans were killed in the war, 105,785 were wounded. Forty-five per cent of all US casualties occurred after the first armistice negotiations began. The British Commonwealth - Britain, Canada, Australia and New Zealand - lost 1,263 killed and 4,817 wounded. The South Korean army lost 46,812 killed and 159,727 wounded. The other UN nations - Belgium, Colombia, Ethiopia, France, Greece, Holland, the Philippines, Thailand and Turkey - lost 1,800 killed and 7,000 wounded between them, of whom almost half were Turks. The North Koreans suffered 214,899 killed and 303,685 wounded. The Chinese sustained 401,000 killed, 486,995 wounded and 21,211 missing, presumed dead. Civilian losses were staggering; two million had died and three million more had been made homeless.[14]

Veterans of Korea came home to discover that very few - outside of their families - cared about the war. It was a war that had not been won. There were few victory parades. Sean Taheny was told it was not a war, but a "police action." Discharged in Fort Dix, in 1953, Sean was given his US citizenship when he left the army. He had a lot of trouble settling down and returned home to Ireland in 1955. He would have stayed in America were it not for the war but Korea had soured his American dream.

Pat Quinn had spent two-and-a-half years as a POW in North Korea. "After thirty-one months in captivity I was released on August 19,1953," Pat Quinn said. "There were no parades; we were just happy to be home and try to pickup where we left off. Unfortunately most were not able to as we suffered from post-stress syndrome. We didn't win and we didn't lose but we stopped the spread of

Communism. I was proud to serve under the American flag even though I was not an American citizen. I knew of twenty-seven, who like myself came from Ireland, and were not US citizens but died in Korea serving under the American flag." [15]

James Dunwoody, 1st Royal Ulster Rifles, said, "I was very proud to have served with our allies who were in the first engagement under the United Nations Flag."[16] At the war's end 14,200 Commonwealth troops were serving in Korea. Over 87,000 servicemen from the United Kingdom served in Korea, along with 26,791 Canadians and 17,164 Australians.

As Edwin P. Hoyt wrote: "There was nothing satisfactory about the Korean War, except that it finally ended."[17] The war left the Korean peninsula divided and in ruins. Now East and West faced each other across another hostile border, adding a tense new flashpoint to an increasingly divided world. The Eisenhower administration embarked on an aggressive policy to contain "Soviet-Communist expansionism" which would eventually lead America into a more costly and soul-destroying war in Vietnam.

While hostilities had ended in Korea the final demarcation line had to be policed by both sides. Irish soldiers continued to end up in Korea helping the UN to keep the peace. Ballyshannon man Peter Daly was posted to the 25th Infantry Regiment in Korea at the end of 1953. He had emigrated to New York in September 1952 and volunteered for the draft. An earlier bid to join the Royal Air Force had failed when the young runaway was found to be underage. Back home in Donegal he bided his time until an uncle in the Bronx claimed him out. He served a year in Korea policing the DMZ (demilitarised zone). "It was still a miserable country then," he said, "very poor."[18] Patrick "Packie" O'Dwyer arrived in Korea with the 1st Royal Irish Fusiliers in November 1954. "The Truce had already been signed when we landed. It was all over apart for a few skirmishes. My first impression was that it was a terrible country. The people had suffered terribly. We landed at Pusan. It was flattened and the people were living in cardboard houses." Packie had emigrated in 1949 to England from Cashel, Co.

Tipperary, when he was seventeen, looking for work. He was called up for National Service towards the end of 1952 and was sent to the Irish Fusiliers. From England he went with the Faughs to Germany and then on to Korea. The Irish Fusiliers spent a year in Korea on the Demilitarised Zone and then went on to Kenya in December 1955 where they helped in the suppression of the Mau-Mau.[19] The last British troops departed Korea in July 1957.

A decade later Jimmy Frawley, from Doolin, Co. Clare, was part of the 50,000 American contingent policing the DMZ. He was drafted a year after arriving in the US and his original orders were for Vietnam, but were changed to Korea, which Jim had little objection to. He found Korea still "was real Third World; poverty everywhere you looked." Jimmy Frawley spent thirteen months in Korea as a medic with the 2nd Engineer Battalion, 2nd Infantry Division. During his tour, 1965-66, there "was an occasional skirmish, though nothing serious." He met several Irish priests from the Columban Fathers who were still working on the missions in Korea. He found "the people very nice, friendly and helpful". Once asked by a Korean local where he was from Jimmy said Ireland and was asked was that near San Francisco! Strange at the time that the people who are known as the Irish of the Orient did not know where Ireland was.[20]

Today, South Korea is the world's eleventh largest economy and home to major car-makers and international electronics firms. By comparison, North Korea's failed economy amounts to only seven per cent of that of the South. South Korea still has 680,000 men in their regular army situated along the border. They also have 2,000,000 men on active reserve. All Korean men have to spend two and a half years in the military forces. North Korea has 1,200,000 men on their side of the border. The DMZ between the two Korea's is four kilomotros wide and the land where possible for seven to ten kilometres behind is considered a war zone and has road blocks, guns, missiles, tanks, troops and tank traps everywhere. There is hope and talk of reunification, but for the moment Korea remains the Cold War's last frontier.

Appendices

Appendix 1

Irish Korean War veterans finally become US Citizens

On Thursday, October 30 2003, fifty years after the end of the Korean War, twenty-eight Irish-born US servicemen were posthumously granted American citizenship. The moving ceremony at the Senate Dirksen Office Building in Washington, D.C., was the culmination of a decades long campaign by other war veterans. The event followed Mass which was celebrated at the National Shrine of the Immaculate Conception by Archbishop Edwin F. O'Brien and was attended by many dignitaries from the political, military and ecclesiastical sections of the Washington community. In attendance at the ceremony were Senator Charles Schumer, sponsor of the bill, Senator Edward Kennedy, Congressman Peter King and Congressman Marty Meehan, and retired Gen. P.X. Kelly, former commandant of the US Marine Corps. Many Korean War veterans from various parts of the US were also in attendance. Thirty-three family members had flown in from Ireland, while others came from all parts of the US.

New York Senator Charles Schumer, main sponsor of the bill that granted the twenty-eight Irish veterans posthumous citizenship said that the bill, which also applies to immigrants killed in action in Iraq, was long overdue. "Few stories are as poignant as those of proud immigrants who fell wearing the uniform of their new home," Schumer said at the ceremony. "Anyone who dies for America deserves to be called an American. These Korean War heroes honoured the United States of America by their service, and returning this honour by giving them official citizenship is the very least we can do. These brave men fell in the field of battle in Korea, but their legacy will live on forever. Because of their example and their love for America, every immigrant who follows in their footsteps and makes the ultimate sacrifice will get our highest honour - being called an American citizen."

In 1953 a Bill was passed granting fast-track citizenship to all immigrant soldiers who served in the US armed forces was passed by the Eisenhower administration. However, this was not made retroactive which meant that those who served from 1950 to 1952 in Korea had to wait for five years from the time of their arrival in the US. As for the Irish and other non-citizens who gave their lives for their adopted country, on the battlefields of Korea before 1952, they of course could not get citizenship. It was John Leahy, a Kerry native and Korean veteran, who spearheaded the campaign for citizenship. Leahy left Derrevrin, Lixnaw, Co. Kerry, in 1949 and ten months after his arrival in America was draft-ed into the US army. He served as a sergeant with distinction on the frontlines in Korea, where he was attached to the 82nd AAA (Anti-Aircraft Artillery) Battalion, 2nd Infantry Division. John Leahy had to wait the full five years for citizenship upon his return from Korea. He was spurred into action in 1976 when the US was celebrating its bicentennial. "I was in New York and saw all the flags and banners and I thought about my fellow Irish who had died and were never recognised, so I decided to do something about it," Leahy said. As Frank Durkan wrote in the *Irish Voice*: "He petitioned, nudged, wrote letters and he probably made a great nuisance of himself, but his efforts bore fruition..." John Leahy was joined in his campaign by Brian McGinn, a Vietnam veteran, who with Marlyn Knapp initiated The Irish in Korea, a website which highlighted all Irish-born casualties in Korea and maintained the citizenship campaign online, and others including Dan Herlihy, a Korean War veteran from Youghal, Cork, and USMC General P.X. Kelly.

Ray O'Hanlon, reporting for the *Irish Echo* on the citizenship ceremony, wrote: "Though all eyes in the room were on the high-profile speakers, it was the words of the relatives that were to strike the most poignant notes on the day. 'I was ten the last time I saw him,' Dubliner Bridie Williams said of her brother, Cork native

William Francis Murphy, who died as a prisoner of war in May of 1951. 'I still remember him going through the gates to go to America and my father said, "Take a good look at your brother because that's the last time you're ever going to see him." This all brings back a lot of memories. He's with me all the time and I'm sure he was very pleased to see this today.'

"Donal O'Connell of Limerick accepted the citizenship certificate on behalf of his brother Alphonsus O'Connell, a corporal in the U.S. Army. 'He finally got recognised,' O'Connell said. 'It's all he would have wanted.' Foncy O'Connell was killed in action in September 1951.

"Michael Fitzpatrick, from Calremorris, Co. Mayo, was killed in action in August 1951 but when his remains were shipped back go Chicago he was not given a military funeral due to his lack of citizenship. A lone officer attended the funeral, saluted and left. The minimal recognition of Michael Fitzpatrick's service and death on behalf of his adopted country infuriated his sister, Mary Doody, and it continued to trouble her for more than fifty years. 'In the beginning it seemed that nobody was interested,' Mary Doody, who still lives in Chicago, said after hearing of the president's signing of the bill. 'But as long as it's signed, it counts. I never thought it would happen and it's kind of hard to believe. But if you wish and pray hard enough, it will happen.'

"Oliver Lynch said that in 1952, he and his family heard of his brother's death in Korea on the radio while in their home near Tuam, Co. Galway. The body of Philip Columba Lynch, an army machine gunner, was later brought back from Korea and is buried in Kilconly parish cemetery near the family home. 'It's very nice, but it comes an awfully long time afterward,' Lynch said.

"After the ceremony, and a reception hosted by the carpenters union - a separate reception the previous evening was hosted by Guinness - the relatives travelled by bus from Capitol Hill to the Korean War Memorial. Under a deep blue afternoon sky, and to the sight and sound of aircraft on the final approach to Ronald Reagan Airport, a lone piper led the relatives past the haunting bronze figures of GIs depicted on a patrol during the Korean War to the flagpole atop which the Stars and Stripes fluttered in a light, balmy breeze. Here the relatives laid a wreath in the colours of Ireland. And here too, at the base of the marble wall that forms part of the memorial, they placed specially printed cards with the names of the twenty-eight men, their military units and the date of the long awaited day that Irish soldiers in the army of America had finally become American citizen soldiers."

Sadly, Brian McGinn, one of the key figures in the campaign, died on July 20 2005, after a long battle with cancer. Ray O'Hanlon wrote in the *Irish Echo*. "Brian McGinn was the primary moving force behind websites devoted to the Irish-born who died in both the Korea and Vietnam conflicts. 'The securing of posthumous citizenship for those Irishmen would not have been accomplished with the ease that it was but for Brian's intelligence and know how,' said John Leahy who initiated the campaign. A tribute on the Korean and Vietnam websites described McGinn as 'a rare combination of intellect, common sense, sweetness and fair-ness. His hard work helped many, not least those families who finally saw their soldiers made posthumous citizens.' McGinn's efforts to document the story of the Korea Irish dead arose from his interest in the Irish who fought in Vietnam. Born in New York, but raised and educated in Ireland, McGinn served with U.S. army intelligence in Vietnam in 1969-70. He later initiated a website called Irish on the Wall, a reference to the Vietnam memorial in Washington D.C. This, in turn, led to the Korean War website. McGinn was laid to rest at Mt. Comfort Cemetery in Alexandria, Virginia."

On Tuesday July 12 2005 James Kenny, U.S. Ambassador to Ireland and Jong Rak, South Korean Ambassador to Ireland, jointly unveiled a monument in the form of a stone arch to the memory of thirty-five Irish people, soldiers and civilians, who were killed in the Korean War in the village of Lixnaw, Co. Kerry, birthplace of John Canty.

Appendix 2

Roll Of Honour

American Armed forces

Pfc. Maurice Angland (Rockchapel, Co. Cork) 8th Engr. Cmbt. Battn. Div. KIA 4/10/1951.

Sgt. Mark Brennan (Kiltimagh, Co. Mayo) 78th AAA Battn. DIA 18/6/1953.

Pfc. John Canty (Lixnaw, Co. Kerry) 13th Engr. Cmbt. Battn.. DIA 26/8/1951.

Pfc. William Collins (Templegelatine, Co. Limerick) 23rd Inf. Regt. KIA 18/5/1951.

Pfc. Michael Conroy (Claremorris, Mayo) 9th Inf. Regt. KIA 19/9/1951.

Pfc. John Corcoran, 32nd Inf. Regt. (Millstreet, Co. Cork) DOW 2/10/1950.

Pvt. John F. Dillon (Kiltealy, Co. Limerick) 32nd Inf. Regt. KIA 9/2/1953.

Pfc. Michael Fitzpatrick (Claremorris, Co. Mayo) 23rd Inf. Regt. KIA 18/8/1951.

Cpl. Bartolmew Glavin (Annascul, Co. Kerry) 23rd Inf. Regt. KIA 1/9/1950.

Cpl. Michael Gannon (Achill, Co. Mayo) 15th F.A. Battn. KIA 13/2/1951.

Pvt. Michael Patrick Hardiman (Ballaghaderreen, Co. Roscommon) 17th Inf. Regt. KIA 6/3/1951.

Pvt. Daniel Christopher Harrington (Eyeries, Co. Cork) 35th Inf. Regt. KIA 6/6/1951.

Pfc. Michael Herlihy (Scartglen, Co. Kerry) 38th Inf. Regt. KIA12/9/1951.

Pvt. Daniel Keogh (Drumlish, Co. Longford) 9th Inf. Regt. KIA 17/3/1953.

Pfc. Michael King (Elphin, Co. Roscommon) 38th Inf. Regt. KIA 13/2/1951.

Pvt. Patrick J. Lavin (Drumkeeran, Co. Leitrim) 17th Inf. Regt. KIA 10/7/1953.

Pvt. Philip Columba Lynch (Kilconly, Co. Galway) 38th Inf. Regt. KIA 27/9/1951.

Pfc. Michael A. McCormack (Taughmaconnell, Co. Roscommon) 658th Quartermaster Coy. DIA 22/7/1952.

Pfc. Patrick McEnery (Glin, Co. Limerick) 19th Inf. Regt. KIA 13/11/1951.

Lt. Terence McLarnon (Belfast) 955th F. A. Battn. KIA 7/10/1951.

Pvt. John Mills (Belfast) 7th Cav. Regt. MIA 5/11/1951.

Pfc. William F. Murphy (Cork City) 38th Inf. Regt. Died as a POW 18/5/1951.

Sgt. Thomas Joseph O'Brien (Emly, Co. Tipperary) 90th F.A. Battn. KIA 26/10/1950.

Cpl. Alphonsus O'Connell (Garryowen, Co. Limerick) 8th Engr. Cmbt. Battn. KIA 29/10/1951.

Pfc. Owen Prior (Ballinamore, Co. Roscommon) 772nd M.P. Battn.. Drowned 21/7/1952.

Pfc. Thomas Stephen Quinn (Ballinlough, Co. Roscommon) 5th Cav. Regt. KIA 6/10/1951.

Pfc. William Scully (Galbally, Co. Limerick) 31st Inf. Regt. KIA 14/1/1951.

Cpl. Patrick Sheahan (Newtown Sandes, Co. Kerry) 7th Inf. Regt. KIA 4/10/1951.

Pfc. Thomas J. Ward (Belfast City) 35th Inf. Regt. KIA 22/8/1950.

Pfc. John Patrick White (Cahirdaniel, Co. Kerry) 7th Mar. Regt. Died as POW 24/9/1952.

Pfc. Patrick Augustine White (Dundalk, Co. Louth) 14th Inf. Regt. KIA 6/10/1951

Australian Armed Forces

Cpl. William Kevin Murphy (Ennis, Co. Clare) 3rd RAR. KIA 24/4/1951.

Pte. Peter White (Cahir, Co. Tipperary) 3rd RAR. KIA 14/1/1953.

British Armed Forces

Cpl. William Adair (Newtownards, Co. Down) 1st Royal Ulster Rifles MIA 5/1/1951.

Lt. C.G. Alexander (Dublin) 8th King's Royal Irish Hussars KIA 3/1/1951.

Rfn. N. Black (Belfast) Duke of Wellington's. KIA 29/5/1953.

Maj. C.A.H.B. Blake (Meelick, Co. Galway) 1st Royal Ulster Rifles. KIA 3/1/1951.

Fus. A.R. Browne (Galway)1st Royal Northumberland Fusiliers. KIA 30/11/1950.

Rfn. J. C. Bustard (Lisburn, Co. Antrim) 1st Royal Ulster Rifles. KIA 15/1/1951.

Sgt. T. Cawley (Sligo) 61st Light Artillery. KIA 18 /11/1951.

Rfn. Charles Clarke (Ballymoney, Co. Down) 1st Royal Ulster Rifles. KIA 25/4/1951.

Tpr. J. Collison (Athy, Co. Kildare) 8th King's Royal Irish Hussars. KIA 4/1/1951.

Pte. M.Connor (Clare) Duke of Wellington Regt. KIA 29/5/1953.

Rfn. Robert Craig (Belfast) 1st Royal Ulster Rifles. Died as POW. 25/6/1951.

Rfn.. R. Cunningham (Roslea, Co. Fermanagh) Died in accident 17/9/1951.

Lt. A. Bruce Samuel Hudson (Dublin) 45th Field Artillery. KIA 23/4/1951.

Cpl. William Davidson (Ballymoney, Co. Antrim) 1st RUR. Died as POW 1/6/1951.

Pte. M. Dempsey (Waterford)1st Arglye&Sutherland Highlanders. KIA 21/9/1950.

Rfn. J. Donnelly (Cork) 1st RUR. KIA 5/1/1951.

Rfn. J. T. Doyle (Clonakilty, Co. Cork) 1st RUR. KIA 19/2/1951.

Capt. R.D. Fleming (Culduff, Co. Donegal) 45th Field Artillery. KIA 3/1/1951.

Rfn. J. Foley (Kilkenny) 1st RUR. Killed in accident 1/10/1951.

Pte. J. D. Foster (Dublin) 1st Arglye&Sutherland Highlanders KIA 5/11/1950.

Sgt. David Gaw (Bangor, Co. Down) 1st RUR. KIA 25/4/1951.

Cpl. J. D. Gibson (Belfast) 1st RUR. Killed in accident 29/11/1950.

Rfn. Cornelius Gouldsborough (Thurles, Co. Tipperary) 1st RUR. KIA 25/4/1951.

Rfn. D. H. Johnson (Belfast) 1st RUR. KIA 4/1/1951.

Sgt. Lawrence Kavanagh (Pollertton, Co. Carlow) 1st RUR. Died as POW 4/9/1951.

Gnr. P. J. Keating (Dublin) 61st Light Artillery. KIA 12/6/1953.

Rfn. Thomas Kennedy (Belfast) 1st RUR. KIA 4/1/1951.

LCpl. G.H. Lawrence (Dublin) 1st Glosters. KIA 25/11/1950.

Sgt. T. Lennon (Bourbridge, Co. Down) 1st RUR. KIA 25/4/1951.

Cpl. W. Lorimer (Ballymena, Co. Down) 1st RUR. KIA 25/4/1951.

Rfn. Edward Lyons (Belfast) 1st RUR. Died as POW 31/8/1951.

Rfn. Daniel Maher (Tipperary) 1st RUR. Died as POW 28/9/1951.

Rfn. Robert Martin (Carrickfergus, Co. Antrim) 1st RUR. Died as POW 22/4/1951.

Rfn. J. P. McCartan (Belfast) 1st RUR. KIA 25/4/1951.

Cpl. William McConnell (Ballyclare, Co. Antrim) 1st RUR. KIA 3/1/1951.

Rfn. Robert McCormick (Belfast) 1st RUR KIA 3/1/1951.

Rfn. Robert McCracken (Belfast|) 1st RUR. KIA 4/1/1951.

Rfn. H. McCracken (Belfast) 1st RUR. KIA 25/4/1951.

Pte. John Patrick McDonell (Monaghan) Army Catering Corps. 4/1/1951

Cpl. Patrick McGeoghegan (Londonderry) 1st RUR. KIA 4/1/1951.

Rfn. Thomas McGivern (Belfast) 1st RUR. KIA 25/4/1951.

Rfn. A. J. McNaughton (Belfast) 1st RUR. KIA 23/4/1951.

Rfn. Michael McSherry (Dublin) 1st RUR. KIA 4/1/1951

Rfn. William McWilliams (Newry, Co. Down) 1st RUR. Died as a POW 12/4/1951.

Rfn Samuel Montgomery (Londonderry) 1st RUR. KIA 23/4/1951.

Cpl. William Moore (Limavady, Co. Londonderry) 1st RUR. KIA 4/1/1951.

Rfn. Samuel Mullan (Belfast) 1st RUR. KIA 25/4/1951.

Rfn. Christopher Murray (Dublin) 1st RUR. KIA 4/1/1951.

Sgt. Frank Nugent (Belfast) 1st RUR. Died as POW 18/4/1951.

Rfn. J. O'Gorman (Cork) 1st RUR. KIA 19/2/1951.

Rfn. James Porter (Derry) 1st RUR. KIA 25/4/1951.

Rfn. C. Ramsay (Templemore, Co. Londonderry) 1st RUR. KIA 3/1/1951.

Rfn. Michael Reidy (Ennistymona, Co. Clare) 1st RUR. Died as a POW

2/8/1951.

Rfn. Samuel Robinson (Ballymena, Co. Antrim) 1st RUR. KIA 4/1/1951.

Cpl. J.M. Rudge (Dublin) Royal Signals. 27/10/1950.

Rfn James Shannon (Ballymena, Co. Antrim) 1st RUR. KIA 5/1/1951.

Pte William Francis Synott (Dublin) 1st Glosters. KIA 24 /4/1951.

Rfn Samuel Wallace (Belfast) 1st RUR. KIA. 20/3/1951.

Rfn James Walshe (Dublin) 1st RUR. KIA 25/4/1951.

Irish Missionaries

Monsignor Patrick Brennan (Chicago, Illinois) Columban Fathers. Murdered 24/9/1950.

Father Frank Canavan (Killursa, Co. Galway) Columban Fathers. Died in Captivity 6/12/1950.

Sister Mary Clare (Enniskerry, Co. Wicklow) Community of St. Peter. Died in captivity 6/11/1950.

Father Anthony Collier (Clogherhead, Co. Louth) Columban Fathers. Murdered 27/6/1950.

Father Thomas Cusack (Ballycotton, Co. Clare) Columban Fathers. Murdered 24/9/1950.

Father James Maginn (Butte, Montana) Columban Fathers. Murdered 6/7/1950.

Father John O'Brien (Dunamon, Co. Roscommon) Columban Fathers. Murdered 24/9/1950.

Father Patrick Reilly (Dunraney, Co. Westmeath) Columban Fathers. Murdered 29/8/1950.

Last Call of the Bugle

In Pusan there is hallowed ground
A simple cross to mark each mound
They brought us there from whence we died
To lie together side by side.

Our Country's call that bugle sound
We answered we were honoured bound
They said the cause was just, you know.
But then was this not always so?

Strange country and a stranger war,
It made no odds we knew the score.
We were blood brothers, truth to tell.
In valiant company when we fell.

Seek not our grave and do not weep
We are not there, we do not sleep.
The life we gave was ours to give
Remember this, and we still live.

For like the tireless wind that blows,
Chilled by endless northern snows
Or warmed in harsher southern lands
Of spinifex and desert sands.

Part of the sound of mornings hush
Kin to the swift demanding rush
Of noisy flocks in searching flight
As sunlight softens passing night.

We touch the fields of ripening grain

Red cattle grazing sun-drenched plain
We span the forest, farm to reach
The towns and cities, oceans beach.

Long gone that bugle's strident blast
We kept the Faith, we were the last.
Seek not our grave, weep not nor cry
We are not there, We did not die.

JFG.

End Notes

Chapter 1. The war begins.

1. Jack Murphy. *History of the US Marines* p.127.

2. *ibid*, p.128

3. Bevin Alexander. K*orea. The Lost War*, p.44-5.

4. *Irish in Korea* website.

5. Edward Fischer, *Light in the Far East*, p.5.

6. Michael Clifford, *Dying for the love of God*; Philip Crosbie, *March till they die*, p.14-5; Irish in Korea.

7. Clifford; Irish in Korea; Columban Fathers.

8. Brian Gallagher, *Ireland and the Korean War*, p.38.

9. Crosbie, p.31, 52; Irish in Korea; Columban Fathers.

10. Clifford; Irish in Korea; Columban Fathers.

11. Clifford; Irish in Korea; Columban Fathers.

12. Fischer, p.97-8; Clifford; Columban Fathers.

13. Columban Fathers Correspondence Col. Robin Charley, 12/8/05.

14. Fischer, p.101-3.

15. *The Splendid Cause 1933-83. Fifty years of Columban Outreach to Korea.*

16. Columban Fathers.

17. Clifford.

18. Crosbie, ps.135, 142, 157.

19. Clifford.

20. Irish in Korea; Crosbie p.173-4.

21. Alexander, p.47.

22. ibid, p.56; Murphy, ps. 515, 518.

23. Alexander p.123; Max Hastings *The Korean War*, p.88-9.

24. Irish in Korea; author interview Liam O'Dubhir 21/3/05.

25. Irish in Korea.

26. Alexander, p.183.

27. Peter Jones, *Argylls in Korea*.

Chapter 2. Army of all nations.

1. *Irish Independent* 8/10/1947.

2. Author interview Gerry Fox 11/6/05.

3. Murphy, p.126.

4. Alexander, p.49.

5. J.T. Jennings address to the Mayo Society of New York. 2004 & correspondence 21/4/05.

6. Author interviews Pat Healy, Mike Keating and Tom Daly 13/6/05.

7. Author interview Billy May 17/10/05.

8. Correspondence Pat Lane 5/10/05.

9. Gerry Murphy 12/8/05.

10. Gallagher, p.4-5.

Chapter 3. On to the Yalu.

1. William Manchester. *American Caeser*, p.530.

2. Alexander, p.169-70.

3. Author interview Charles Dennehy, 6/5/05.

4. *ibid*; 32nd Infantry history, untitled document.

5. Irish in Korea.

6. Edwin P. Hoyt *On to the Yalu*, p.163.

7. Dennehy; Alexander p.216-7.

8. Manchester, p.543-4.

9. *ibid*, p.542.

10. *ibid*, p.541.

11. *ibid*, p.544.

12. Irish in Korea.

Chapter 4. Red storm.

1. 32nd infantry; Dennehy.
2. *ibid.*
3 Dennehy.
4. Murphy, p.139-40.
5. Robin Neillands *By Land and Sea*, p. 278-9.
6. *ibid*, 286-92.
7. Joseph R. Owen *Colder than hell*, p. 140-1.
8. *ibid,* p.253-4.
9. Murphy, p.144.

Chapter 5. A winter of discontent.

1. Henry O'Kane. *O'Kane's Korea*, ps. 3,6.
2. Correspondence Robin Charley 19/10/05
3. Correspondence Hans Milligan 12/8/05.
4. H. Hamill. *Royal Ulster Rifles in Korea.*
5. *ibid.*
6. Milligan.
7. Correspondence James B. Dunwoody 12/8/05.
8. Richard Doherty *Sons of Ulster*, p.150.
9. Hastings, p.95.
10. Hamill.
11. Charley.
12. Hamill.
13. *ibid.*
14. Dunwoody.
15. O'Kane, p.17-8.
16. Charley.
17. Doherty, p.152-3.
18. O'Kane p.19.
19. *ibid*, p.19.
20. Hamill.

21. *ibid.*

22. Correspondence Turtle Bunbury 19/7/05; correspondence Mrs. Joyce Green 3/19/05.

23. Hastings, p.200-1.

24. O'Kane p.21.

25. Charley.

Chapter 6. War at Sea.

1. O'Kane, p.7.

2. Interview and correspondence with Tom O'Keefe, 5/05.

3. Hoyt, p.252.

4. O'Keefe.

5. Author interview Tony Lynch 17/10/05.

Chapter 7. American frontline.

1. Hastings, p.227.

2. Irish in Korea.

3. *ibid*; 15th FA history, untitled document.

4. Breandán MacGearailt & Mike Shaughnessy. Dúthaigh Duibhneach, p. 131-2.

5. 15th history.

6. Western People 12/12/01.

7. Irish in Korea.

8. Manchester, p.600-02.

9. Hastings, p.246.

10. Murphy, p.148.

Chapter 8. The Ulsters and Irish on the Imjin.

1. Edwin P. Hoyt *Bloody road to Panmunjom*, p.301.

2. O'Kane, p.26.

3. Hamill.

4. O'Kane p.14.

5. Hastings, p.253-5.

6. Correspondence Pat Lynch 6/7/05.

7. Dunwoody.

8. O'Kane, p.38.

9. Hastings, p.264.

10. John Dyer interview, Imperial War Museum.

11. O'Kane, p.32-3.

12. Doherty, p.158-9.

13. Hamill.

Chapter 9. Duty First.

1. Robert O'Neill. *Australia in the Korean War.*

2. Author interview John Hawkins 4/05.

3. Hawkins.

4. O'Neill.

5. *ibid*; Hawkins.

6. *ibid*; Hawkins.

7. Hawkins.

8. O'Neill.

9. Hawkins.

10. *ibid.*

11. O'Neill.

12. Hawkins.

13. O'Neill.

14. Hawkins.

Chapter 10. To the trenches.

1. Hastings, p.272-3.

2. Author interview Mike Kelly 6/9/05.

3. Irish in Korea.

4. Kelly.

5. ibid.

6. Irish in Korea.

7. 23rd Infantry history.

8. Irish in Korea.

9. Kelly.

10. Hamill.

11. Correspondence Robin Charley 19/10/05.

12. Author interview Pat O'Connor 8/7/05.

13. Author interview Pat Kelly 8/7/05.

14. Canadians in Korea, untitled; correspondence Tom O'Sullivan 29/9/05.

15. Correspondence Mary Doody 25/9/05.

16. Irish in Korea.

17. *ibid.*

18. Alexander, p.442.

19. Dennehy.

20. Jennings.

21. Irish in Korea.

22. John Fitzgerald, *Western People.*

23. US Senate Proclamation, courtesy John Leahy 22/8/05.

24. Coyne family, correspondence and interview 10/5/05.

25. Irish in Korea.

26. *ibid.*

27. *ibid.*

Chapter 11. Over there.

1. Excerpts from Harry O'Mara's unpublished memoirs of the Korean War.

2. Author interview Harry O'Mara 12/10/05.

3. Excerpts of interview of Paddy Sheehy by Denis O'Shaughnessy from his book *A spot so fair.*

Chapter 12. The hills of Korea.

1. Australian War Memorial.

2. Irish in Korea.

3. *ibid.*

4. Author interview Michael McCormick 4/9/05.

5. Author interview Jack Clarke 18/7/05.

6. Cecil Blacker and H.G. Woods *Change and Challenge*, p.96.

7. Clarke; 1st Welch history, untitled document.

8. Clarke.

9. Blacker, p.96.

10. May.

11. Hamill.

12. Blacker, p.96-7.

13. *ibid*, p.97.

14. Australian War Memorial.

15. Blacker, p.98.

16. Clarke; 1st Welch.

17. AWM; Roll of honour.

18. Blacker, p.104-6.

19. *ibid*, p.108.

20. *ibid* 112-4.

21. *ibid*, p.114.

22. Harry O'Mara *Recollections of Christmas Eve*.

23. Irish in Korea.

24. Author interview Ron Price 1/8/05.

25. Billy McLeer *Unit Pride*, p.73-5.

26. AWM.

27. Jennings.

28. Author interview Sean Taheny 4/5/05.

29. Hoyt, p.274.

Chapter 13. POWs.

1. Crosbie, p.61.

2. *ibid*, p.112.

3. *ibid*, p.135.

4. *ibid*, p.139-40.

5. *ibid*, p.141-51.

6. *ibid*, p.157.

7. Johnson List.

8. Crosbie, p.119-20.

9. Clifford.

10. Crosbie, p.173.

11. *ibid*, p.174.

12. *ibid*, p.183.

13. Doherty, p.155-6; Hamill.

14. Hastings, p.330-1.

15. Doherty, p.153-55.

16. *Whittier Daily News* interview with Henry Contreras.

17. MacGearailt, p.131-35.

18. Irish in Korea.

19. O'Kane, p.32; Hastings, p.334.

20. *ibid*, p.35.

21. *ibid*, p. 36-7.

22. *ibid*, p.42.

23. US POWs, untitled document.

24. Hastings, ps 336, 352; O'Kane, p.40; Monasterevin Local History.

25. Sarah Herlihy.

26. Albert Tyas, Imperial War Museum.

27. O'Kane, ps 43, 52.

28. US Dept. of State letter to Columban Foreign Mission 26/1/52.

29. *Irish Independent* 30/12/52.

30. Crosbie, ps 217, 221.

31. Clifford.

32. O'Kane, p.55.

33. Pat Quinn Irish in Korea.

34. MacGearailt, p.135.

35. O'Kane p.56-7.

Chapter 14. Dying for peace.

1. Medal of Honour Citations.

2. Irish in Korea.

3. Correspondence Jack McCabe, *Tampa Morning Tribune* 1/11/52, p.2.

4. Taheny.

5. Irish in Korea.

6. *ibid.*

7. Eric Donnelly, *I was a prisoner in North Korea.*

8. Hawkins.

9. Irish in Korea.

10. Correspondence J. T. Jennings 30/5/05.

11. Irish in Korea.

12. *ibid.*

13. Taheny.

14. Alexander, p.483.

15. Quinn.

16. Dunwoody.

17. Hoyt, p.303.

18. Author interview Peter Daly 14/8/05.

19. Author interview Packie O'Dwyer 28/3/05.

20. Author interview Jimmy Frawley 21/8/05.

Bibliography

Alexander, Bevin. *Korea. The Lost War.* London. 1989.

Blacker, General Sir Cecil & Woods, Major-General H.G., *Change and Challenge. The Story of the 5th Royal Inniskilling Dragoon Guards. 1928-1978.* 1978.

Crosbie, Philip. *March Till they Die.* 1955.

Doherty, Richard. *The Sons of Ulster. Ulstermen at war from the Somme to Korea.* Belfast. 1992.

Fischer, Edward. *Light in the Far East. Archbishop Harold Henry's forty-two years in Korea.* New York. 1976.

Hastings, Max. *The Korean War.* London. 1987.

Hoyt, Edwin P., *On to the Yalu.* New York. 1984.

Hoyt, Edwin P., *The bloody road to Panmunjom.* New York. 1985.

MacGearailt, Breandán "Brandy", & Shaughnessy, Mike. *Dúthaigh Duibhneach.* Dublin 2004.

Manchester, William. *American Caeser. Douglas MacArthur 1880-1964.* London. 1979.

McLeer, John & Dickson, Billy. *Unit Pride.* London. 1982.

Murphy, Jack. *History of the US Marines .* New York. 1984.

Neillands, Robin. *By Sea and Land. The Story of the Royal Marine Commandos.* London. 1987.

O'Dwyer, Martin. *A Biographical Dictionary of Tipperary.* Cashel, Tipperary. 1999.

O'Kane, Henry. *O'Kane's Korea.* London. 1988.

O'Neill, Robert. *Australia in the Korean War 1950-53*, Volume 2: *Combat*

Operations.
O'Shaughnessy, Denis. *A spot so fair. Tales from St. Mary's.* Limerick.. 1998 .
Owen, Joseph P., *Colder than hell. A Marine rifle company at Chosin reservoir.* New York. 1996.

Journals and Periodicals.

Argylls in Korea, Peter Jones.
The Morning Calm. Journal of the British Korean Veterans Association.
Dying for the Love of God. Michael Clifford. (Article in The Big Read, Sunday Tribune, 29/5/2005.)
I was a prisoner in North Korea, Eric Donnelly, from *Korea Remembered.*
Ireland and the Korean War, Brain Gallagher.
The Royal Ulster Rifles In Korea. Capt./Adjt. H. Hamill. Belfast: Wm. Mullan & Son (Publishers) Ltd., Donegall Place. 1953.

Veterans interviewed.

John Hawkins, (Enniscorthy, Wexford) 3rd Royal Australian Regiment.
Packie O'Dwyer, (Cashel, Tipperary) 1st Royal Irish Fusiliers.
J.T. Jennings, (Knockmore, Mayo) US 32nd Infantry Regiment.
Charles Dennehy, (Staigue, Kerry) US 32nd Infantry Regiment.
Sean Taheny, (Gurteen, Sligo) US 179th Infantry Regiment.
J.T. Jennings (Long Island, NY) US 32nd Infantry Regiment.
Tom O'Keefe, (Wexford) HMS *Cockade.*
Jack Clarke, (Dublin) 1st Welch Regiment.
Pat O'Connor, (Tralee, Kerry) US 2nd Infantry Division.
Pat Kelly, (Millstreet, Cork) US 445th Ordinance Ammunition Company.
Jimmy Frawley, (Ennis, Clare) US 2nd Engineer Battalion.
Peter Daly, (Ballyshannon, Donegal) US 25th Infantry Regiment.
James B. Dunwoody, (Belfast) 1st Royal Ulster Rifles.
Hans Milligan, (Belfast) 1st Royal Ulster Rifles.
Robin Charley (Newtownards, Down) 1st Royal Ulster Rifles.

Mike Keating (Mitchelstown, Cork) US 8186 Army Unit.

Ron Price (Dublin) 12th Field Squadron, Royal Engineers.

Gervase Murphy, (Bangor, Down) Royal Army Chaplain's Department.

Mike Kelly (Eyeries, Cork) US 8th Cavalry Regiment.

Michael McCormick (Loughrea, Galway) US 21st AAA Battalion.

Harry O'Mara (Ballinrobe, Mayo) US 31st Infantry Regiment.

Tony Lynch (Cobh, Cork) HMS *Consort*.

Index

Albrecht, Lt. A., 163.

Alexander, Lt. Godfrey, 75.

Almond, Gen. Edward, 45-6, 52, 56.

Amey, Snowey, 109.

Angland, Maurice, 137.

Anthis, Dewey, 166,168.

Anzac Day,111,112.

Austin, Warren, 14.

Australian forces in Korea,
K Force, 41; National Service, 41;
34th Infantry Brig., 106; 1st Royal
Australian Regt., 168, 209;
2nd RAR, 106, 209; 3rd RAR, 29, 49,
106-20, 148, 161-2, 169, 206; 67th
Battn., 106; RAAMC, 148.

Beard, Capt., 114.

Belgian Battalion, 94-6, 98, 103.

Berlin Complex, 212.

Bertrand, J., 153, 158, 163.

Blackstock, Cpl., 75.

Blake, George, 196.

Blake, Maj. Tony, 73-5.

Bloody Angle, 138.

Bloody Ridge, 129-30, 132, 136.

Blowick, Fr. John, 15.

Booth, Fr., 178.

Bousfield, Lt. Brian, 207-8.

Boyle, Paddy, 37.

Boyle, Richard, 148.

Brady, Dave, 57-8.

Braithwaite, Maj. Archie, 67.

Brennan, Sgt. Mark, 212.

Brennan, Mnsg. Patrick, 19, 21-2,
195.

Brennan, Helen & Martin, 212.

British Army,
Army Emergency Reserve, 39;
National Service, 39-40;
Territorial Army, 39;
Royal Armoured Corps, 104;
Royal Army Chaplain Dept., 41;
27th Brig., 29-30, 49, 51, 69, 76, 106-
8, 111-2, 120; 28th Brig., 111;
29th Brig., 62, 67-8, 70-1, 76, 94-5,
103-4, 112, 121, 159, 189; North Irish
Brigade, 158; Border Regt., 153;
Highland Light Infantry, 153;
Inniskilling Fusiliers, 64; Irish Fusiliers,
39, 102; Irish Rifles, 65, 155; Ulster
Rifles, 64, 70, 153, 190, 193-5; 1st
Argyll and Sutherland Highlanders,
29-31, 76, 111-2; 1st Black Watch,
164; 1st Glosters, 62, 94-8, 104, 154;
1st King's Own Scottish Borderers,
111, 153; 1st Kings Shropshire Light
Infantry, 111; 1st Middlesex, 29, 110-
1, 114-5, 117; 1st Royal Irish
Fusiliers, 214; 1st Inniskillings, 153;
1st Leicesters, 168; 1st Norfolks, 156;
1st Northumberlands, 62, 94, 97-8;
1st Tank Regiment, 164; 1st Royal
Ulster Rifles, 62-4, 66, 68, 76, 98,
104, 113, 126, 155-7, 181, 189, 194,

214; 1st Welch, 153-4, 160-1; 2nd Inniskillings, 102; 2nd ulster Rifles, 20; 5th Royal Inniskilling Dragoon Guards, 153, 158-9, 162, 164; 8th Kings Royal Irish Hussars, 62-3, 72, 75-6, 94-5, 97, 104, 158-9; 12th Field Squadron, 165; 41st Independent Commando, 52, 57, 191; 45th Field Artillery, 73, 95, 97; 176th Battery, 67; Cooperforce, 73-4; Lowertherforce, 95.

British Occupation Force Japan, 106.
Brodie, Brig. Tom, 94, 98, 156.
Buckley, Michael, 194.
Bunker Hill, 199.
Burke, Brig., 111, 117.
Bush, Pres., 183.
Byrne, Bishop Patrick, 18, 174, 177-8, 196.

Cadman, Sgt. Jack, 99.
Campbell, Sgt.,75-6.
Canavan, Fr. Frank, 17, 22, 24, 174, 177, 195-6.
Canadian forces in Korea, 42, 111, 128; Canadian Infantry Brigade Group, 128, 156, 160; Princess Patricia's Own Light Infantry, 160.
Canty, John, 212.
Carr, Lt. Col. Arthur, 158.
Carson, Col. Jack, 73, 157.
Charley, Capt. Robin, 64, 68, 71, 76, 127.

Chinese Communist forces in Korea, 64th Army, 104; 124th Division, 50; 1st Phase Offensive, 50; 1st Step 5th Offensive, 113; New Year's Offensive, 86, 156; Spring Offfensive, 90, 112, 122, 156; 2nd Spring Offensive, 124.
Church, Brig. Gen. John H., 14.
Clare, Sis. Mary, 8, 23, 174, 177, 196.
Clarke, Jack, 153-4, 160-1.
Clarke, Gen. Mark, 166, 195, 201.
Clayton, Sgt. Maj., 163.
Coey, Rev. D.S., 164
Collier, Fr. Anthony, 16-8.
Collier, Kieran, 16.
Collier, Teresa, 16.
Collins, Billy, 123-5.
Collins, Martin & Mossie, 124-5.
Collison, Joseph, 75.
Columban Fathers, 14-23, 174.
Compo Canyon, 70.
Commonwealth forces in Korea, 1st Commonwealth Division, 128, 148, 155, 159, 162, 197, 205, 209.
Commonwealth Task Force 91, 80.
Condron Andrew, 193.
Connor, Michael, 209.
Conroy, Michael,136.
Contreras, Henry, 182-3.
Cooper, Capt. Donald-Astley, 73, 75.
Corcoran, Pte. J., 155.
Corcoran, John, 46-7.
Cork Examiner, 125.

Coyne, Brian, 137.
Coyne, John, 137.
Craig, Lt. Hedley, 96.
Craig, Robert, 193.
Crawford, Davey, 190.
Crosbie, Fr. Philip, 18, 23-4, 174-8, 195-6.
Culligan, John, 131.
Cusack, Fr. Thomas, 20-2, 195.
Custer, Gen., 126.

Daly, Peter, 214.
Daly, Tom, 38.
Daniel, Ivor, 71, 95.
Davidson Line, 30.
Davidson, William, 193.
Davie, Cpl., 116.
Deane, H. H. "Dixie", 153.
Dempsey, Michael, 31.
Dennehy, Charles, 43-7, 53-6, 60, 133, 201.
Dickson, Billy, 166, 168, 180.
Dillon, John F., 204.
Dillon, Patrick & Mary, 204.
Donnelly, Eric, 207-8.
Doody, Mary, 130-1.
Doyle, Rear-Admr. James H., 42, 61.
Drysdale, Douglas B., 57.
Dunwoody, James B., 67, 70, 98, 214.
Durney, Jimmy, 39.
Dutch forces in Korea, 49.
Dyer, John, 100.

Eisenhower, Dwight D., 202.

Far East, 22.
Ferguson, Col., 114-5.
Fields, Vernon, 131-2.
Filipino Battalion, 97.
Fisher, Col. Henry G., 28.
Fitzgerald, Brendan, 197.
Fitzpatrick, Michael, 129-32.
Fitzsimons, Sgt. Maj. Sean, 69.
Fleming, William, 169.
Fogarty, Ray, 194.
Ford, Aubrey St. Clair, 95.
Fox, Gerry, 33.
Frawley, Jimmy, 215.
French Battalion, 125.
French Navy, 42.

Gale, Richard, 95.
Galvin, Bartholomew, 29, 30.
Galvin, Fr. Edward, 14, 15.
Gannon, Michael, 87, 88.
Gannon, John, 212.
Geraghty, Fr. Brian, 18, 19.
Gloster Hill, 97.
Grahame, Denis, 162.
Gravener, Capt. Norm, 113, 118.
Griffin, Fr. Cornelius. J., 58-9.
Greek Battalion, 49, 126-7.
Greene, Col. C. H., 108, 109.
Hamill, Capt. H., 65-6, 69, 72-3, 94, 126.
Happy Valley, 71, 98, 193.

Hardiman, Michael, 90-1.
Harrington, Daniel, or Donal, 122-23, 165.
Harrington, Eileen, 165.
Harris, Billy Joe, 163.
Harrison, Gen. William, 212.
Hassett, Jeremy, 195.
Hawkins, John, 106-20.
Hawkins, Paddy, 106, 209.
Healy, Pat, 38.
Heartbreak Ridge, 133-4, 137, 152, 171-2.
Herlihy, Diarmuid O'Sullivan, 194.
Herlihy, Michael, 136.
Hinge, The, 148, 209.
Hogge, Col., 15.
Hook, The, 154, 162.
Hope, Bob, 82.
Hoyt, Edwin P., 172, 214.
Hudson, Lt. A. Bruce, 97.
Huth, Maj. Henry, 97, 99.

Irish Echo, 138.
Irish Independent, 195.
Iron Triangle, 82, 122, 201, 212.
Invasion Valley, 128.

Jamestown Line, 137, 199.
Jennings, John T., 34, 132-6, 169-70, 210-1.
Jennings, Ned, 37.
Jennings, Tom, 37.
Johnson, James M., 206.
Johnson, Johnnie, 176, 177.
Johnson's List, 177.

Kansas Line, 122, 129.
Kavanagh, Lawrence, 193.
Kavanagh, Lt. P.J., 96.
Kavanagh, Michael, 37.
Keating, Mike, 38.
Kelly, Jack, 194.
Kelly, Mike, 121-3, 125-6.
Kelly, Pat, 128.
Kennedy, Nat, 179-80.
Keogh, Daniel, 204-6.
Kim, Gabriel, 17.
King George, 106.
King, Michael, 87-8.
Korean Military Advisory Group (KMAG), 13.

Laing, Chaplain, 114.
Lane, Tom, 40.
Lavery, Joe, 180.
Lavin, John, 210.
Lavin, Nellie, 210.
Lavin, Pat, 210-1.
Leany, John, 137.
Lee, John, 89, 183, 185-7, 197.
Lee, Mary, 187.
Lemass, Sean, 196.
Line Minnesota, 202.
Little Gibraltar, 162, 204, 206.
Lord, Commiss. Herbert, 22, 175-6.
Luke's Castle, 171.

Lynch, Philip Columba, 129-32.
Lynch, Tony, 84.
Lyons, Edward, 179-80, 193.

MacArthur, Douglas, 14, 28, 30, 35,
42, 46, 47-49, 50-3, 55, 59, 61, 78,
80, 90-1.
Maginn, Fr. James, 18-9, 195.
Maguire, Patrick, 164.
Maher, Daniel, 193.
Makarounis, Lt. Alexander, 22.
Malenkov, Georgi, 204.
Manchester, William, 42.
Mannett, Lt. 118.
Manning, Capt., 163.
Mao, Chairman, 50.
Marshall, George, 49.
Martin, Robert, 193.
Massey, Cpl. 181.
May, Billy, 39, 155-
May, Paddy, 194.
McAleer, John, 168.
McCallum, Ensign E.A., 81-82.
McConnell, Joseph, 151.
McConville, Andy, 64.
McCord, Lt. Mervyn, 75, 95.
McCormack, Michael, 212.
McCormick, Maureen, 152.
McCormick, Michael, 151-3.
McEnery, Patrick, 149.
McHale, Carmel, 196.
McLarnon, Terence, 201.
McLoughlin, Pfc. Alford, 199-200.

McNab, Andy, 194.
McWilliams, William, 193.
Milligan, Hans, 64-5, 67.
Mills, John, 149.
Missions, 23, 177.
Mole, Lt. John, 99.
Montgomerie, Lt., 116.
Moore, May, 88.
Mosley, Ted, 109.
Mount, Col. Charles McNamara, 132.
Muir, Major, 31.
Murphy, Stephen, 183.
Murphy, William, 87-8, 182-3.
Murphy, William Kevin, 107, 116, 119.
Murray, Gavin, 99.
Murphy, Gervase, 40-1.
Murray, John, 90.

Nam Il, Gen., 212.
NATO, 164.
Neligan, Fr. Tom, 20.
Nicholls, Lt., Max, 99.
North Korean Peoples Army, 13, 15,
17, 20, 25, 47, 108, 149, 173, 191,
196; 7th Division, 17.
No Name Line, 122, 124.
Nugent, Frank, 193.

O'Brien, Fr. John, 20-2, 195.
O'Brien, Pte, R.G. 107.
O'Brien, T.W. 107.
O'Brien, Thomas, J. 27, 50, 51.
O'Connell, Alphonsus, 147, 148-49.

O'Connell, Joe, 40.

O'Connor, Frank, 138, 165.

O'Connor, Pat, 127-8.

O'Dowd, Maj. Ben, 119.

O'Duibhir, Liam, 27, 50.

O'Dwyer, Patrick, 214.

O'Grady, Fr, 149.

O'Kane, Henry, 63-4, 70, 72, 75-6, 94, 96, 98, 101-2, 189-92, 194-5, 197-8.

O'Keefe, Tom, 78-82.

O'Keefe, Raymond, 78.

Old Baldy, 164, 171, 204, 210.

Olivier, Paul, 47.

O'Mara, William Harry, 141, 146, 164.

Operation Chromite, 40.

Operation Commando, 137, 148, 156.

Operation Jehu, 162.

Operation Showdown, 201.

Operation Killer, 91.

Operation Ripper, 91-2.

Operation Yo-Yo, 82.

Ormond, Capt. Peter, 99.

O'Shaughnessy, Kevin, 128.

Ovens, Capt. Pat, 57.

Phillips, Chaplain, 114.

Pork Chop Hill, 164, 171, 210-11.

POW Camps, Bean Camp, 181, 184-5, 188;

Chongsong Camp1 186-9, 191-2, 194, 196; Death Valley, 191; Hanjang-ni, 24, 178; Manpo, 174; Peaceful Valley, 191; Valley Camp, 191.

Punchbowl, 133, 152, 172, 212.

Pusan Perimeter, 21, 26, 29, 43, 48-9, 52.

Prior, Owen, 212.

Pratt, Rfn.179-80.

Price, Ron, 165-6.

Quinlan, Mons. Thomas, 15, 18, 22, 24, 174, 176, 178, 195, 196.

Quinn, Pat, 188, 197, 213.

Quinn, Thomas, 137.

Quinn, Col. William "Buffalo Bill," 90-1.

Reidy, Michael, 193.

Reilly, Fr Patrick, 19.

Rhee, Syngman, 47.

Rickord Maj. Gerald, 67, 98, 104.

Ridgway, Gen. Matthew B., 53, 85-7, 93, 123, 149-50, 166.

Robertson, Maj. 114-5.

Roche, Billy, 125.

ROK Army, 13; II Corps, 54, 68; 1st Div., 71, 137; 5th Div., 87, 124; 6th Div., 112, 120; 7th Div., 124; 8th Div.,87; 1st Regt., 153; 17th Regt., 46; 36th Regt.,129-30.

ROK Navy, 42.

Rowland, Mark, 37.

Royal Air Force (RAF) 827 Squadron, 79.

Royal Australian Air Force (RAAF) 77 Squadron, 106, 109

Royal Australian Navy,

Shoalhaven, 78; *Bataan*, 78, 80; *Devonshire*, 169.
Royal Navy, Far East Fleet, 78; *Ark Royal*, 78; *Belfast*, 78, 82, 95; *Black Swan*, 78; *Ceylon*, 80; *Charity*, 80; *Chevron*, 78; *Cockade*, 78-82; *Comus, 82; Comet*, 78; *Concord*, 80, 82;
Consort, 78, 84; *Cossack*, 78, 84; *Devonshire*, 82; *Dilwara*, 82; *Empire Fowey*, 153, 156; *Empire Halladale*, 157, 164; *Empire Pride*, 63-5;
Glory, 83; *Jamaica*, 78; *London*, 81; *Thesus*, 83; *Triumph*, 83.
Royal New Zealand Army Corps, 16th Field Regt., 111, 114.
Royal New Zealand Navy, 42.
Ryan, Capt. Mick,107, 118.
Ryan, Maj. Joe, 74.

San Francisco Chronicle, 170.
Scully, Billy, 86.
Scully, Denis, Jack, 86.
Shaw, Maj. John, 76.
Shaw, John, Rfn., 195.
Sheahan, Pat, 138-9.
Sheehy, Paddy, 146-7.
Shenon, Ron, 208.
Shirver, D. S., 206.
Sinnett, Tommy, 107.
Skelton, Mick, 81.
Slag Heap Hill, 179.
Smith, Capt Tom, 70, 94.

Smith, Lt. Col. Charles B., 24-5.
Smith, Rfn., 179-80.
Spears, Tommy, 102.
Spence, Jack, 194.
St. Columban's Order, 14.
Stalin, Joseph, 204.
Standard, 18.
Steele, Gen., 157.
Sutherland, Lt., 162.
Sweetlove, Cpl. Norman, 102.
Synott, William, 98.

Taheny, Sean, 170-1, 202-3, 212-3.
Task Force Drysdale, 57.
Task Force Smith, 24.
Taylor, Brig. G., 111.
Taylor, Lt. C.,162-3.
Taylor, Maxwell D., 204.
T-Bone Hill, 203-4.
Thai Battn, 49.
Thorburn, Charley, 110.
Tiger, 22-3, 175, 178.
Tiger March,174-5.
Truman, Harry, 14, 33, 86, 90-1.
Turkish Brig, 68-9, 111.
Tyas, Rfn. Albert, 194.

UN Blockading & Escort Force, 79.
East Korean Support Group, 79.
West Korean Support Group, 79.
8th Destroyer Flotilla, 82.
United Nations General Assembly, 49.
UNSEC Council, 14.

United States Air Force, 13.

39th Fighter-Interceptor Squadron, 151.

United States Army,

Eighth Army, 26-7, 30, 52, 60, 66, 68, 85-6, 91, 93, 108, 121, 149, 204;

I Corps, 69, 94, 148, 171, 203; IX Corps, 86; 91; 111; 133; 201;

X Corps, 50, 52, 54-5, 59-60, 69, 82, 85, 93, 148;

1st Cav. Div., 24, 26, 29, 37, 47, 107-9, 122, 126, 137, 140, 148;

2nd Inf. Div.29-30, 61, 68, 88, 124, 129, 133, 136, 188, 191, 203-4, 215;

3rd Inf. Div., 43, 55, 61, 137-8, 160;

6th Inf. Div., 152;

7th Inf. Div., 21, 24, 37, 42-8, 52-6, 60-1, 132-4, 137, 145-6, 203-4, 210-1;

9th Inf. Div.,43; 24th Inf. Div., 24, 26, 29, 149-50;

25th Inf. Div., 24, 26-7, 50-1, 123, 137, 140, 152;

31st Inf. Div., 40th Inf. Div., 171, 202; 45th Inf. Div., 171, 202; 101st Air. Div., 204; 5th RCT, 26;

187th Airborne RCT, 108; 2/15th Infantry, 160; 5th Cavalry, 109;

7th Cavalry,126-7, 137, 149; 8th Cavalry.,109, 121, 137;

9th Infantry., 29, 125, 132, 136, 204;

14th Infantry, 140;

17th Infantry, 37, 48, 53, 56, 90, 210-1; 19th Infantry, 149;

23rd Infantry, 29, 124, 129, 131-2;

24th Infantry, 26; 25th Infantry, 214;

31st Infantry, 21, 86, 145, 164, 210;

32nd Infantry, 37, 43-8, 52-6, 132-4, 169, 201, 204; 35th Infantry, 27, 73, 122-3; 38th Infantry, 87-8, 124, 132, 136, 184, 203; 179th Infantry,171-2, 202; 180th Infantry, 172, 202; 2nd Eng. Btn, 215;

8th Eng. Cbt Btn, 137, 148-9; 13th Eng. Cbt Btn, 212; 15th FA Btn, 87-8; 21st AAA Btn, 152; 89th Tank Btn., 108; 90th FA Btn, 27, 50-1; 78th AAA Btn, 212;

555th FA Btn, 27; 772nd MP Btn, 212; 955th FA Bty, 201; 658th QM Coy, 212;

445th Ord. Ammo. Coy, 128; 56th Army Band, 66; 8186th Army Unit, 38.

US Marine Corps, 33; Fleet Marine Force, 33; 1st Marine Div., 42, 45, 48, 52, 55, 57, 60-1, 191; 1st Mar. Prov. Brig., 26; 1st Marine Regt., 212; 5th Marine Regt., 43, 199; 7th Marine Regt., 43, 50, 58, 89, 200, 212.

US Navy, 42; US 7th Fleet, 13, 78; *Aiken Victory*, 106; *Breckenridge*, 126; *General Black*, 169; *General Collins*, 169; *Marine Adair*, 171; *Marine Phoenix*, 36; *Missouri*, 45; *Rendova*, 79.

Van Fleet, Gen. James A., 91, 121,

149, 201, 204.
Veasey, Tpr. P., 162.
Vinegar Hill, 106.

Wagner, Capt., 76.
Walker, Gen. Walton, 27, 30, 60, 85,
93.
Ward, Lt. Johnny, 117.
Ward, Pfc. Thomas, 27-8.
Ward, Tom, Snr., 28.
Welles, Gordon, 208.
White, John, 43, 200-1.
White, Michael, 140.
White, Patrick, 140.
White, Peter, 206-8.
Whittier Daily News, 183.
Williamson, Sgt., 159.
Woods, Fr. Frank, 20.

Zeg, Stephen, 26.